IMAGES
of America

Southern Maryland's Historic Landmarks

On the Cover: An elderly woman and a chicken share the front porch of Stagg Hall (constructed c. 1739–1746) in the village of Port Tobacco, Charles County, in 1936. (Courtesy of the Frances Benjamin Johnston Photographic Collection, Library of Congress.)

IMAGES
of America

SOUTHERN MARYLAND'S HISTORIC LANDMARKS

Christopher R. Eck

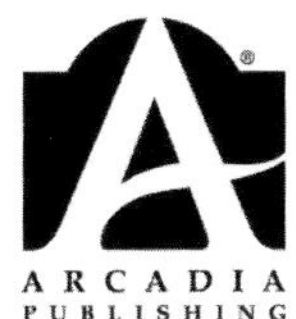

ISBN 978-1-4671-1722-7

Published by Arcadia Publishing
Charleston, South Carolina

Printed in the United States of America

Library of Congress Control Number: 2016931628

For all general information, please contact Arcadia Publishing:
Telephone 843-853-2070
Fax 843-853-0044
E-mail sales@arcadiapublishing.com
For customer service and orders:
Toll-Free 1-888-313-2665

Visit us on the Internet at www.arcadiapublishing.com

To all the members of my family, for their tireless gifts of love, faith, joy, and patience

Contents

Acknowledgments

The author would like to thank the many people whose work preceded this book and who devoted themselves to documenting and preserving the history of Southern Maryland. Anyone who studies the history and historic architecture of this region owes a debt of gratitude to the decades of invaluable research prepared by J. Richard Rivoire, architectural historian. Similarly, for those studying Southern Maryland's archaeology, a tremendous effort has been accomplished for years by Dr. Julia King.

Among the pioneering organizations that documented and helped save Southern Maryland's historic landmarks are the following: the Historic American Buildings Survey (1933), the Restorers of Mount Carmel (1935), the Smallwood Foundation (1939), the Society for the Restoration of Port Tobacco (1948), the St. Mary's County Historical Society, the Calvert County Historical Society (1953), the Historical Society of Southern Maryland (1961), the Maryland Historical Trust (1966), the St. Mary's City Commission (1966, which became the Historic St. Mary's Commission in 1991), and the Southern Maryland Studies Center (1976) at the College of Southern Maryland. Also, I extend a personal expression of gratitude to my fellow members of the History Committee of St. Ignatius Church at Chapel Point whose dedication to understanding the area's ancient heritage has been inspirational.

The historical images in this book primarily come from two collections held at the Library of Congress (LOC): that of the Historic American Buildings Survey (HABS), which began in 1933, and the Frances Benjamin Johnston Photograph Collection (FBJPC), made for her work on the Carnegie Survey of the American South, mostly in the mid-1930s. Unless otherwise noted, all images appear courtesy of the author's collection.

INTRODUCTION

Southern Maryland's historic landmarks are comprised of sites that stretch back over centuries, reflecting the region's fascinating past, diversity of peoples, and distinctive location. From Indian villages to grand Colonial estates, from humble cabins to churches that have survived the ravages of time and wars, Southern Maryland's historic landmarks reflect the development of Maryland and the region's great influence on the story of American history.

Southern Maryland is composed of the state's three southernmost counties, St. Mary's, Calvert, and Charles, which are situated between the Potomac River and the western shore of the Chesapeake Bay. Geologically, these counties are uplands of the Atlantic coastal plain, characterized by low rolling hills and punctuated by numerous small rivers and creeks (locally known by the archaic English term "freshes"), as well as numerous forests, fields, and swamps. Each county is fully or partially separated from the others by rivers: the Patuxent River (colloquially called the "Pax") is between St. Mary's and Calvert Counties, and the Wicomico River is between northwest St. Mary's and southeast Charles Counties.

As a result of this physical and geological separation of the land and its close association with the water, Southern Maryland developed a distinctive culture based on its relationship between water and land, as well as its reliance on farming and maritime trades. With the limited number of roadways leading north to the rest of Maryland, its relative isolation from the daily influence of the larger urban centers of Annapolis, Baltimore, Alexandria, and Washington led to the creation of the region's cultural identity, patterns of speech, and history.

Nevertheless, Southern Maryland built upon its position as the foundation of Colonial Maryland. Before becoming the landing and settlement place of the first English colonists to arrive on the *Ark* and the *Dove* in 1634, the area was home to more ancient Algonquian Indian communities, such as the larger Patuxent and the Piscataway tribes, as well as several other smaller groups. The combination of Europeans, Native Americans, and Africans, both enslaved and free, all contributed to crafting Southern Maryland's unique character, one not devoid of hardship or strife, but which left a lasting legacy for the region.

This combination of peoples was also greatly shaped by religious convictions, as evidenced from the very beginning in their establishment of numerous churches and religious institutions. This was born of the belief of George Calvert, 1st Baron Baltimore (better known to most as the first Lord Baltimore or Lord Calvert), that the colony granted to him by his friend King Charles I could be a refuge for persecuted English Catholics, while also welcoming English Protestants among its settlers.

Though the first Lord Baltimore died in 1631 before he could see his dream come to fruition, his son Cecil, the 2nd Baron or Lord Baltimore, would pick up where his father had left off. The first colonists aboard the two ships landed at St. Clement's Island on March 25, 1634. To celebrate the event, the Reverend Andrew White, a Jesuit priest and confidant of the Calverts, celebrated the first Catholic mass in the English colonies. Soon thereafter, the colonists purchased land from the Yaocomico tribe, allied with the Piscataway Indians, for what would become the first Colonial settlement, St. Mary's City.

In the decades that followed, the late George Calvert's ideal of a refuge for Catholics with toleration for its Anglican settlers was severely tested. Using his younger brother Leonard to act as proprietary governor in the new colony, Cecil Calvert had to weather the storm of Protestant rebellions in his colony, such as the uprising led by William Claiborne from 1635 to 1638 and the repercussions of the Puritan-led English Civil War (1642–1651) at home in Britain. During this time, the colony passed the Act of Toleration (1649) for all Christians, the basis for the Constitutional freedom of religion today.

Through it all, the Calverts managed to remain the proprietors of Maryland until the Glorious Revolution of 1689. During this time, the Lords Baltimore held extraordinary powers to grant titles to land, including the creation of large manors with near-feudal powers. Many of Southern Maryland's historic landmarks resulted from the grant of manor lands in the 17th century.

Always striving to regain their colony after its loss to royal control, the Calverts succeeded in being returned to their proprietorship in 1715 after Benedict Leonard Calvert converted from Catholicism to Anglicanism. Dying shortly before the colony's turnover, his son Charles Calvert became the 5th Baron Baltimore and served as proprietor of Maryland until his death in 1751. His son Frederick became the 6th and last Baron Baltimore, but he led an extravagant and scandalous life and never came to Maryland before his death in 1771. His illegitimate son Henry Harford was allowed by the crown to become the last proprietor of Maryland, but he did not have much chance to enjoy the fruits of his control before it was lost in the independence gained during the American Revolution.

Despite chronic political turmoil, life in Southern Maryland continued. Homes and churches were built, farms were planted, and commerce was sustained. With the coming of the American Revolution, Southern Maryland produced an extraordinary number of patriots and leaders. Among them were Gen. William Smallwood, who bravely led Maryland troops under Gen. George Washington in the New York and New Jersey campaigns; attorney Thomas Stone, who was a signer of the Declaration of Independence and helped draft the Articles of Confederation; John Hanson, a signer of the Articles of Confederation and a president of the Continental Congress; Dr. James Craik, chief physician of the Continental Army; and many others.

Others, less well known, led lives that also shaped the Southern Maryland landscape. Known as the "Apostle of Maryland," Fr. Andrew White was an English Jesuit who preached to several Indian communities, converted several tribal leaders to Catholicism, and translated the catechism into Piscataway. Among the converts was Mary Kittamaquund, the daughter of the *tayac* (emperor) of the Piscataway tribe, who later married the English settler Giles Brent. Along with her sisters-in-law Margaret and Mary, the Brents acquired over 30,000 acres of land in Virginia after 1647, and Giles became the only Catholic ever elected to the House of Burgesses during the Colonial period.

Another extraordinary Southern Marylander was Matthew Henson. Born into a family of black farmers after the end of the Civil War, Henson, along with Robert Peary, became famous as an explorer of the Arctic on seven expeditions over 23 years. Dr. Barton Tabbs, a surgeon's mate under General Smallwood during the American Revolution, created Maryland's first medical school at his home in Great Mills. The Reverend Thomas John Claggett became the first American-born Episcopal bishop to be consecrated.

Places touched by the men and women of Southern Maryland's history have left a physical legacy, an inheritance of historic landmarks for future generations to learn about past lives, understand the roots of their culture, and reflect upon who created the place they live in today. To paraphrase the preservationist James Marston Fitch, the present must learn from the *originals*.

One

St. Mary's County

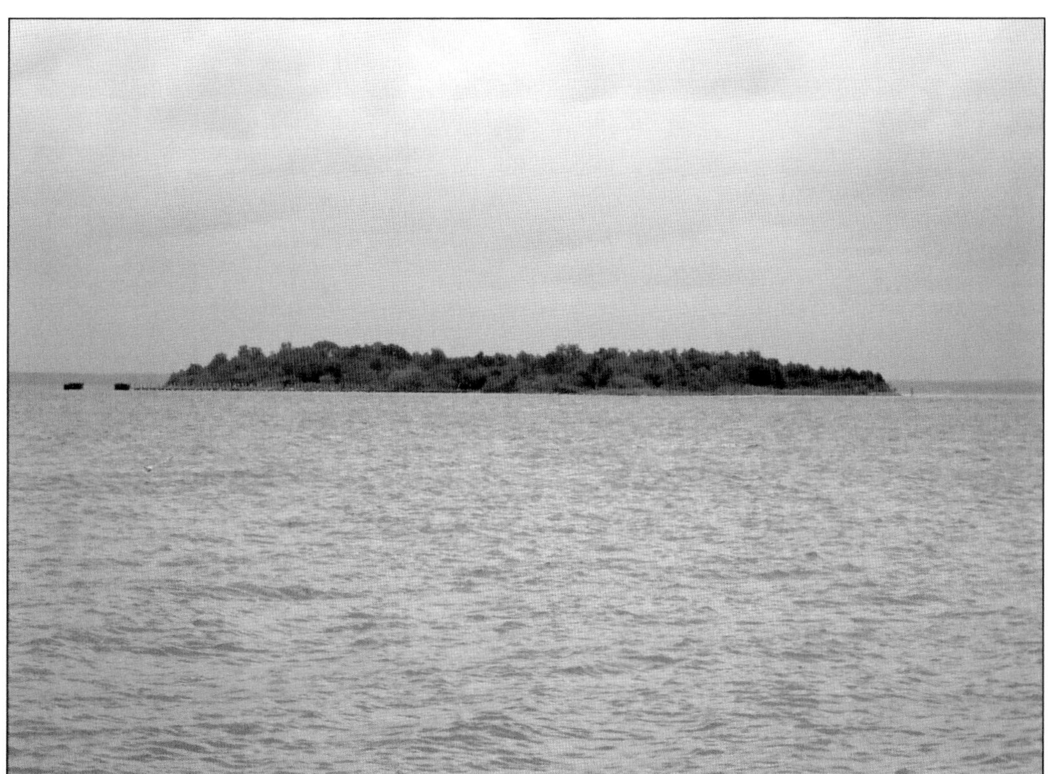

On March 25, 1634, the English colonists aboard the *Ark* and the *Dove* landed on St. Clement's Island, named for the saint whose feast day was the day that the ships departed from England. Known after 1669 as Blackistone Island for the family that acquired it, the island was a British base during the War of 1812, and its lighthouse was damaged by Confederates in the Civil War.

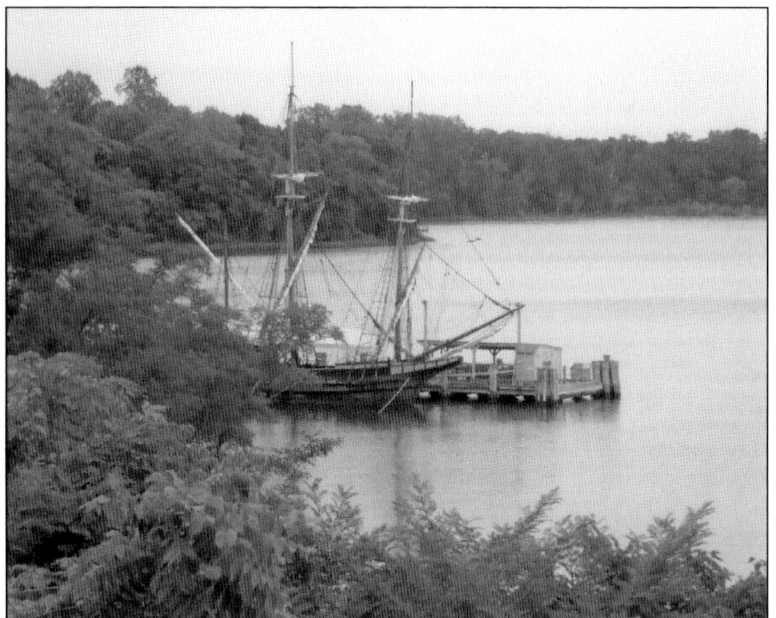

After negotiating with the local Yaocomico tribe for a site to establish their settlement, the colonists sailed to what would become St. Mary's City, about 20 miles southeast and down the Potomac River from St. Clement's Island and 5 miles north up the St. Mary's River. This replica of the *Dove* is docked at Historic St. Mary's City, a living history museum at the site of Maryland's first settlement.

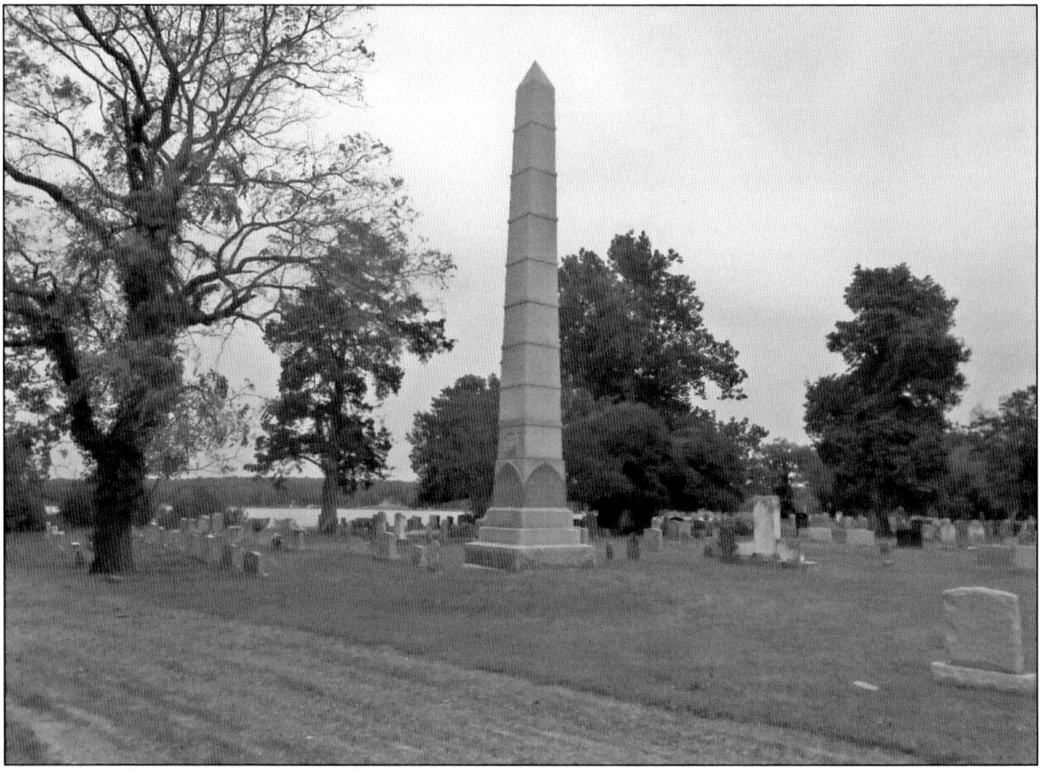

In the cemetery of Trinity Episcopal Church is this monument to Leonard Calvert (1606–1647), the first proprietary governor of Maryland and the second son of George Calvert (1579–1632), the 1st Baron Baltimore, whose desire it was to establish an American colony that would provide religious freedom for English Catholics. After Lord Baltimore's colony at Avalon, Newfoundland, had failed, Governor Calvert successfully pursued his father's dream in Maryland.

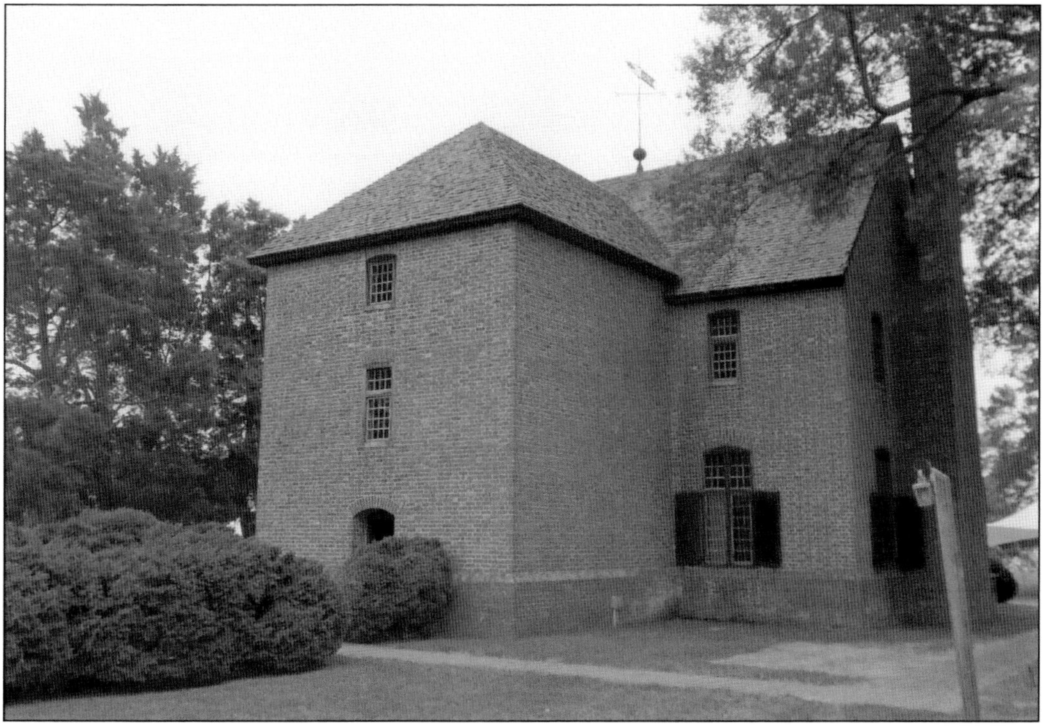

Rebuilt as part of Maryland's 300th anniversary commemoration in 1934, the statehouse originally stood in the nearby Trinity Episcopal Church cemetery. Architects Herbert G. Crisp and James R. Edmunds Jr. of Baltimore and Horace W. Peaslee of Washington designed the reconstruction using archaeological and historical data. The original was built in 1676 and used until the capital was moved to Annapolis in 1694. It was demolished in 1829.

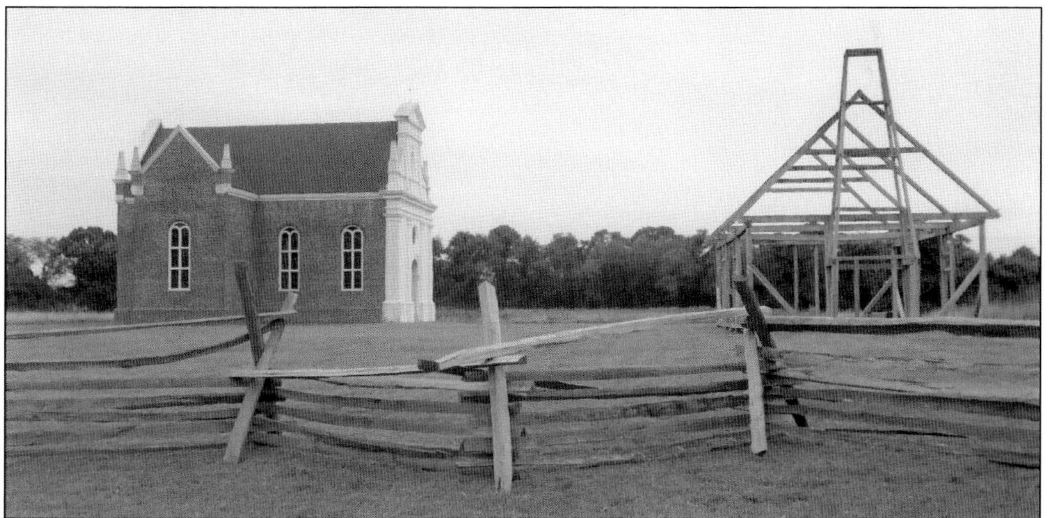

In 1667, Jesuit priests built a brick chapel on the site where another chapel had stood before being burned by Protestant rebels during the English Civil War. Closed by the royal governor in 1704, the Jesuits dismantled it. In 1990, prior to its reconstruction (2002–2009), archaeologists found the lead coffins of Philip Calvert (1626–1682), Lord Baltimore's youngest son; his wife, Anne Wolsey Calvert; and an unidentified child in the church floor.

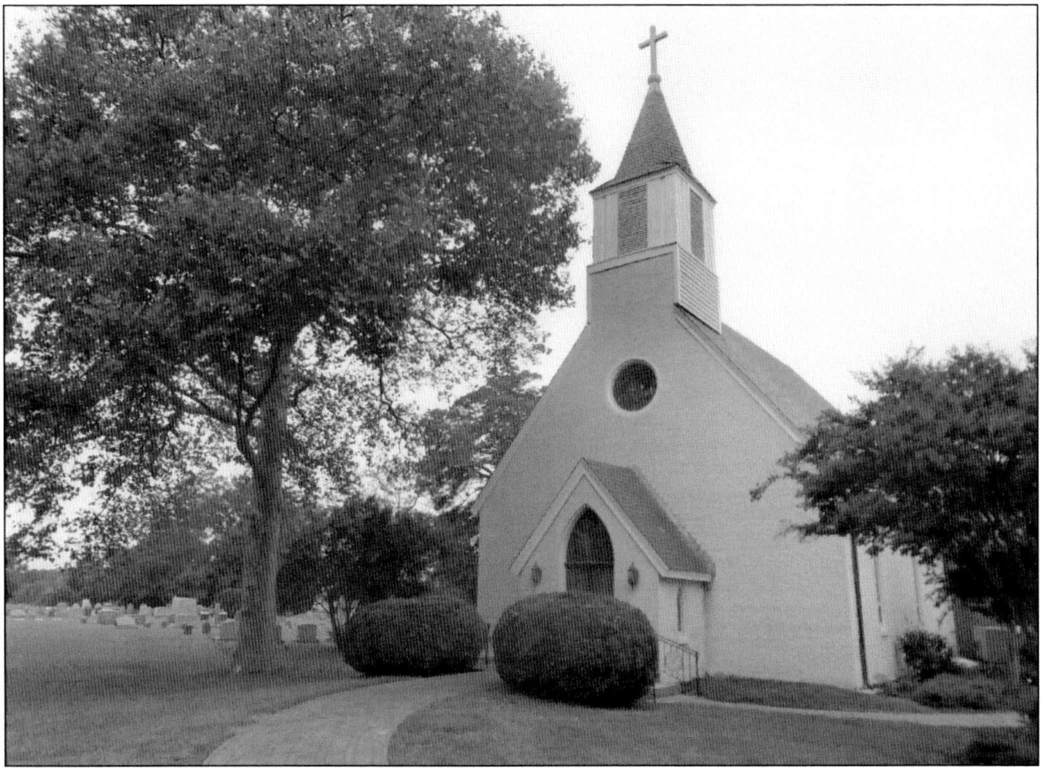

Trinity Episcopal Church was built in 1829 using bricks salvaged from the demolition of the 1676 statehouse. Following the departure of the government to Annapolis in 1694, the former statehouse, which originally stood in the cemetery, was given to the parish in 1720. Though renovated over time, the Victorian Gothic style of the present church is among the earliest in the region.

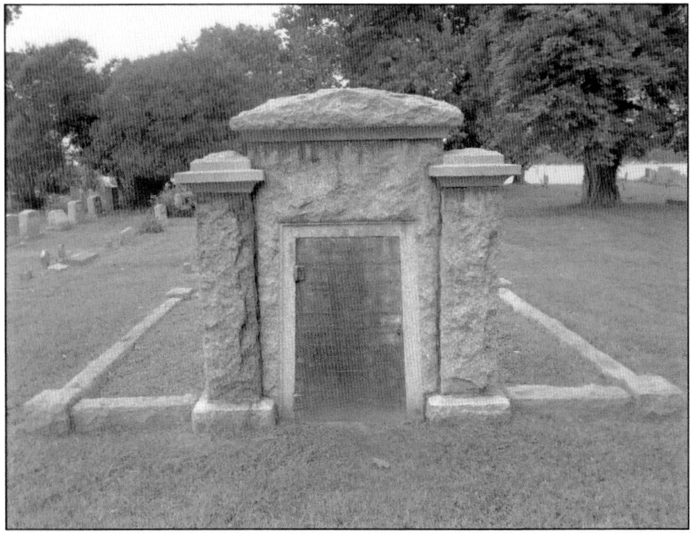

With the loss of the Calvert family's proprietorship of Maryland in the Glorious Revolution (1689), the Anglican Church was made the colony's official religion, with its first royal governor Sir Lionel Copley (1648–1693). Arriving in the colony in 1692 and working at the statehouse, Copley became sick and died and his remains are in this tomb in the Trinity churchyard along with his wife, Anne Boteler Copley, who died in 1692.

North of St. Mary's City is this monument to Rev. Andrew White, SJ, or the "Apostle to Maryland." Father White (1579–1656) was the Jesuit priest who accompanied the colonists aboard the *Ark* and the *Dove* and who served as a missionary to many local Indian tribes. This monument was first erected in 1934 by the Order of the Alhambra, a Catholic fraternal organization, in a nearby park that has since closed.

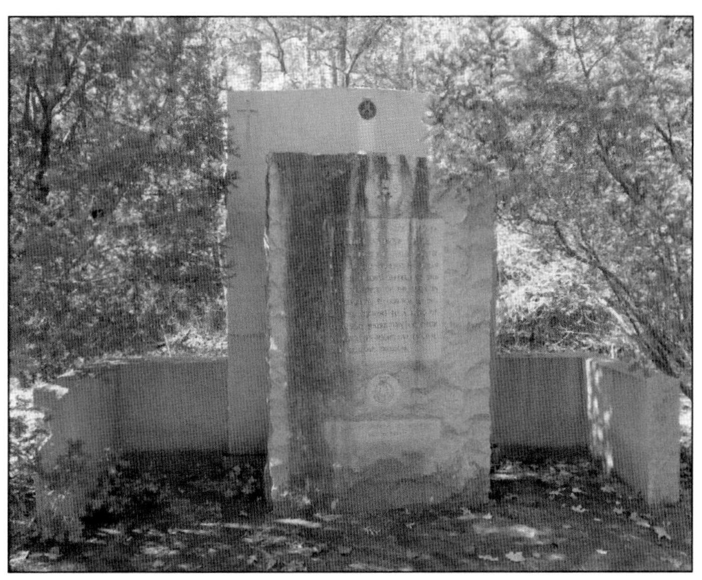

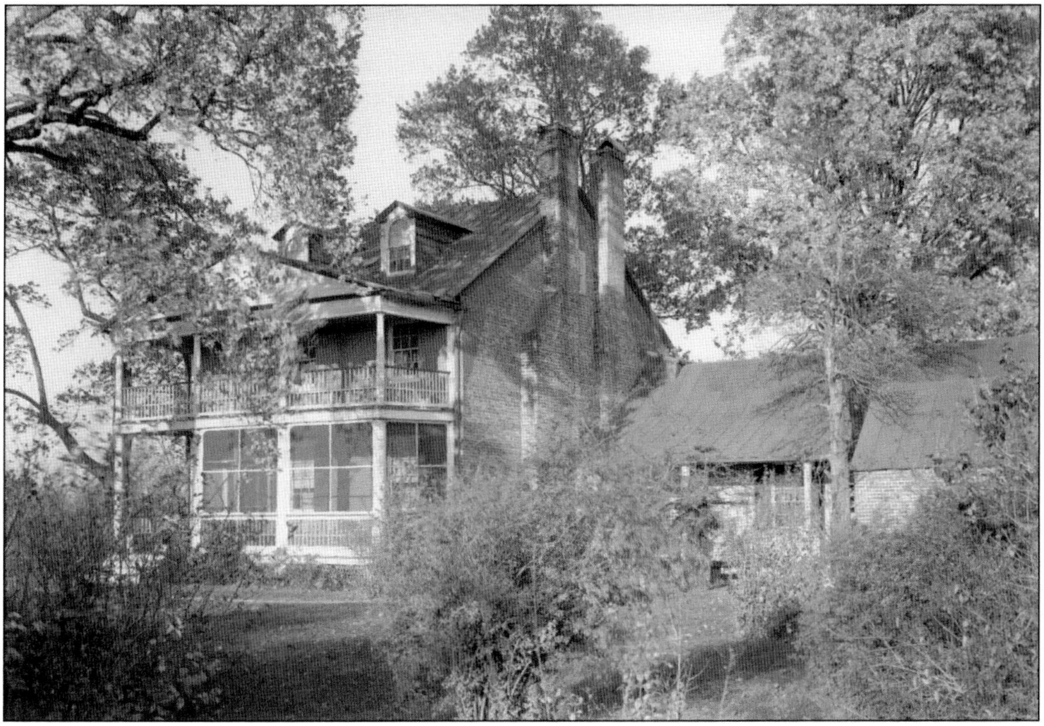

The two-and-a-half-story brick Cross Manor is believed to incorporate the original homesite of settler Thomas Cornwaleys (Cornwallis), who came to Maryland with Gov. Leonard Calvert in 1634 and who suffered greatly in raids during Richard Ingle's revolt of 1644–1645. The earliest part of the house was built in the 1760s, then expanded in the 1790s, and a frame wing was added between 1828 and 1840. (E.H. Pickering, HABS.)

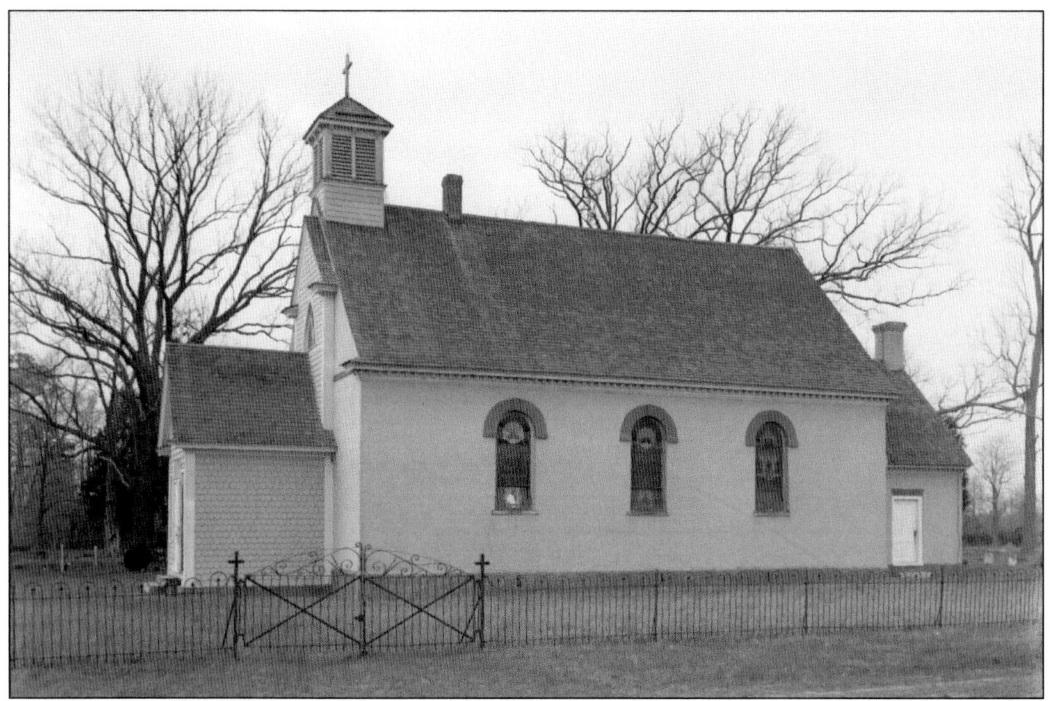

In 1637, Rev. Thomas Copley, SJ, acquired the Jesuit manor lands south of St. Mary's City along St. Inigoe's Creek where St. Ignatius Catholic Church would be built after the American Revolution, once Catholics could freely worship again. The main block of the church was constructed of brick from 1783 to 1785, with a brick sacristy added in 1817 and a wooden entrance vestibule added in 1886. (Charles E. Peterson, HABS.)

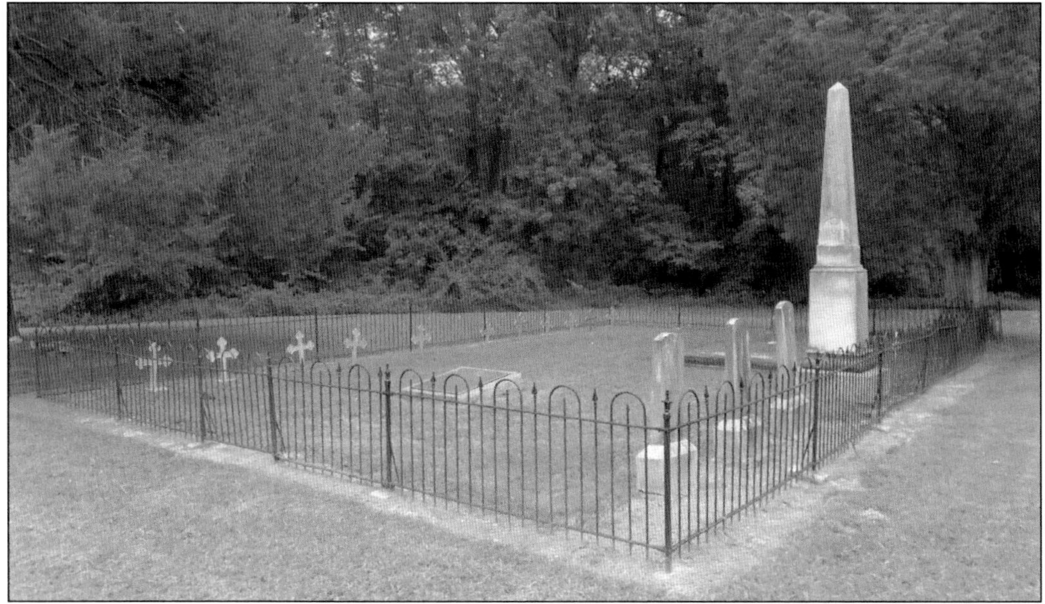

Among the graves of early parishioners, there is a section of the St. Ignatius churchyard that is dedicated to the 28 members of the order who labored in the Maryland province and who were buried here between 1637 and 1891.

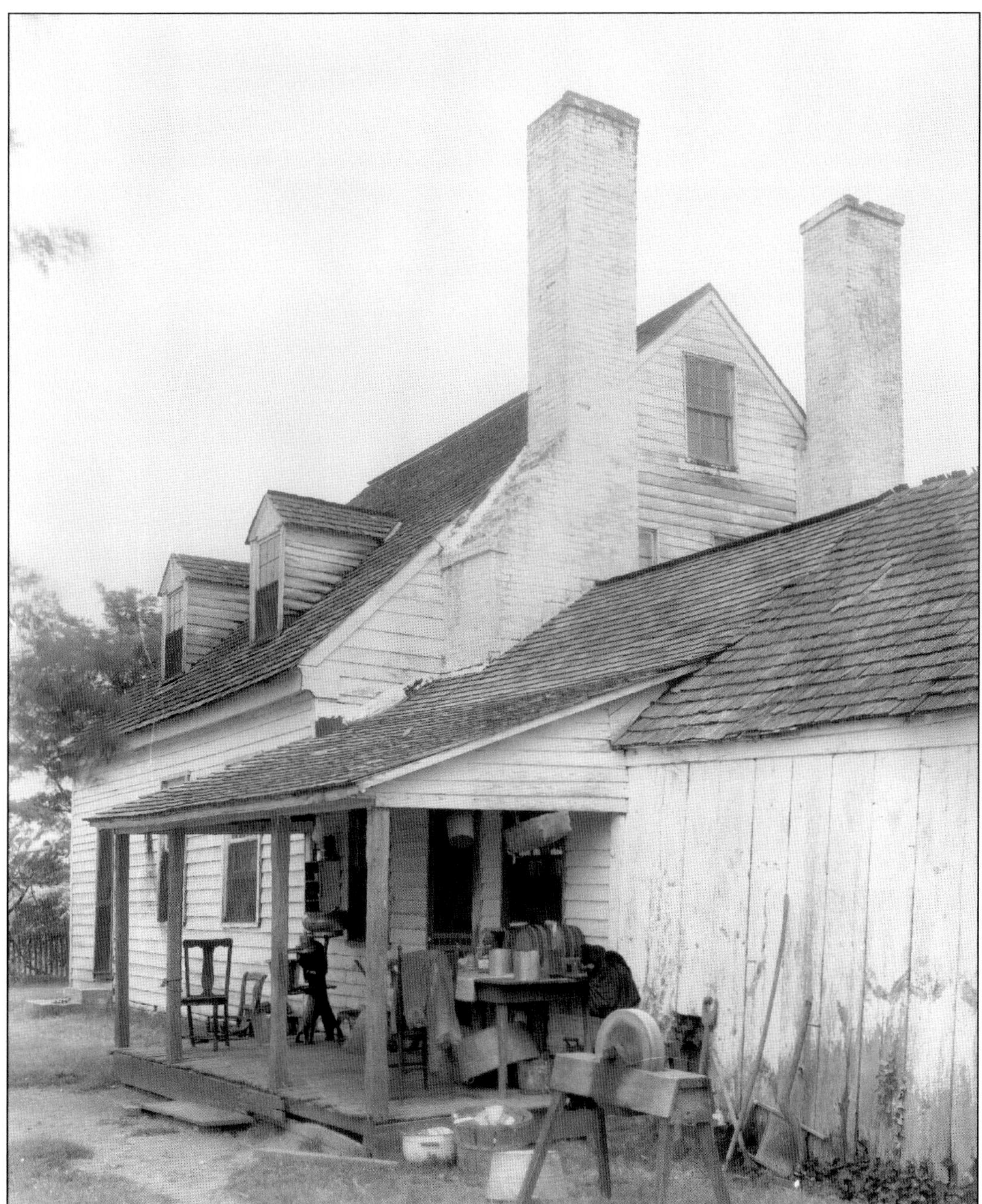

Located on the grounds of the Naval Electronic Systems Engineering Base (Webster Field) in St. Inigoes is the Priest's Manor House, an early-18th-century residence. Although once part of the Jesuit-owned St. Inigoe's Manor, it was not a true manor house. The one-and-a-half-story wood structure had a detached kitchen that joined the residence through a 19th-century hyphen. (FBJPC, LOC.)

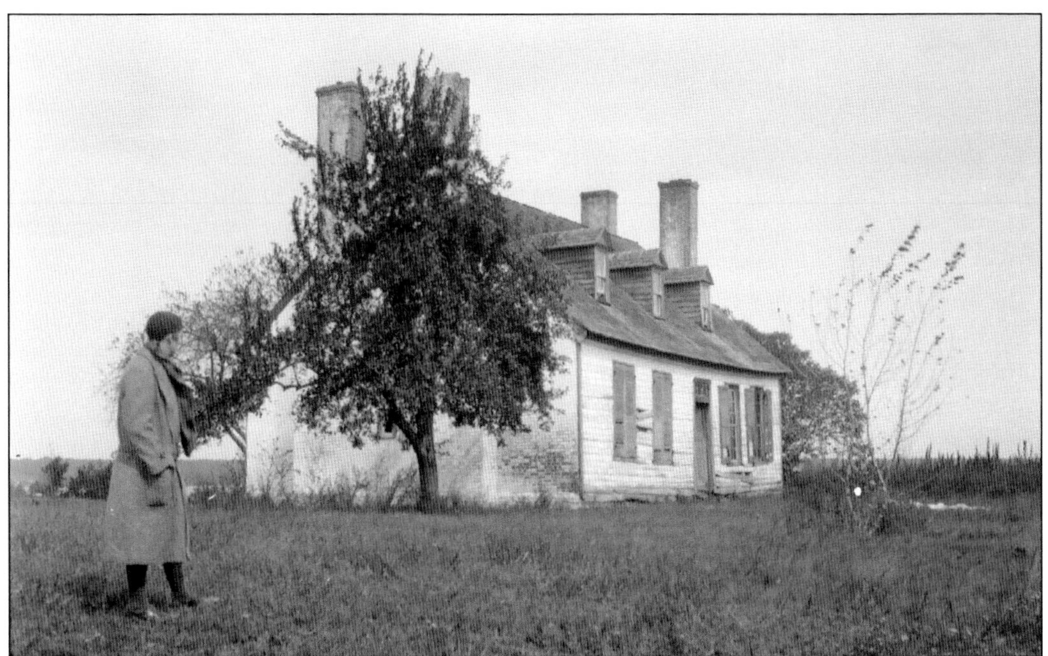

Built on Maryland's first land grant acquired by Capt. Henry Fleet in May 1634 and then acquired by Governor Calvert's councillor Thomas Cornwaleys in 1640, West St. Mary's Manor in Drayden was not the first house on the property. However, it is an early one-and-a-half-story brick and frame home with a central hall and four rooms built between 1700 and 1730. (FBJPC, LOC.)

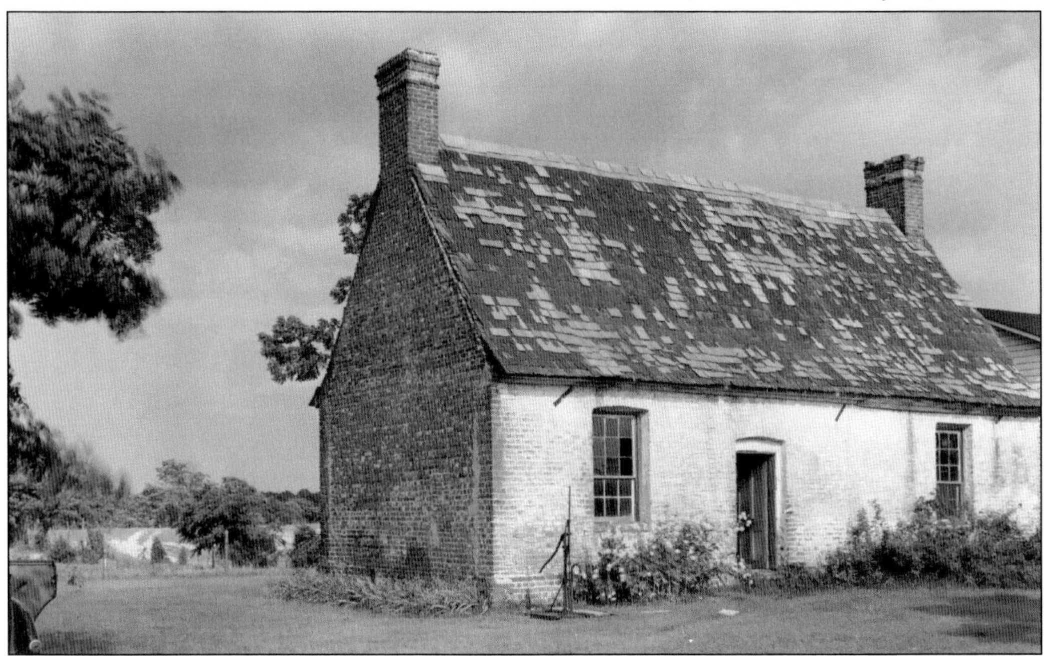

On the estate acquired by Thomas Cornwaleys in 1650, the house known as Resurrection Manor and documented by the Historic American Buildings Survey in 1940 was built on the portion of the property known as Scotch Neck around 1720. The three-bay, one-and-a-half-story brick residence was designated as a National Historic Landmark in 1970. (Thomas T. Waterman, HABS.)

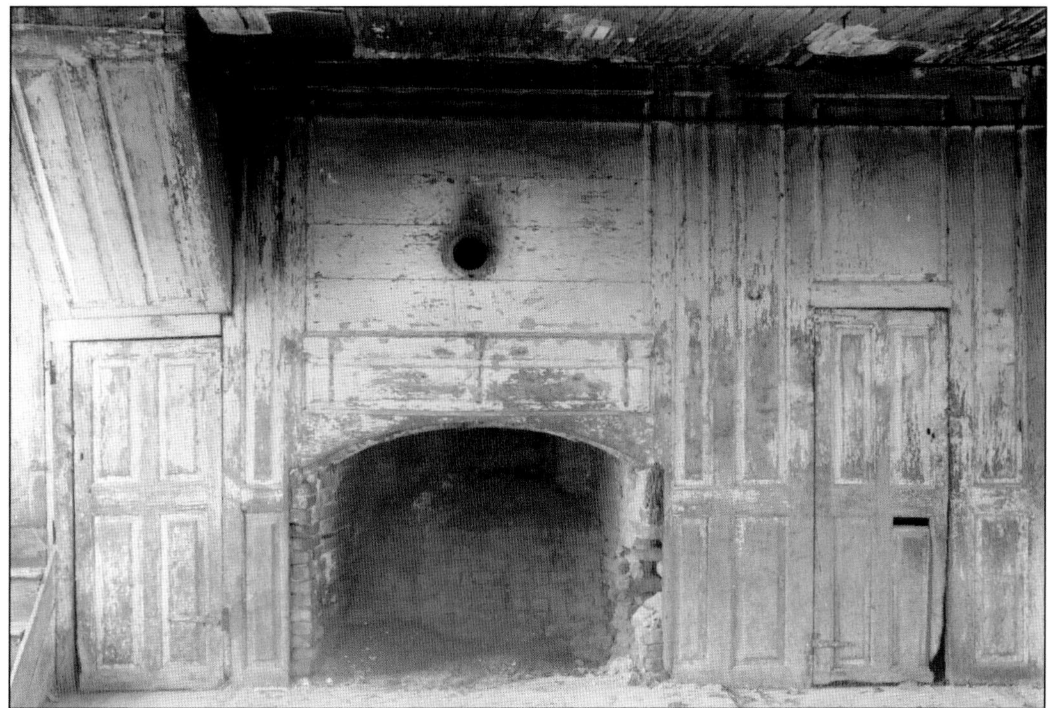

Though much neglected by 1940 when this photograph was taken, Resurrection Manor exhibited significant interior detailing, such as this wood paneling around the fireplace. Unfortunately, by the late 1990s, the home had significantly deteriorated, and in 2002, it was torn down by recent landowners who built a new house on the site. (Thomas T. Waterman, HABS.)

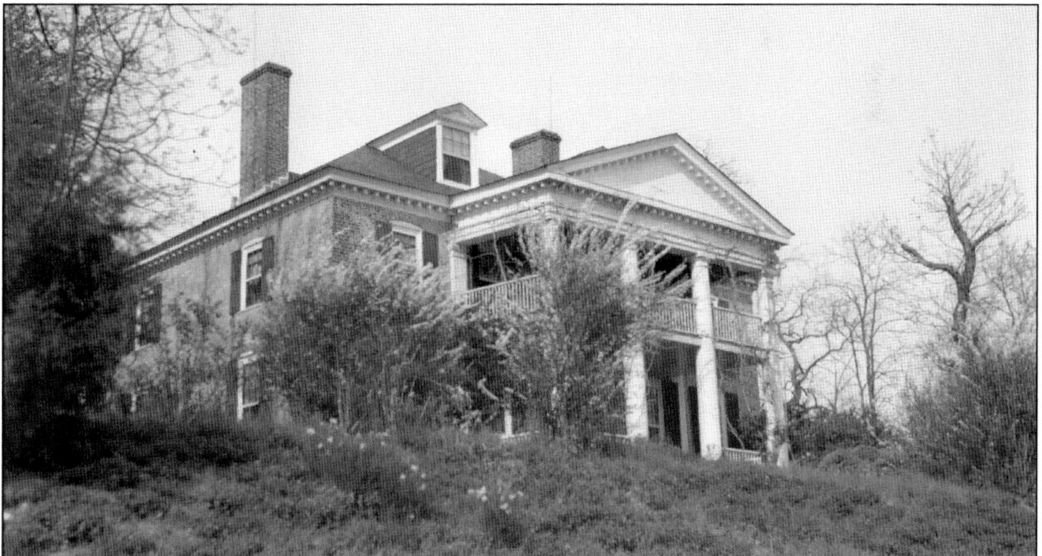

Built by prosperous planter John Attaway Clarke around 1767, Mulberry Fields west of Valley Lee is an impressive five-bay, two-and-a-half-story Georgian hip-roofed mansion that has a one-mile cedar tree allée that stretches from this view to the Potomac River. The home remained in the Clarke and related Somerville family until 1822. A subsequent owner, Thomas Loker, added the two-story Doric portico after his purchase in 1832. (Thomas T. Waterman, HABS.)

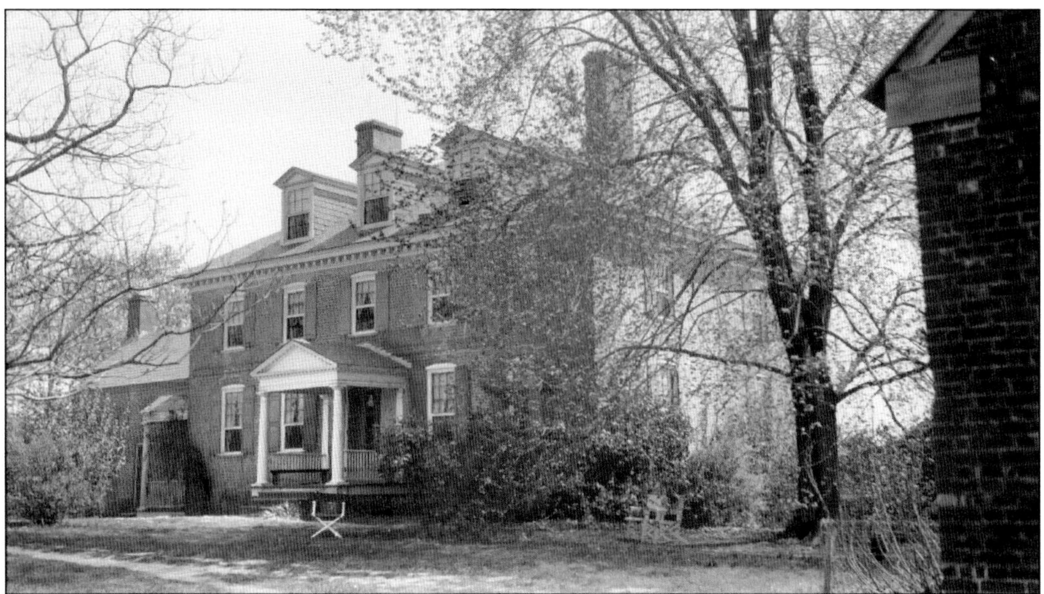

Mulberry Fields' most famous resident was John Attaway Clarke's great-nephew William Clarke Somerville (1790–1826), who was an Army major during the War of 1812. Somerville traveled to Europe, where he befriended Lord Byron and the Duke of Wellington. Pres. John Quincy Adams appointed him as minister to Sweden, but he became ill while traveling and died. Somerville was buried at the Marquis de Lafayette's estate in Courpalay, France. (Frederick D. Nichols, HABS.)

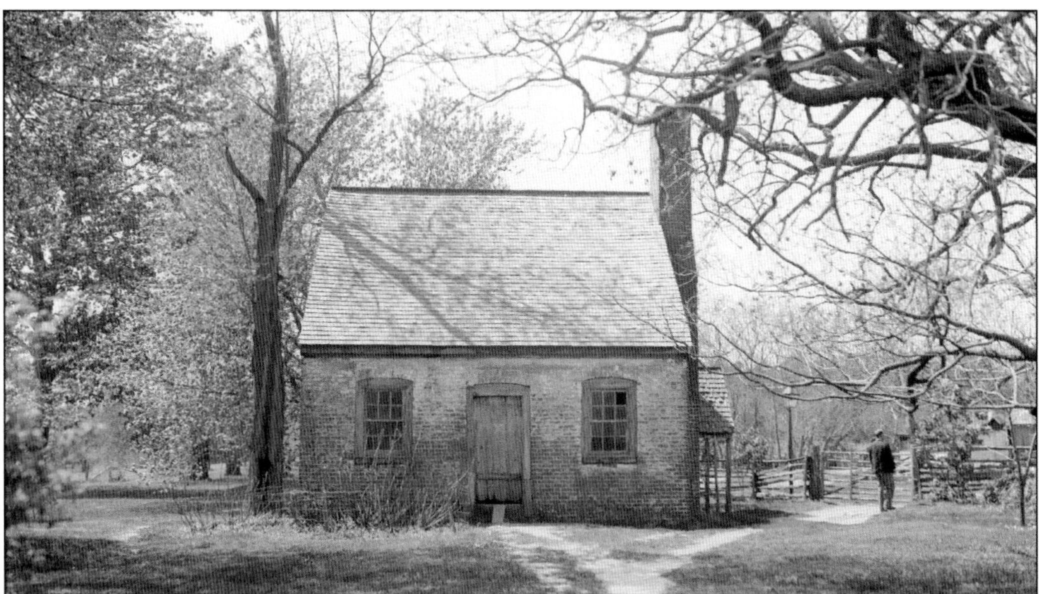

The prosperity of the owners of Mulberry Fields allowed them to afford well-constructed outbuildings on the estate. Built around 1801 (as dated on interior plaster work), this weaving house replaced an earlier frame structure but also functioned as a storehouse and smokehouse. (Frederick D. Nichols, HABS.)

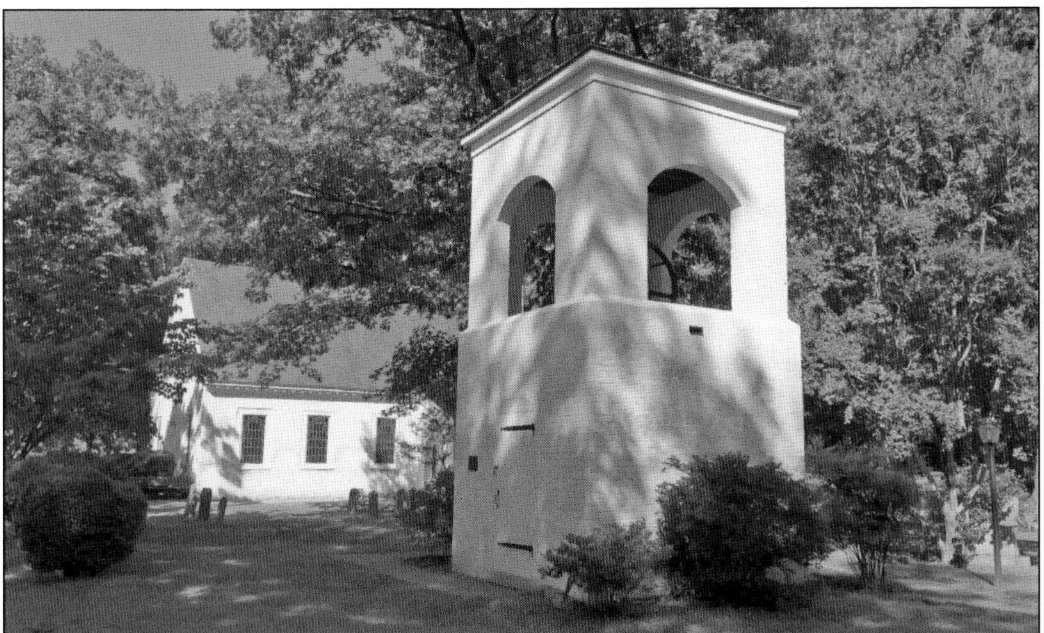

Located in William and Mary Parish (established in 1638), St. George's Episcopal Church in Valley Lee is the fourth church to be built here and is the oldest continuous Episcopal parish in Maryland. It is a one-story, gable-front rectangular brick structure built in 1799, with a separate bell tower in the churchyard. The interior was altered in 1830, 1884, and again in 1958, but the pews appear to be original.

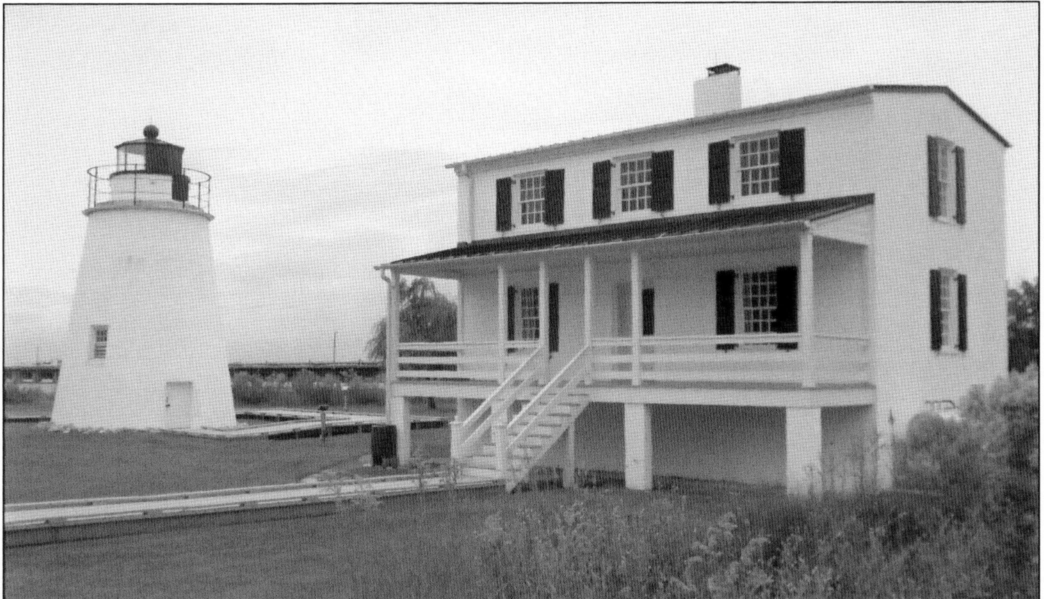

In 1836, John Donahoo erected the brick Piney Point Lighthouse on land purchased by the federal government on Christmas Eve 1835. It was the first lighthouse built entirely on the Potomac River, replacing a lightship in service there since 1821. Donahoo established the raised brick keeper's quarters as a single story, but a second story was added in 1884. Discontinued as a light in 1964, it is now a park.

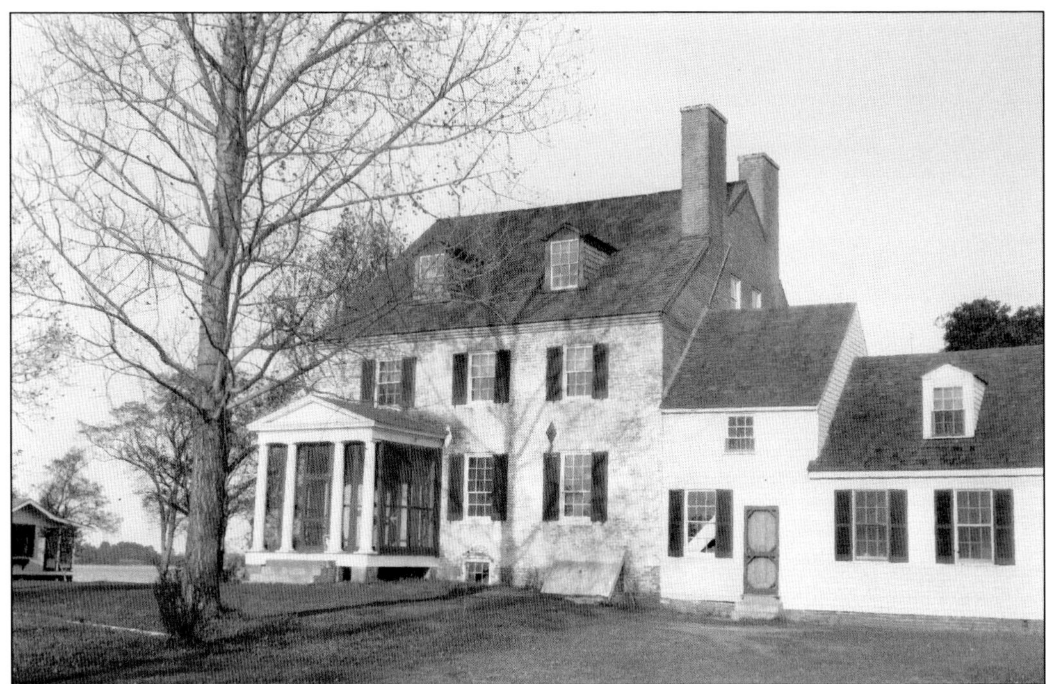

Rebuilt in 1835 following a fire in the 1818 home, Cherryfields is a two-and-a-half-story telescoping brick house with frame additions. Col. William Coad, a Maryland delegate who donated a cannon from the *Ark* and the *Dove* to the Annapolis statehouse in 1840, rebuilt the Federal-style structure on the west bank of the St. Mary's River, south of Drayden and opposite of St. Inigoes. (Delos H. Smith, HABS.)

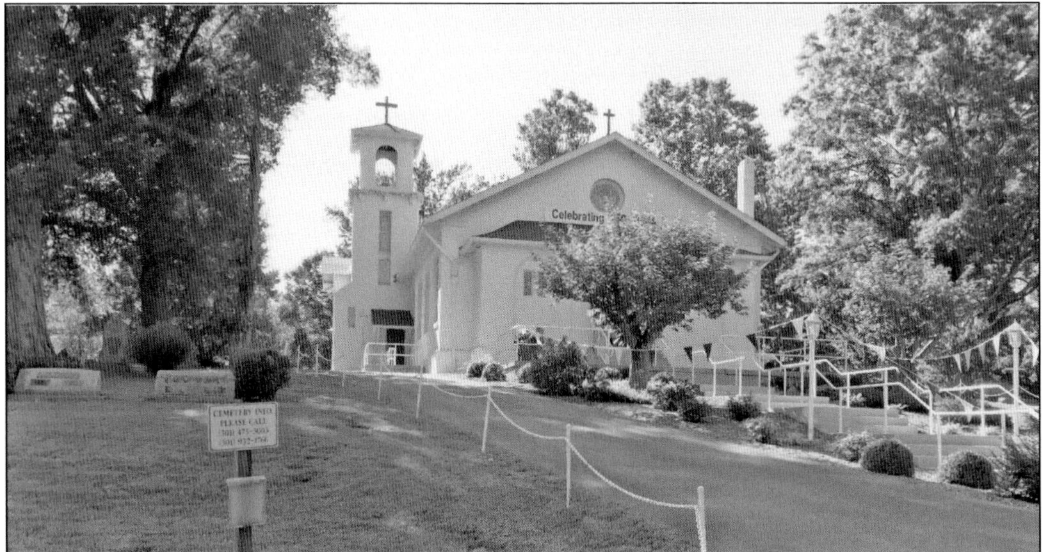

In 1765, Jesuit superior Fr. George Hunter purchased a two-acre parcel with a private chapel called St. Barnard's from the Gough family in Beauvue, near Leonardtown. A brick chapel replaced it in 1831, followed by the current hollow-tile block and concrete church of Our Lady's Chapel, built from 1910 to 1911. Designed by renowned Washington architect Leon Emil Dessez, it is a rare local example of the Spanish Mission style.

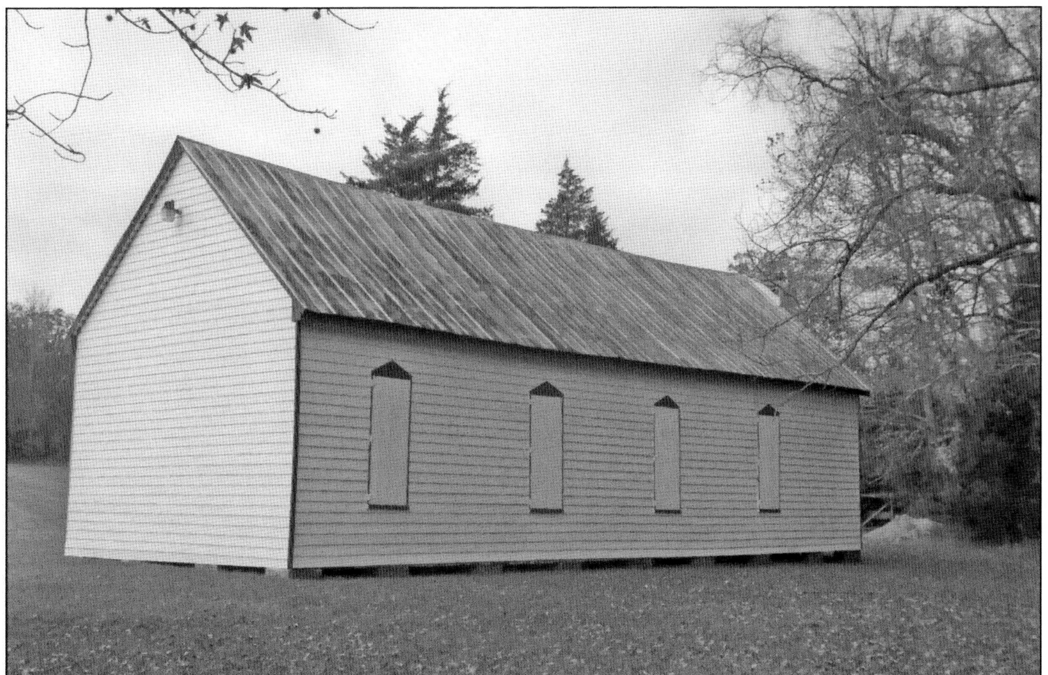

Mill owner John T. Cecil donated land for the construction of the original Holy Face Catholic Church. Built by Fr. Pye Neal in 1887, the single-story frame church was four bays long with weatherboard siding and a steeple, now missing. The building suffered from years of neglect after the new Holy Face church was built in 1940. Now stabilized, it is a contributing structure of the Cecil's Mill Historic District in Great Mills.

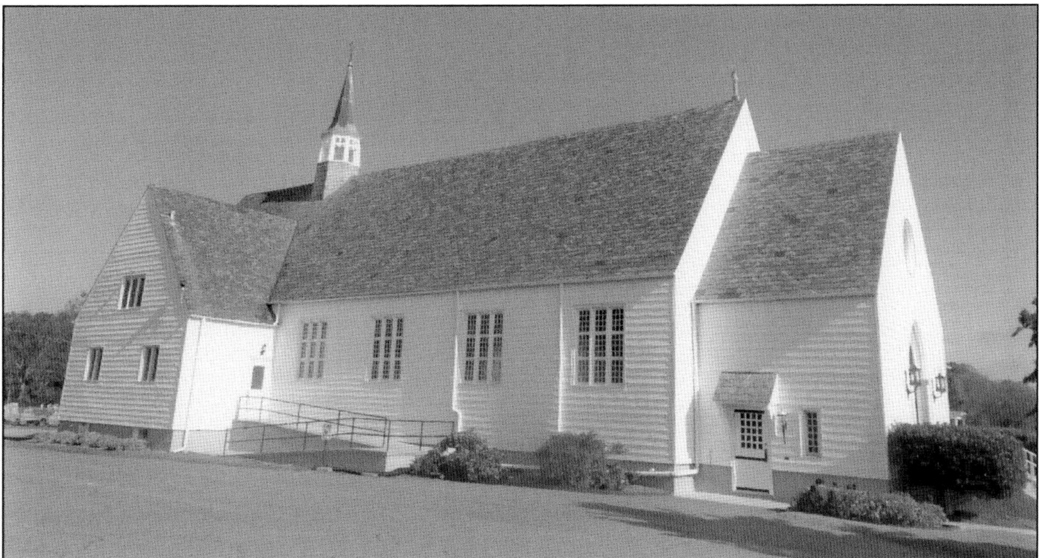

Realizing the original Holy Face church was too small, the parish contracted Baltimore architect Lucien E.D. Gaudreau, who consulted with architect and Catholic convert Philip Frohman, known for the Episcopal National Cathedral in Washington, and local builder Benjamin Unkle for its construction. Built of wood on a medieval English cruciform plan, the church was dedicated by Michael J. Curley, the first archbishop of Washington.

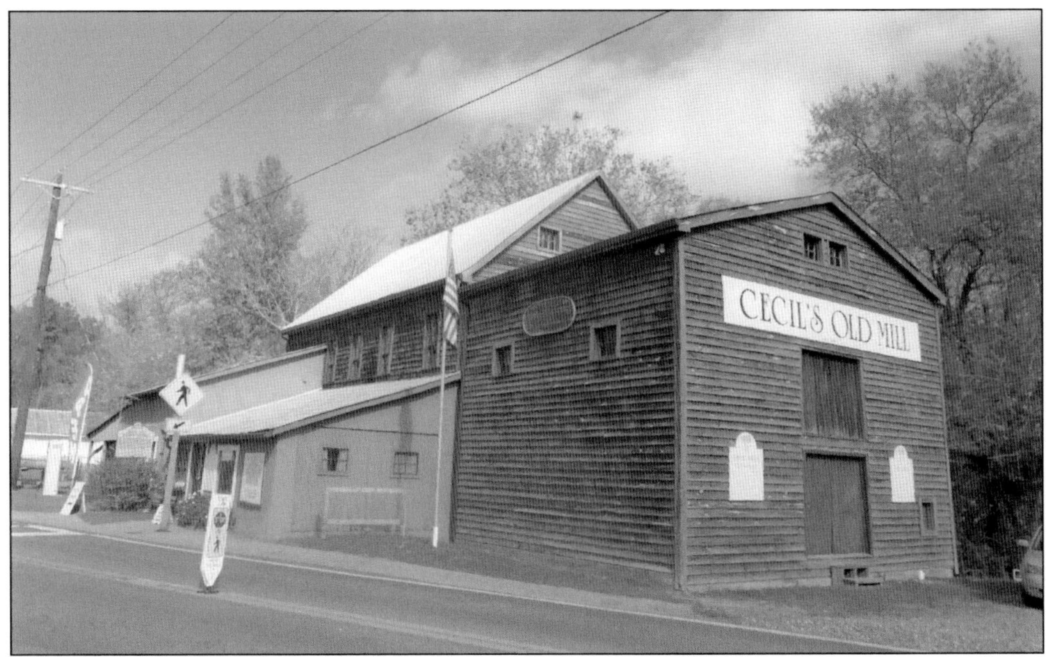

The Clifton Factory was originally built in 1812 as a water-powered textile mill to promote cotton farming in the area. John T. Cecil rebuilt the two-and-a-half-story frame structure as a flour mill in 1900. The mill remained in operation until 1959, when a member of the Cecil family was killed from a piece of mill gear that broke off and struck him.

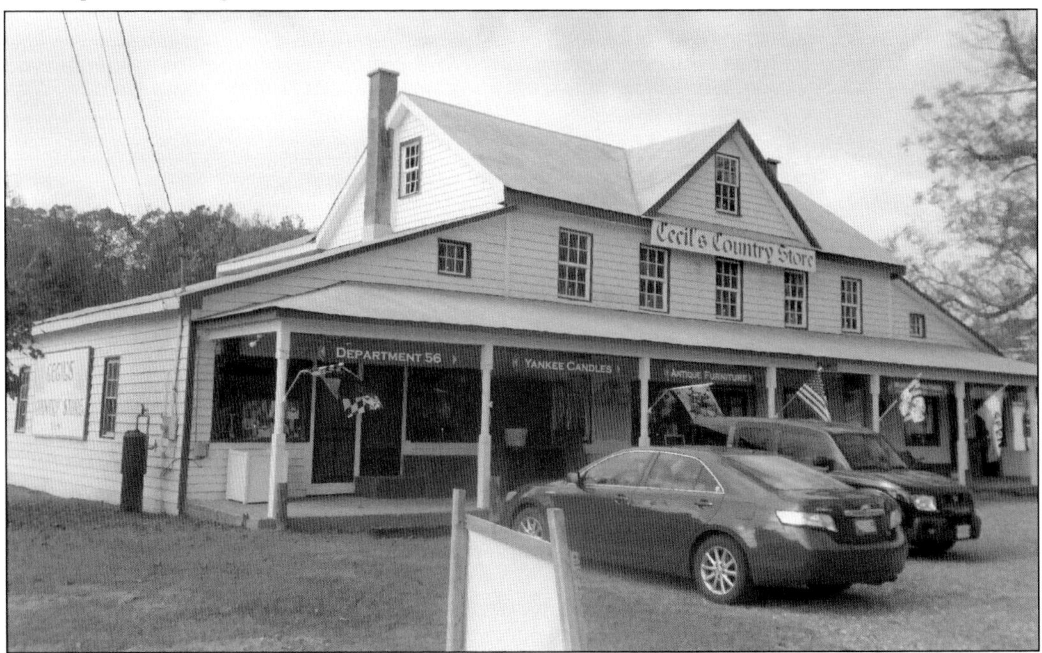

Cecil's Store, part of the Cecil's Mill Historic District, is a five-bay-wide, two-and-a-half-story frame structure with flanking gable-end shed additions and a porch that runs the length of the front elevation. Built in the 1920s and still functioning as a store, the building is a well-preserved example of a rural store in Southern Maryland.

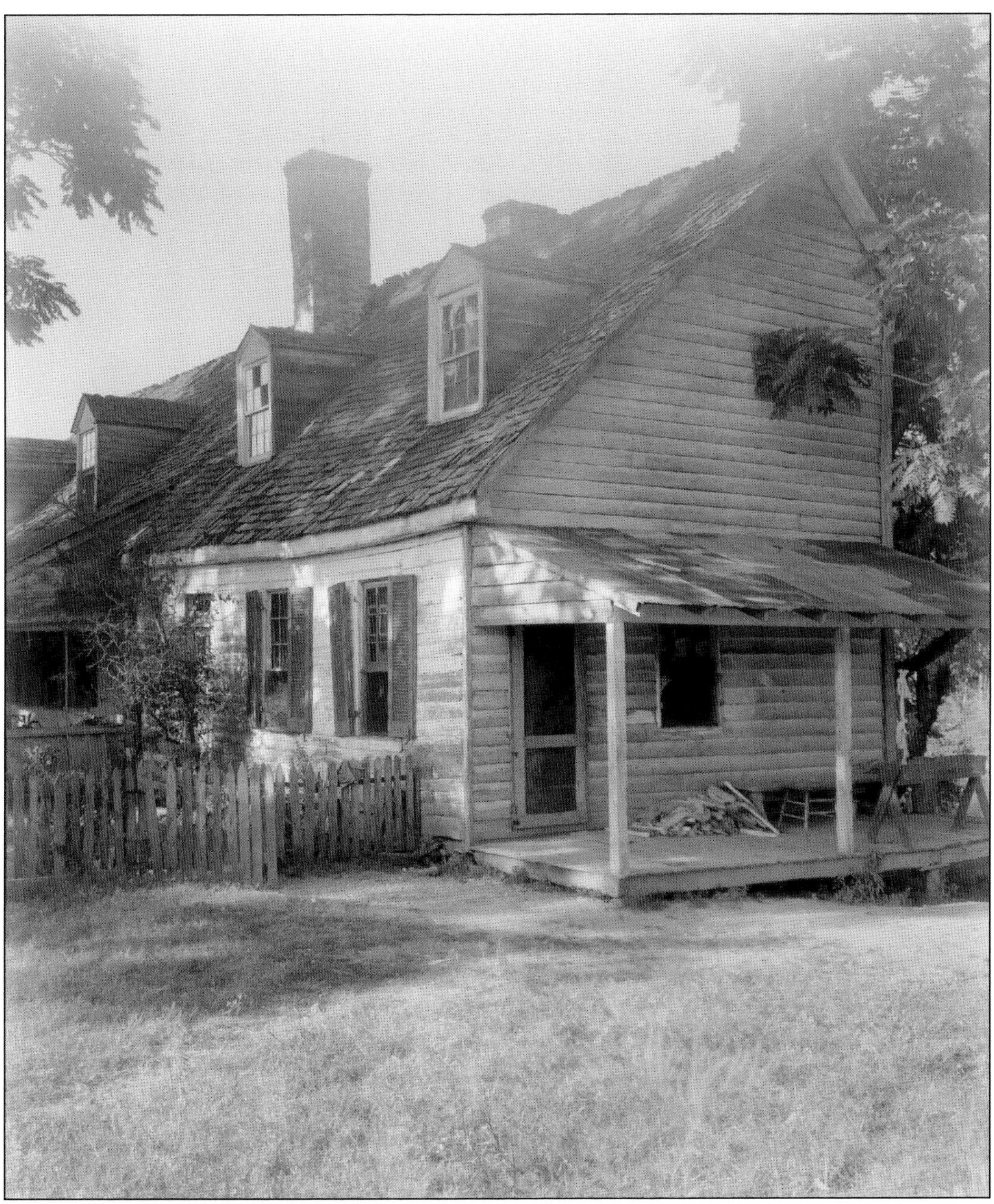

Mistaken by architectural historian Henry Chandlee Forman as Wolseley Manor, the Great Mills Farmhouse was built between 1779 and 1798 by Dr. Barton Tabbs, who was a surgeon's mate under Gen. William Smallwood during the American Revolution. It is significant as the site of Dr. Tabbs's Great Mills Medical College, one of the first places in Maryland to teach medicine. Still standing in 1936, it is now a ruin. (FBJPC, HABS.)

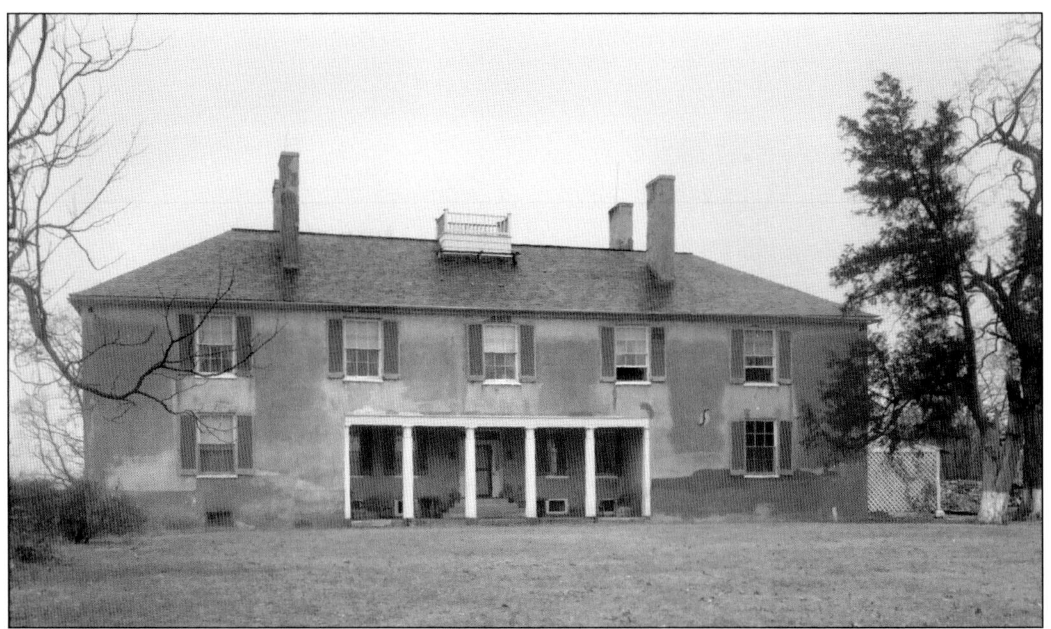

First built by Maj. Abraham Barnes around 1756, Tudor Hall in Leonardtown has undergone several extensive alterations. In 1798, it was a one-and-a-half-story, wood-frame central block with flanking one-story brick wings. Purchased after 1804 by Philip Key, uncle to national anthem author Francis Scott Key, the building was remodeled by Philip's son Henry, who added the second story and its distinctive recessed loggia on the south elevation in 1818. (E.H. Pickering, HABS.)

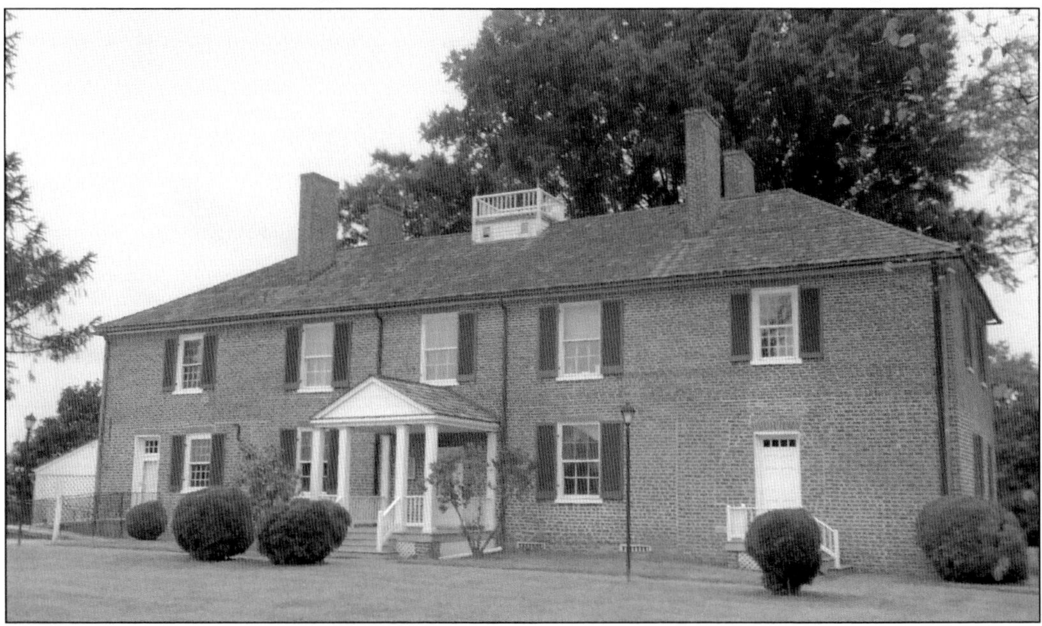

Once the centerpiece of a 1,096-acre estate, Tudor Hall was kept by the Key family heirs until 1947. When a real estate development company threatened to demolish the building in 1950, renowned Washington architect Gertrude Sawyer (1895–1996) was hired to restore it. Sawyer removed the stucco that had been in place since Henry Key's 1818 renovation, and the building was repurposed as a memorial library dedicated to local military veterans.

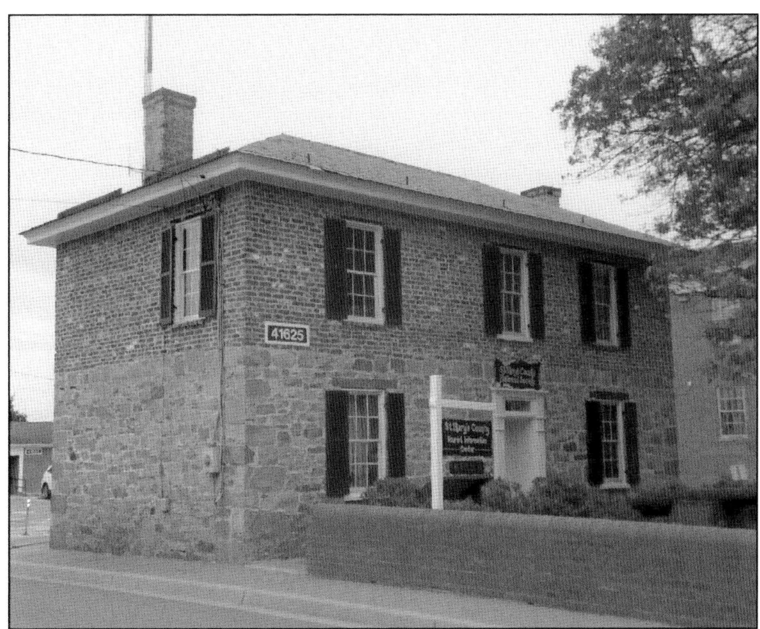

Now the headquarters of the St. Mary's County Historical Society, the old St. Mary's County Jail was built in 1876 on the foundation of a previous jail from 1858. The ground floor, where the jailer's family lived, was constructed with granite blocks, and the second floor, which housed the prisoners, was composed of bricks reused from a dismantled local harness shop.

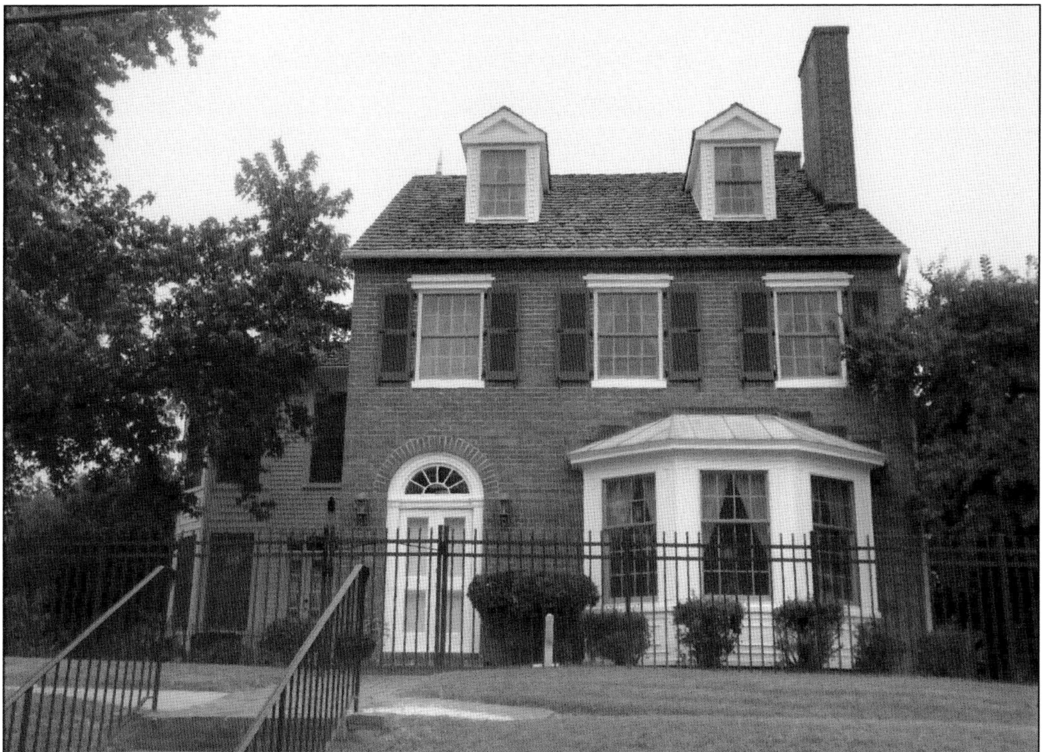

The second-oldest structure in Leonardtown is the Spalding-Camalier House, built for Dr. Andrew Jackson Spalding in 1835. Erected as a three-bay, side-hall town house, it is two and a half stories tall with two later wood additions. The home was purchased by attorney John Alexander Camalier, who successfully petitioned for a presidential pardon in 1865, overturning the conviction of Congressman Benjamin Gwinn Harris of Leonardtown for "harboring" Confederate parolees.

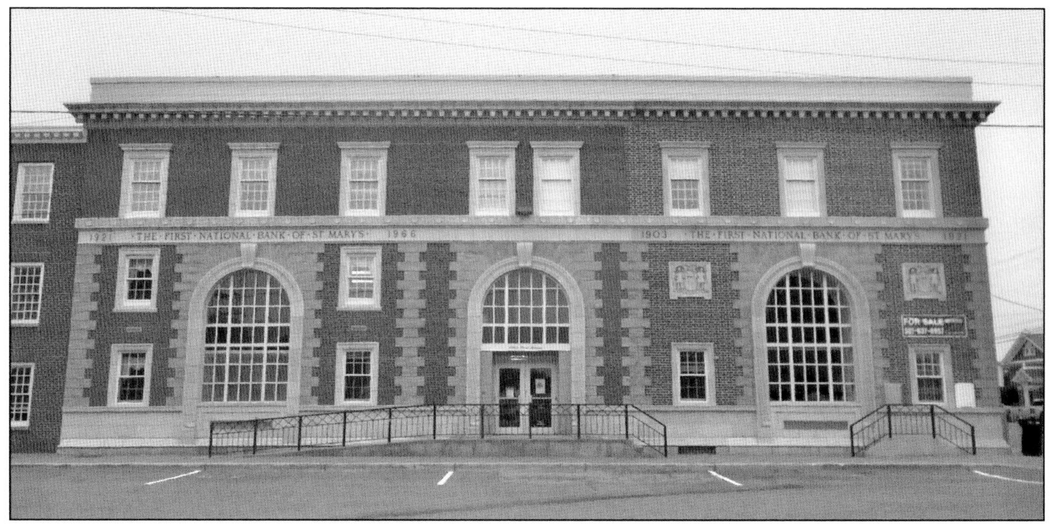

Designed in the Classical Revival style by Baltimore architect Robert L. Harris in 1921, the First National Bank of St. Mary's was constructed by Frainie Brothers & Haigley, also of Baltimore. Built of brick and decorative terra-cotta, the three-story bank quickly achieved its place among the most prominent commercial structures in Leonardtown. A 1966 expansion was gracefully achieved through the use of like materials and design motifs.

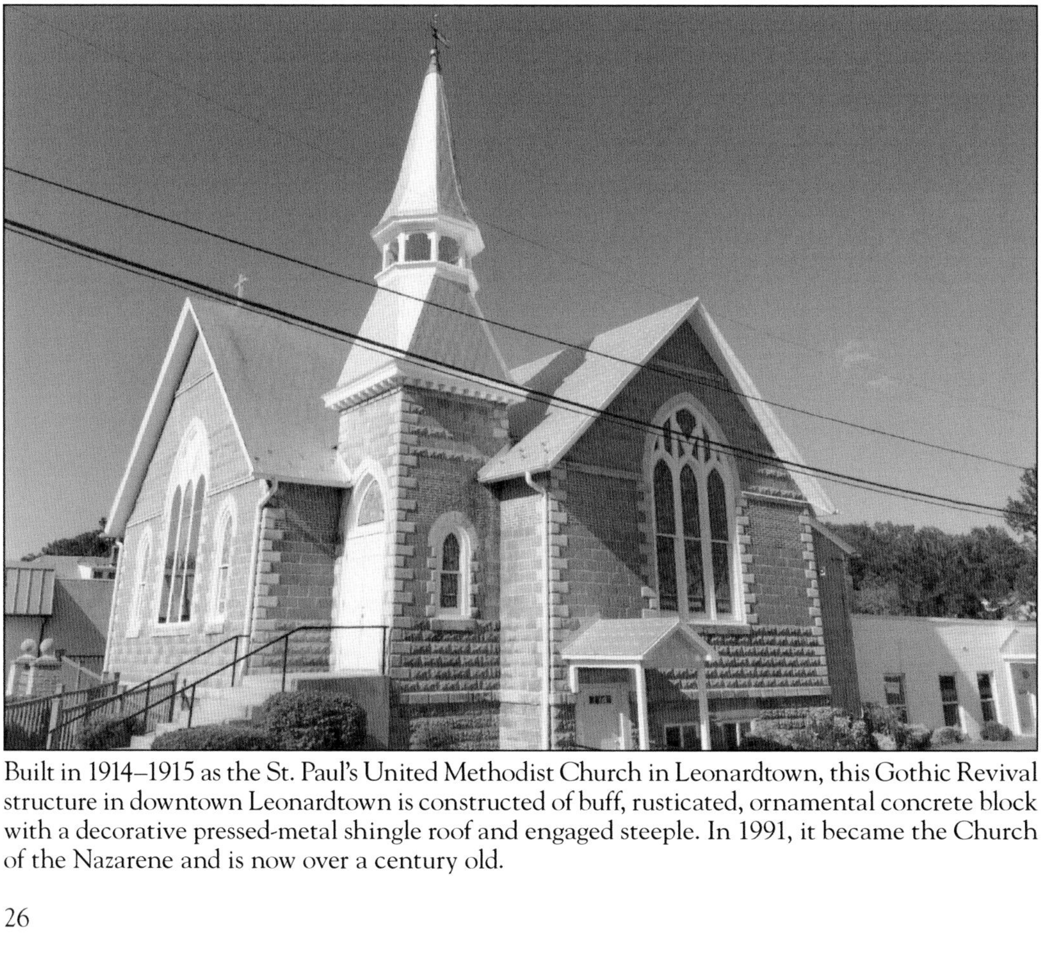

Built in 1914–1915 as the St. Paul's United Methodist Church in Leonardtown, this Gothic Revival structure in downtown Leonardtown is constructed of buff, rusticated, ornamental concrete block with a decorative pressed-metal shingle roof and engaged steeple. In 1991, it became the Church of the Nazarene and is now over a century old.

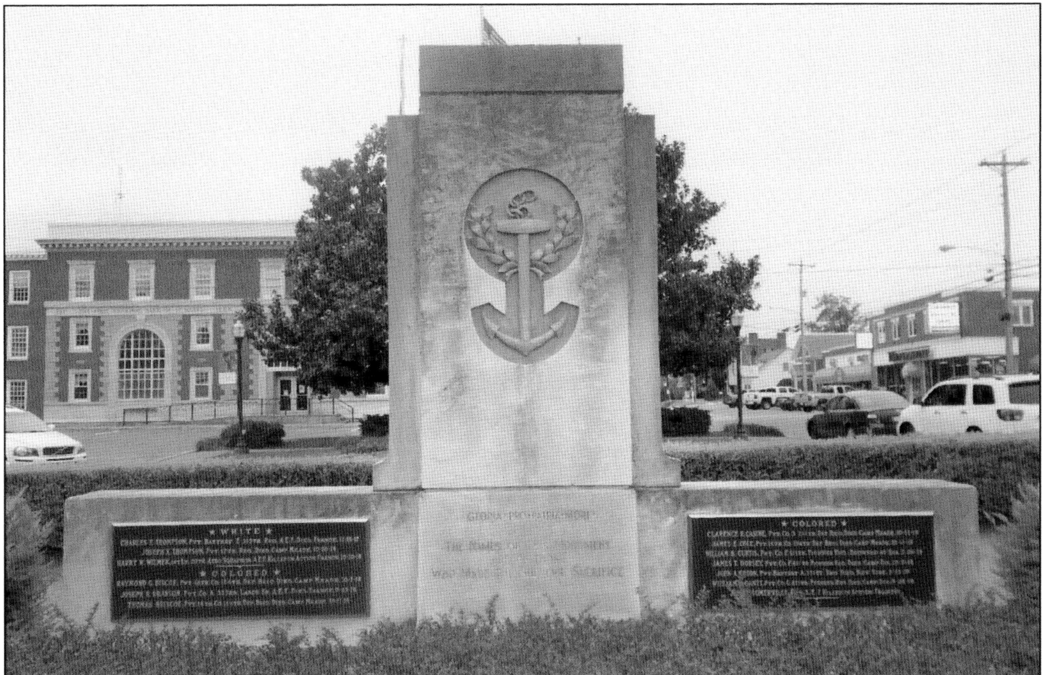

Dedicated on the anniversary of Armistice Day in November 1921, the St. Mary's County World War I Memorial occupies a central location in the square of downtown Leonardtown. The monument honors 27 white and black servicemen from St. Mary's County who died during World War I.

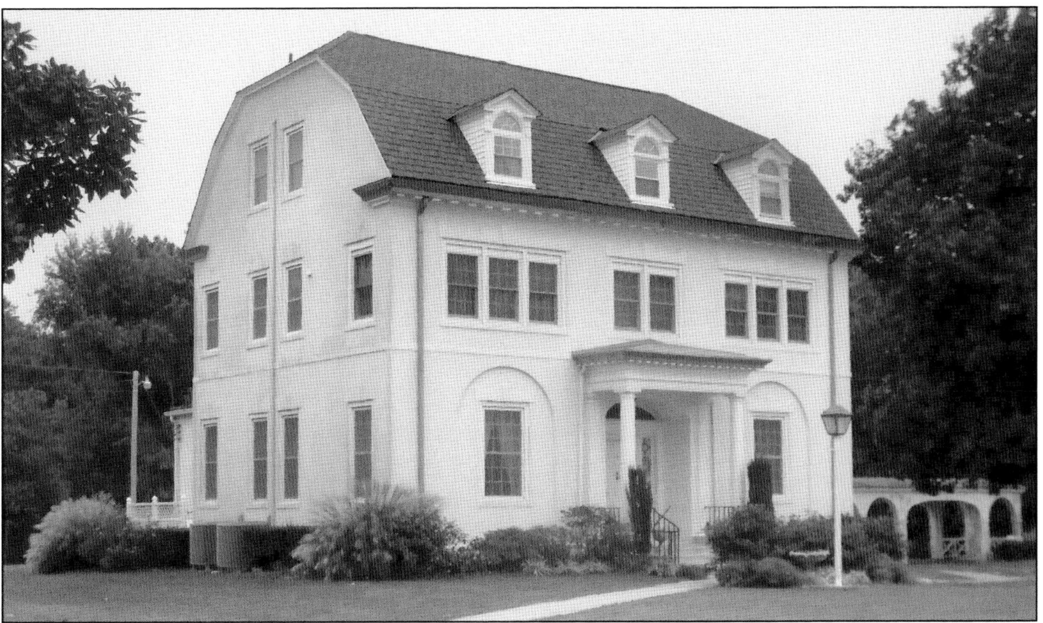

In 1766, Rev. James Walton, an English Jesuit, established the St. Aloysius Catholic Church. The rectory was built in 1920 and retains a high degree of architectural integrity. The two-and-a-half-story Colonial Revival residence is made of stuccoed brick with a clipped-gable gambrel roof of slate tiles. A mile north of the rectory and present church, the parish cemetery has remained in use since the 18th century.

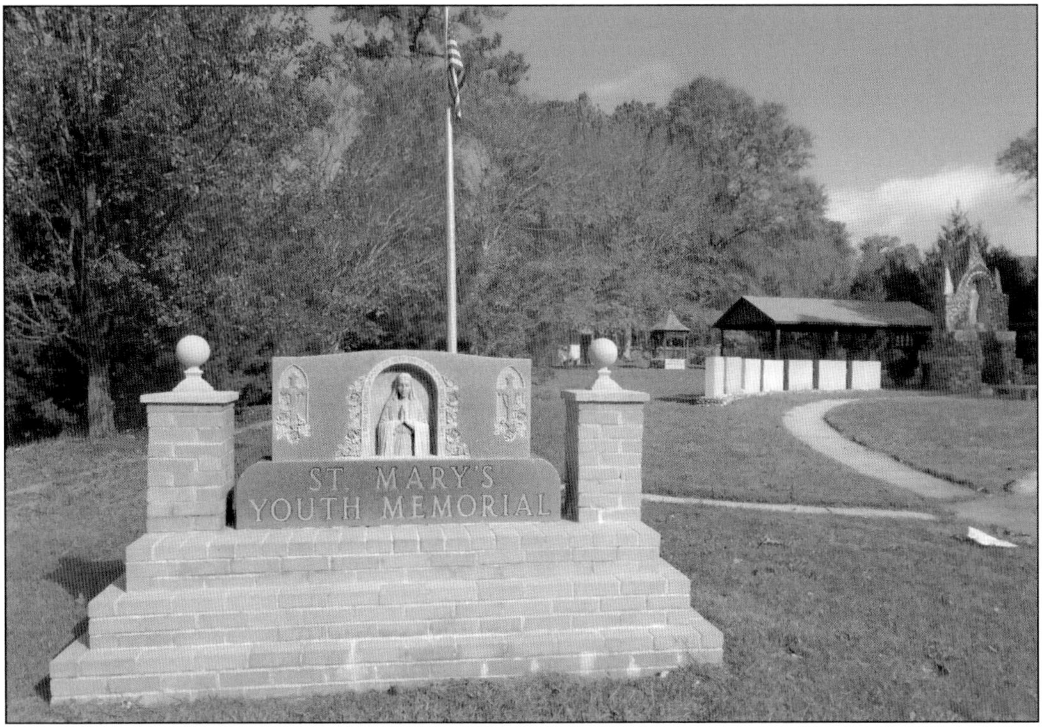

The St. Mary's Youth Memorial was first constructed in 1902 on the campus of St. Mary's Academy (now St. Mary's Ryken High School), located south of Leonardtown, to commemorate the lives of local children killed in tragic circumstances. It consists of a stone grotto dedicated to Our Lady of Lourdes with inscribed granite markers. In 1985, a mass pavilion was established at its present location in Great Mills.

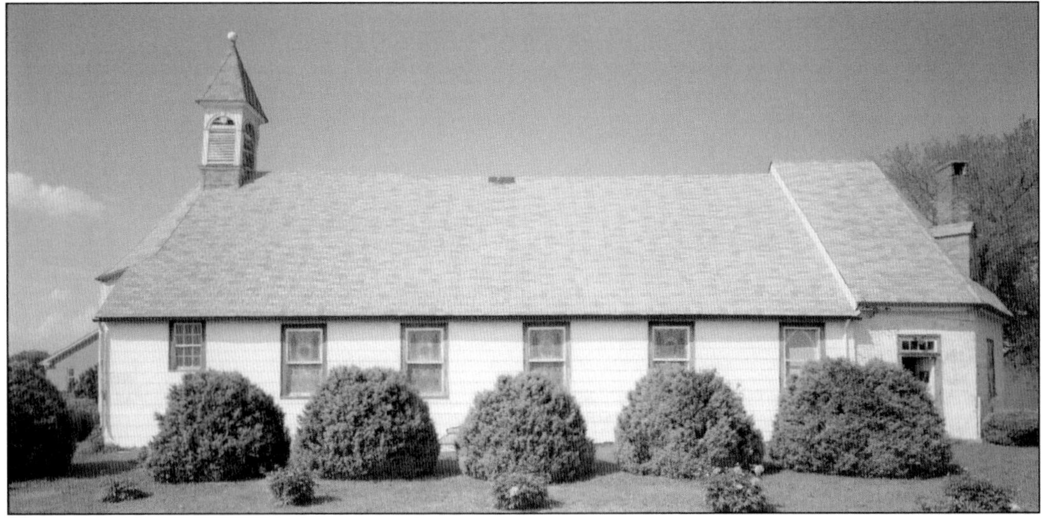

Established as a Jesuit mission south of Compton in 1649, St. Francis Xavier Catholic Church was built about 1731 on land acquired by the order in 1668. An earlier church, built about 1662, once existed at the site of the parish cemetery, less than a half-mile north. The church has a six-bay, wood-frame central block with two octagonal ends—a vestibule (1767) and a sacristy (1816). (Jet Lowe, HABS.)

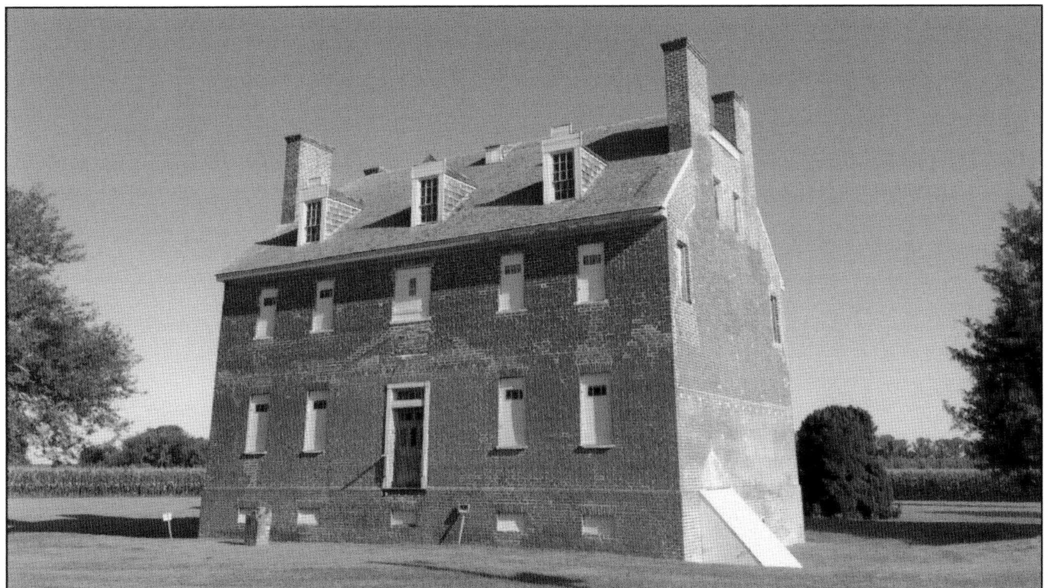

Once part of the Jesuit's 700-acre farm at Newtown Manor, this two-and-a-half-story brick manor house, built around 1789, stands a short distance south of St. Francis Xavier Catholic Church, one of the oldest English Catholic parishes in the United States. The roof of the home was changed from a gambrel to a clipped-gable or jerkinhead form in 1816. Unoccupied for years, it now requires extensive renovation.

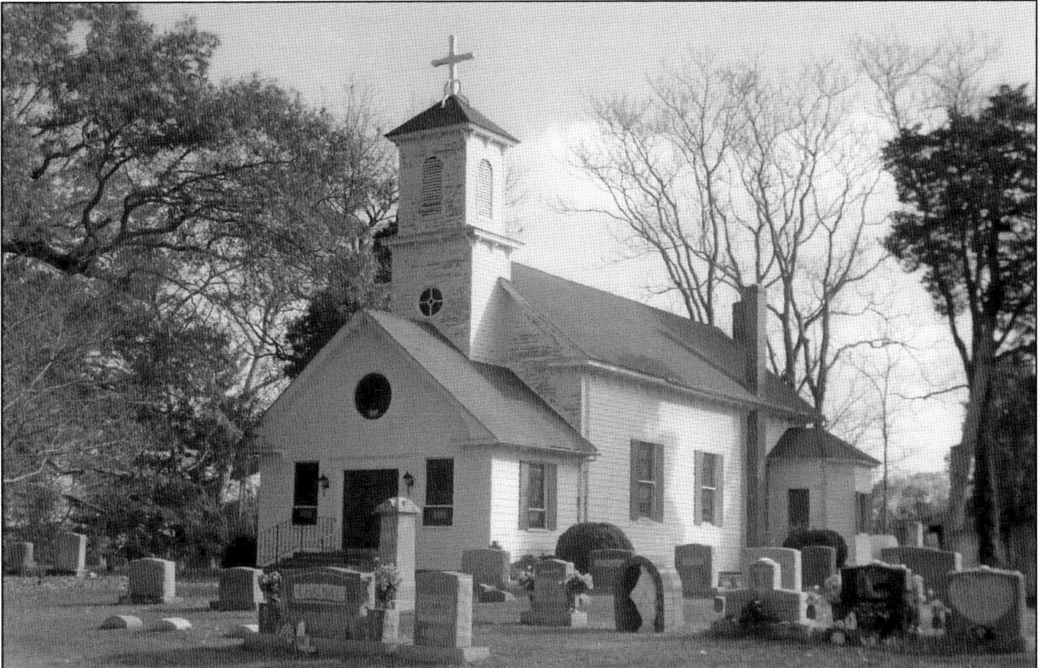

As part of a parish established in 1642, the All Saints Episcopal Church in Oakley is the second church to stand on this site. Constructed in 1846, this small wood-frame church is three bays deep and three bays wide with a frame bell tower at the west entrance. It is the oldest frame Episcopal church in the county.

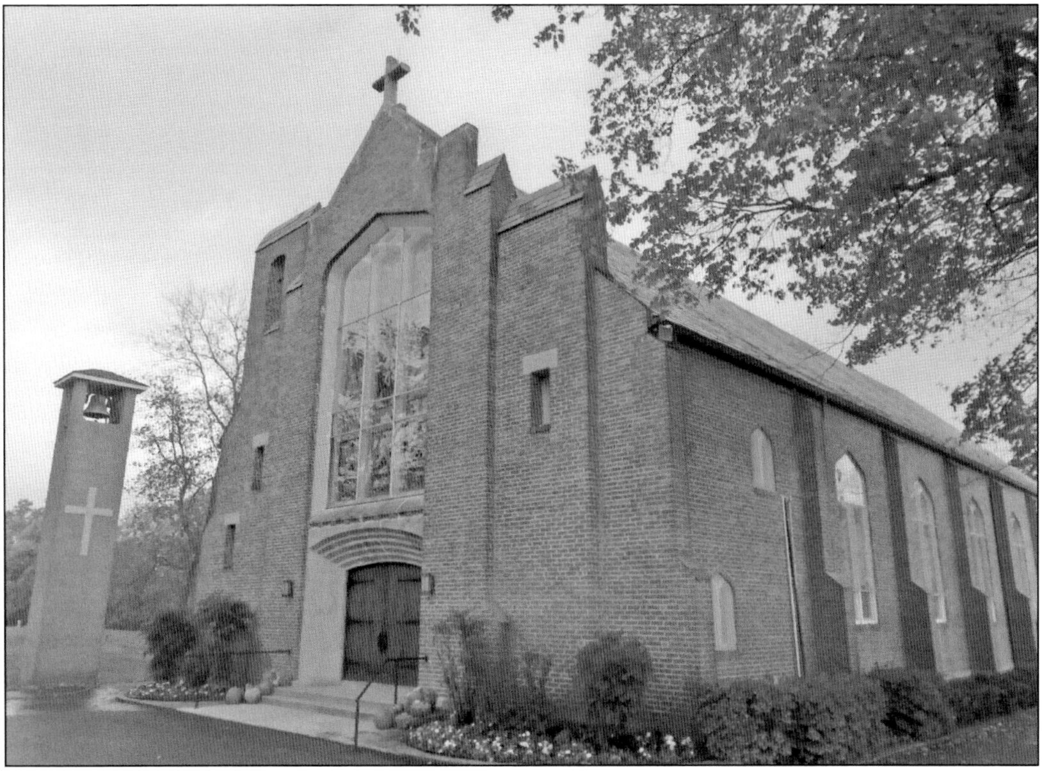

A Catholic chapel and cemetery was first established in Bushwood on the property of Capt. George Slye in 1755. The original chapel was replaced by a frame church built on its foundation in 1892. Following a lightning strike that burned the wooden church in April 1944, the brick Gothic Revival Sacred Heart Catholic Church was designed by Washington architect John M. Walton and completed in 1945.

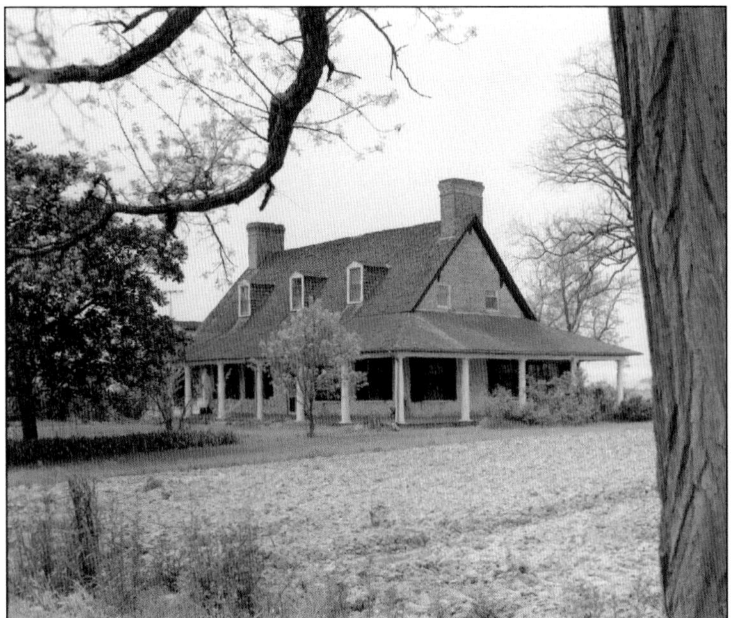

Around 1670, Robert Slye, a wealthy merchant, judge, and assemblyman, began construction on the one-and-a-half-story brick Ocean Hall in Bushwood Manor, once part of Dr. Thomas Gerrard's 16,000-acre grant of St. Clement's Manor of 1639. The interior of Ocean Hall was significantly altered around 1725, followed by other modifications in the 19th century. The porches were added in the 1920s. (R. Randolph Langenbach, HABS.)

Constructed in the mid-18th century as a one-story, brick-ended, and weatherboard-sided home overlooking the mouth of Smith Creek at the Potomac River, Manning's Hold (also known as Smith Creek Farm) was expanded to two stories after 1845 by owner Dr. Sydney Evans. Its most notable feature is the massive end chimney with an exterior opening, once used as the fireplace for a demolished kitchen wing. (FBJPC, LOC.)

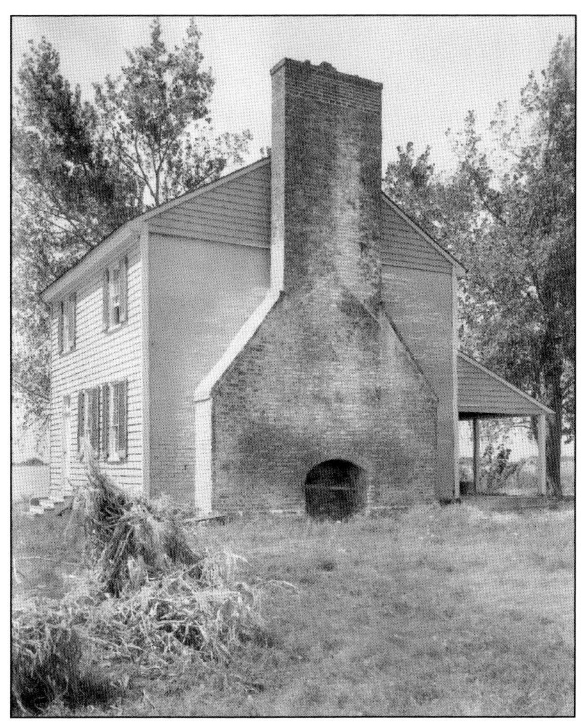

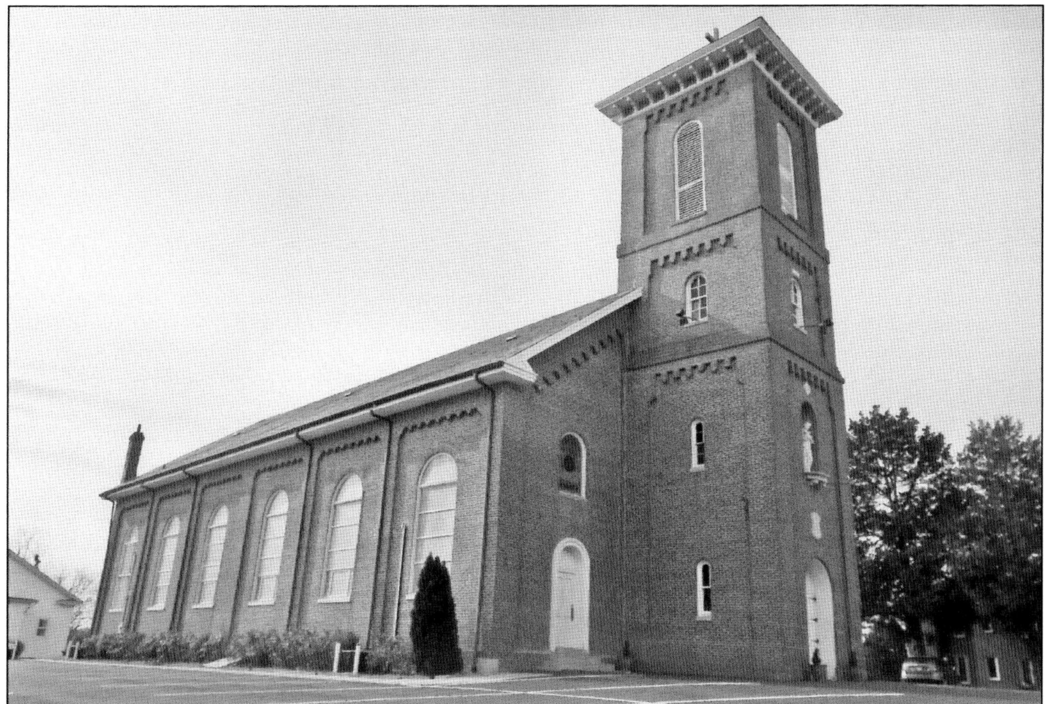

Built between 1858 and 1864 on land donated by the Morgan family, St. Joseph's Catholic Church in Morganza replaced an earlier frame church that was used from about 1759 until the completion of the present brick church. With arched windows and doorways set into recessed panels on all sides and a four-story bell tower, this is the only High Victorian Italianate structure in the county.

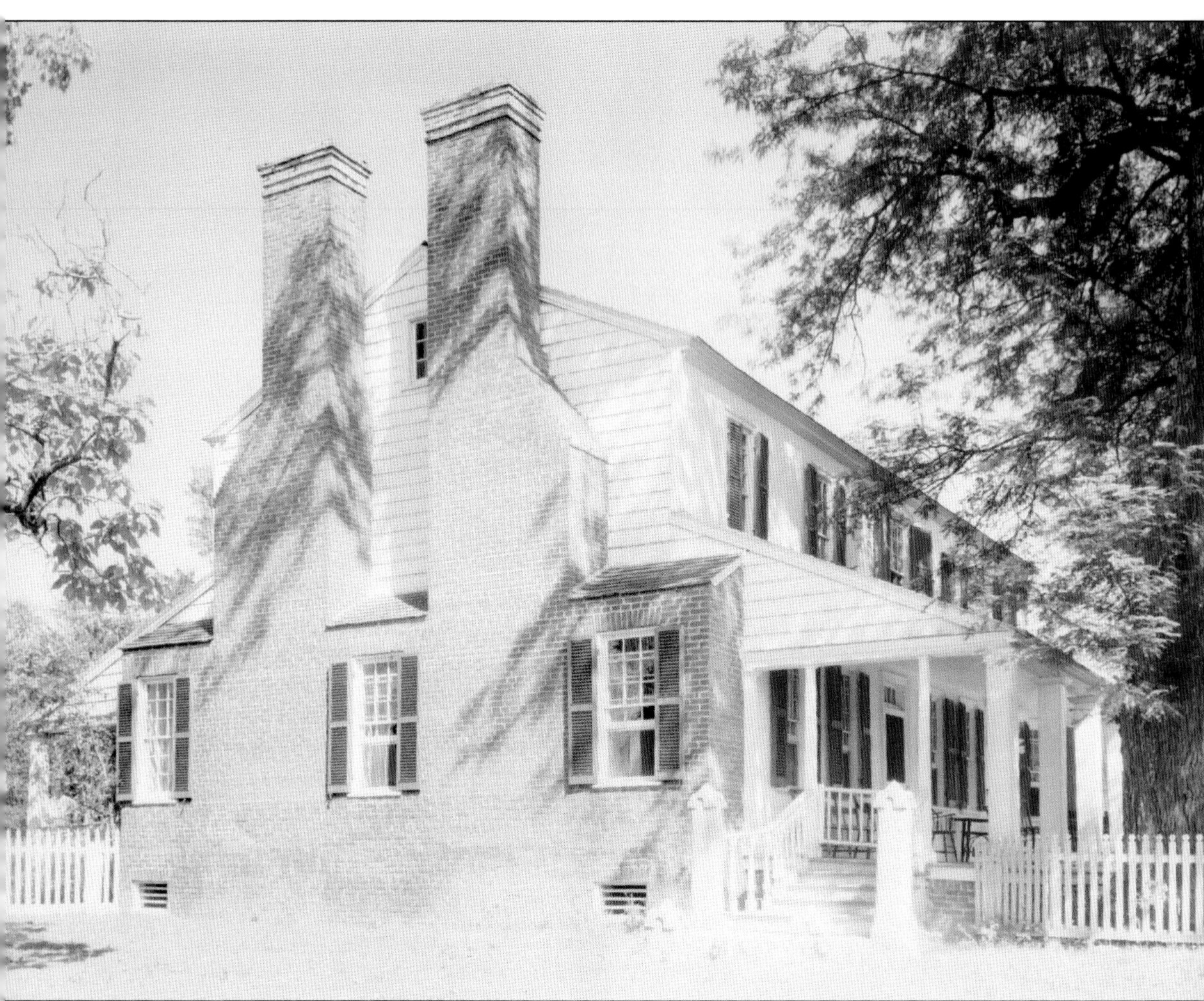

Deep Falls, a two-story frame structure with an attic, was constructed in 1745 on land granted to Thomas Thomas, a Welshman, in 1680 and called Wales. Its design shared a triple pent with windows and double end chimneys similar to nearby Southampton and thus is likely from the same master builder. Once the home of Gov. James Thomas (1785–1845), the property remains in the Thomas family. (FBJPC, LOC.)

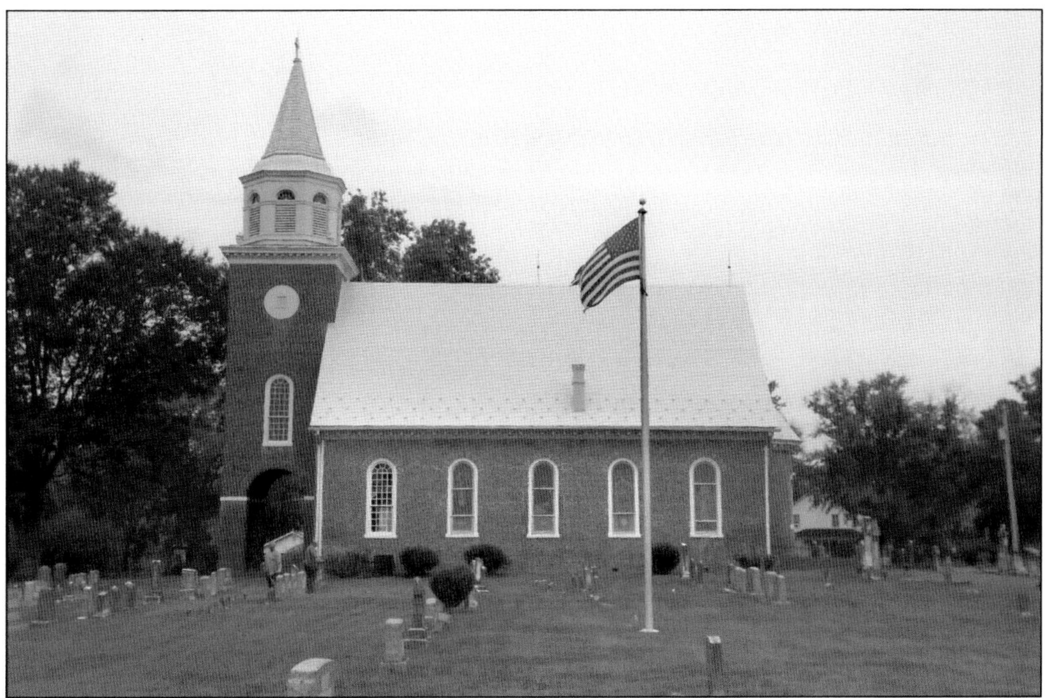

Built in the port of Chaptico in 1736, Christ Episcopal Church has a nave and side aisles, a semicircular rear apse, arched windows and doorways, and gabled ends. A bell tower was added to the entry in 1913. Damaged by British soldiers in July 1814, it required extensive renovations. An 18th-century marble baptismal font still stands inside, and the granite crypt of Francis Scott Key's grandfather, Philip Key, is outside.

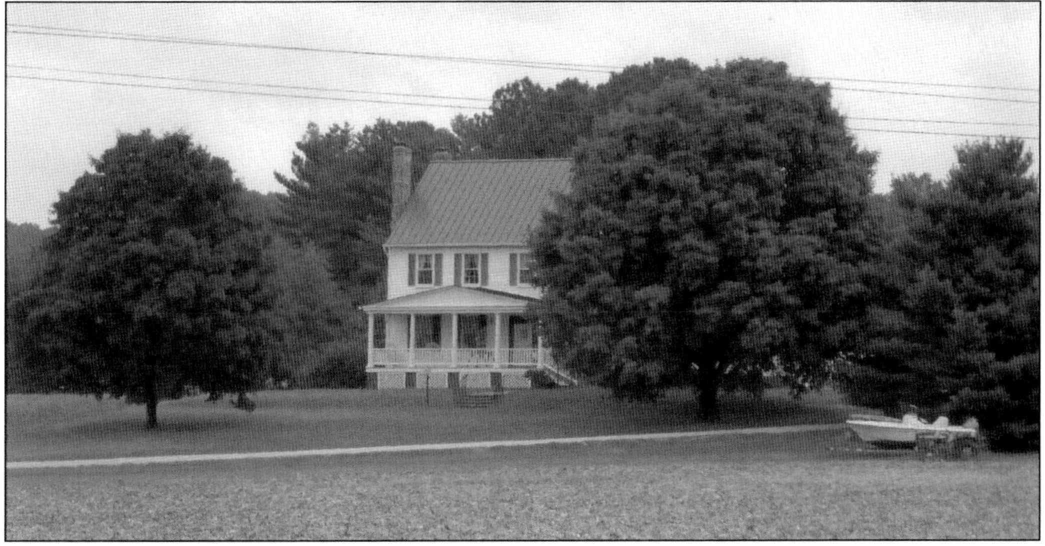

In 1849, Henry Green Garner built Locust Grove in the village of Chaptico on land that was once owned by Philip Key. Set on a raised basement, the two-and-a-half-story frame house replaced an earlier home of the same name from around 1820. Garner was a prosperous Chaptico merchant, the village postmaster, and a vestryman of the nearby Christ Episcopal Church, where he was buried.

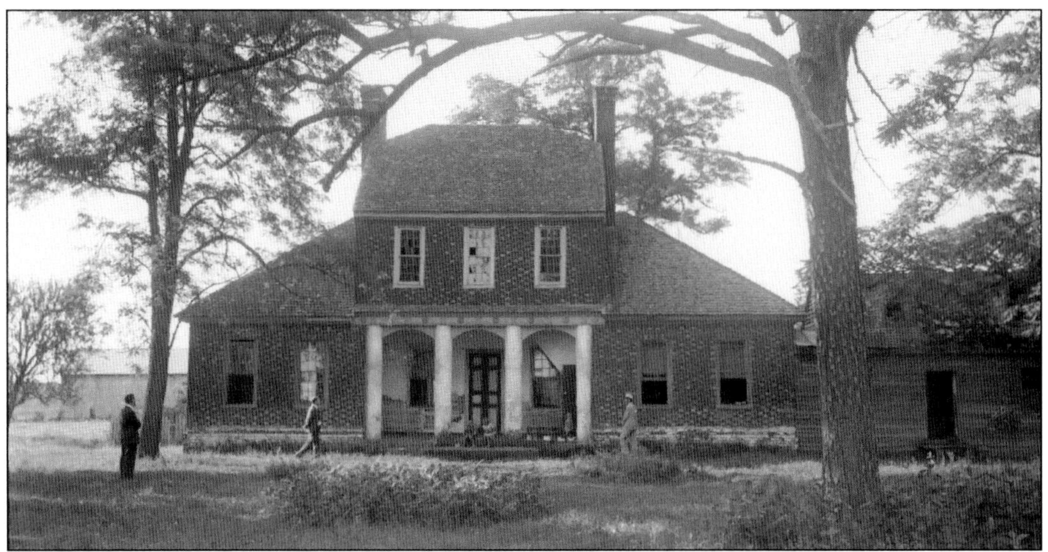

Built on a 1651 land grant to Dr. Thomas Gerrard, Bachelor's Hope has a unique design with no existing analogues; the destroyed Jesuit manor of St. Inigoes was the only similar structure. William Hammersley constructed the home in 1749 with a two-and-a-half-story brick great hall, which is fronted by a recessed columned loggia, topped by a jerkinhead roof, and flanked by a pair of one-story, two-room wings. (Thomas T. Waterman, HABS.)

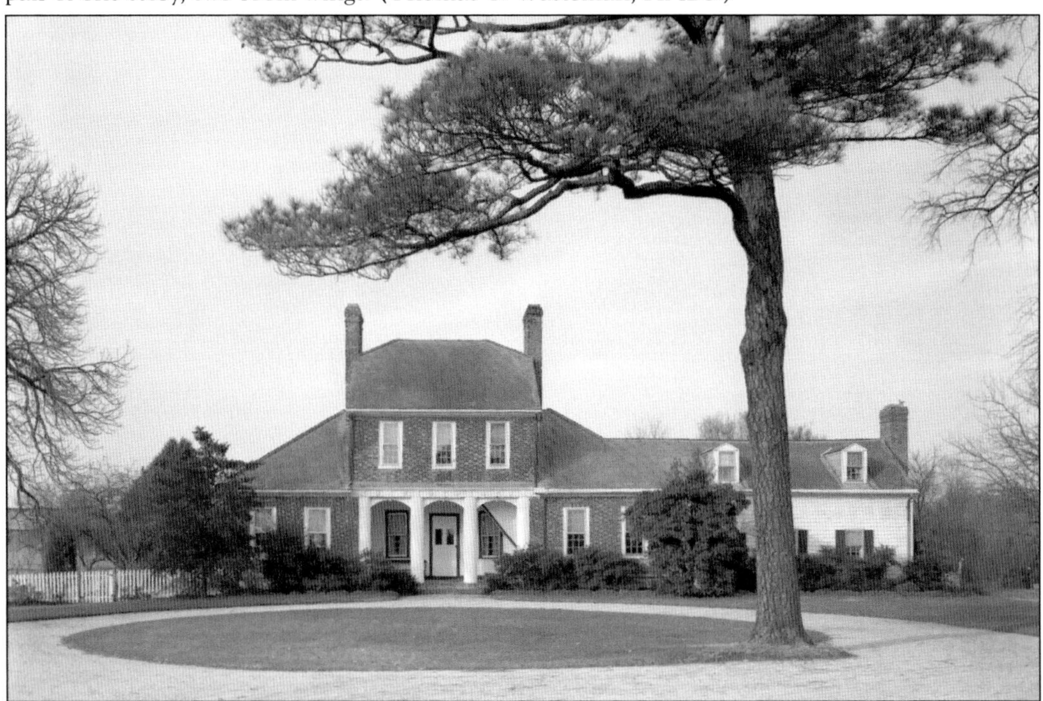

Bachelor's Hope was owned by a number of prominent local families from the 1660s to the 1930s. Acquired by the Turners in 1826, it remained in family ownership until it was sold to Col. Walter Linton Simpson, a retired Army engineer and federal official, and his wife, Elizabeth, in 1937. The Simpsons restored the house and deeded the property to the National Trust for Historic Preservation in 1975. (Frederick D. Nichols, HABS.)

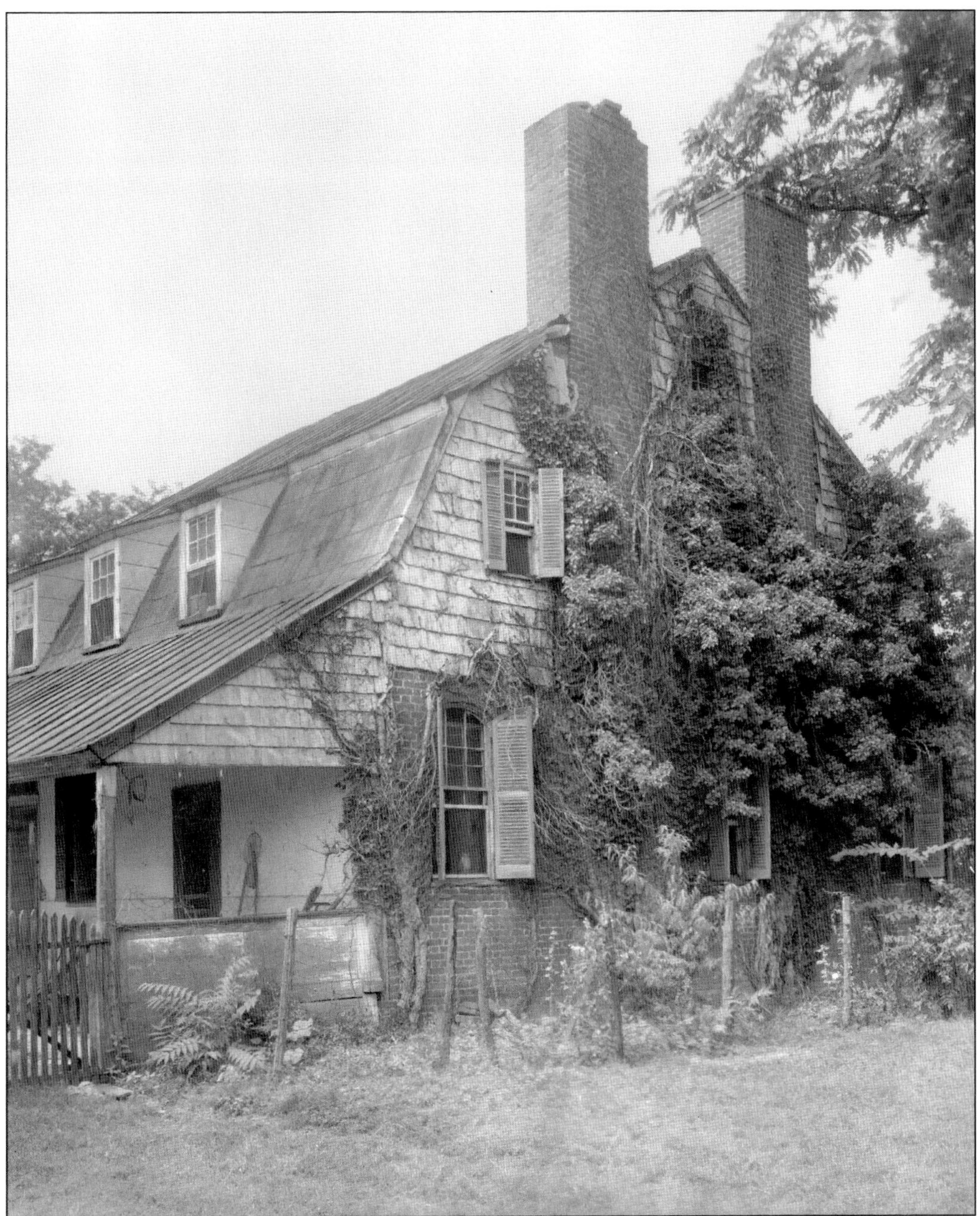

Built in the mid-18th century, Southampton was noted for its large brick triple pent pierced by arched windows that joined the double end chimneys. Clad in weatherboard with a gambrel roof, the home was occupied by the Bond family in the late 1700s and later by Dr. James Waring, who married Anna Maria Thomas, daughter of Maryland governor Dr. James Thomas, in 1838. A fire destroyed the house in 1943. (FBJPC, LOC.)

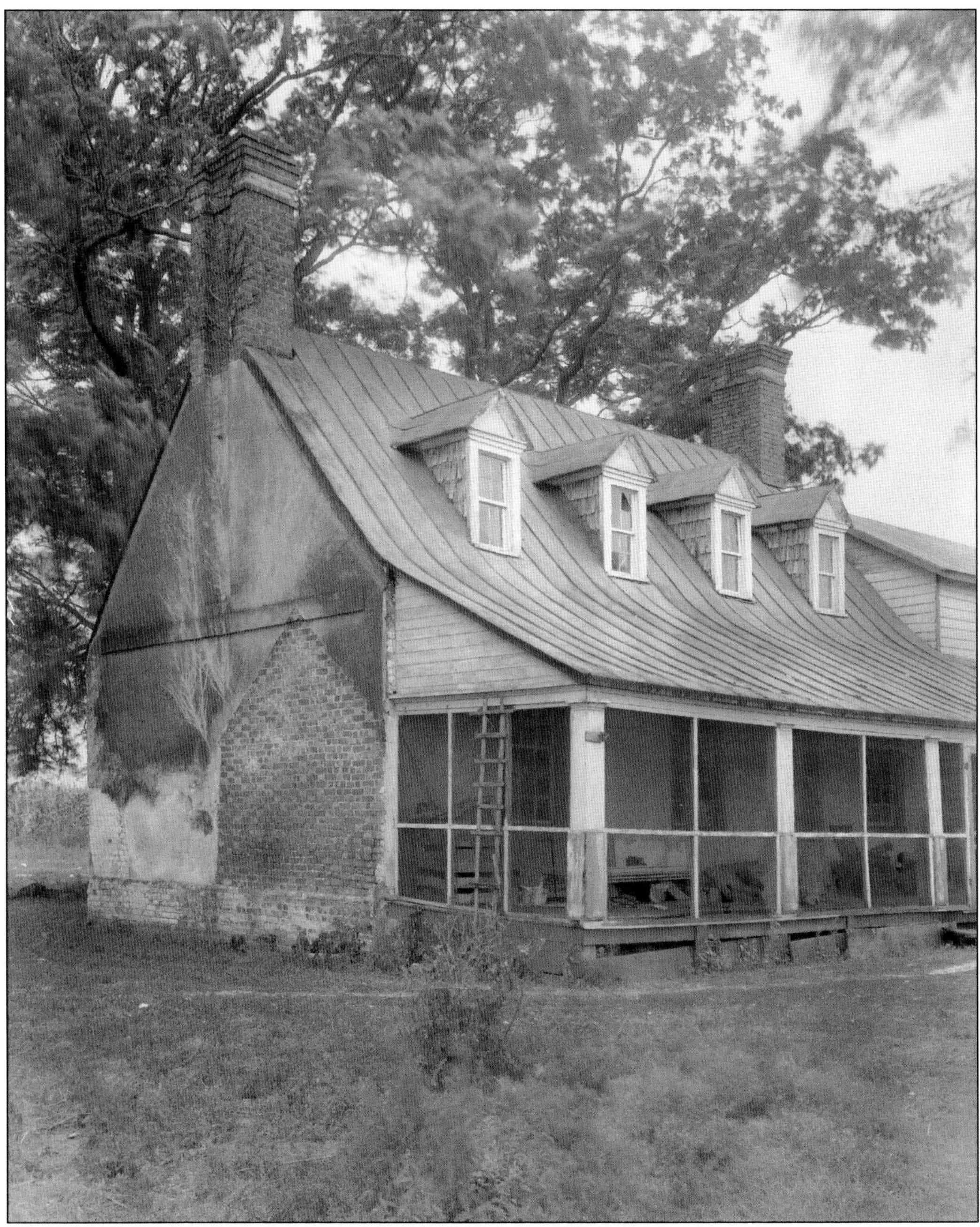

Capt. John Mills built Mills Point near Chaptico in the 1750s. It was a simple one-and-a-half-story, four-bay-wide brick home. Captain Mills had served in the American Revolution, and his wife, Elizabeth, was reportedly the daughter of a French naval officer. Before 1940, the house had a 19th-century porch along its front elevation, as seen in this image. (Delos H. Smith, HABS.)

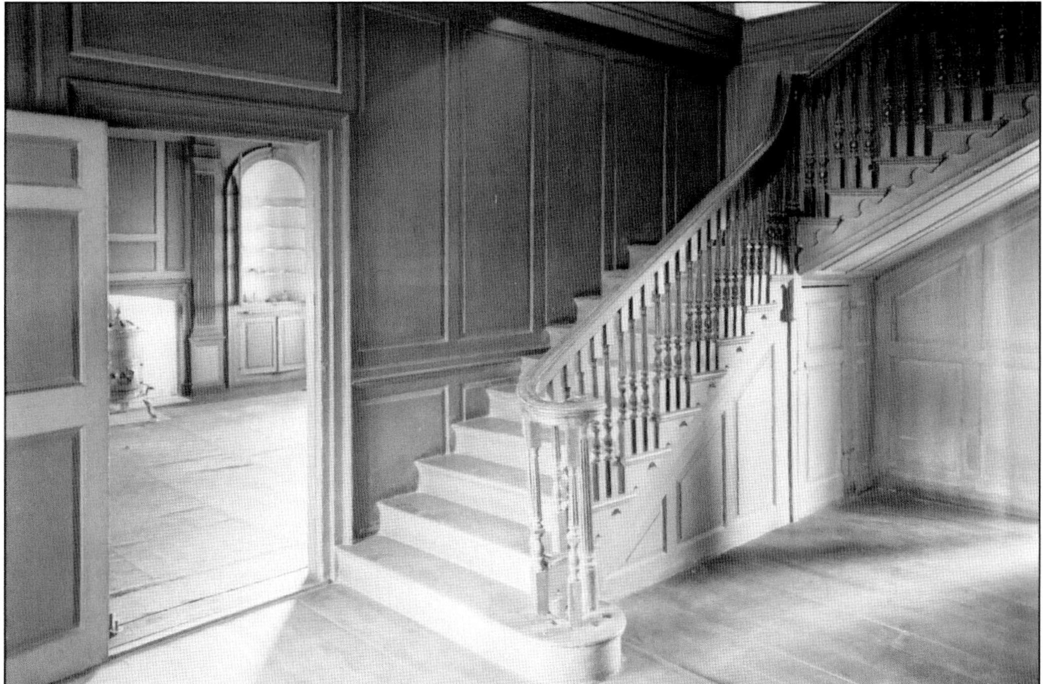

After suffering decades of neglect, Mills Point was demolished in the 1950s. Before it was razed, the interior woodwork seen here was removed and placed in Keechland, a Georgian Revival mansion in Charles County. Similarly, the stairway was repurposed in the restoration of Smallwood's Retreat, the former home of Gen. William Smallwood, also located in Charles County, as assisted by Col. Walter Simpson of Bachelor's Hope in Chaptico. (FBJPC, LOC.)

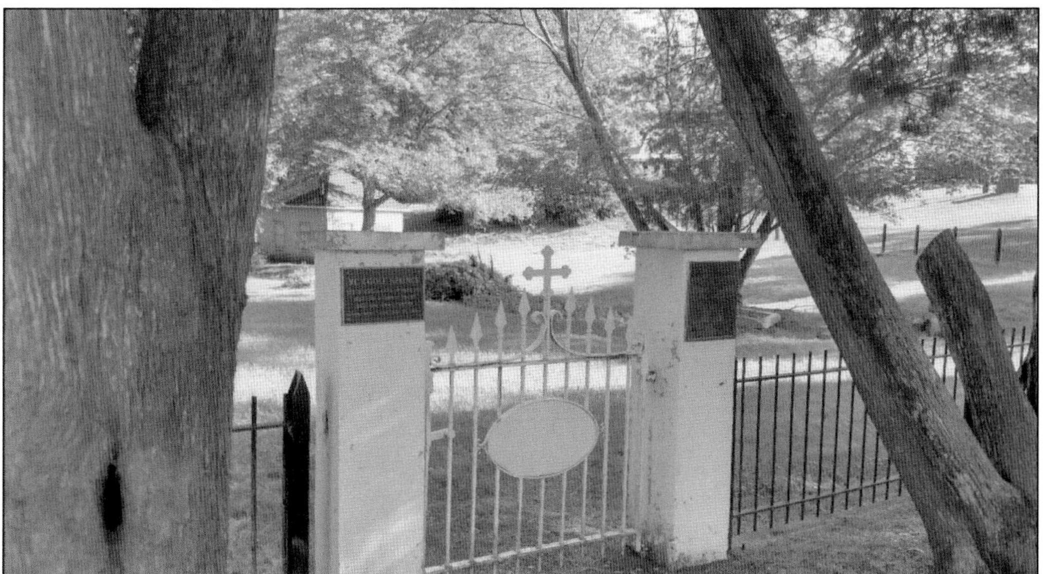

After receiving news that cures were being wrought at a source in Charlotte Hall, royal governor Francis Nicholson (1655–1728) ordered the purchase of approximately 50 acres of Capt. John Dent's land that surrounded "ye Coole Springs" for the construction of facilities to care for the sick. Cool Springs became, in effect, one of the first public hospitals in English America.

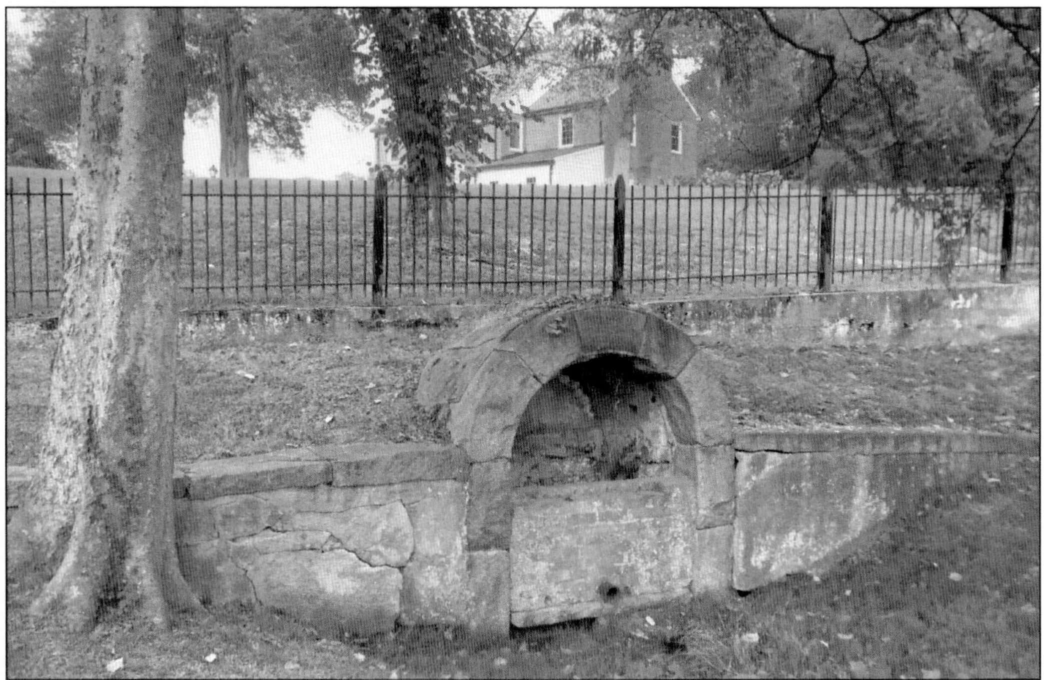

Though the spring is no longer considered medicinal or even potable, the waters of Cool Springs still usher forth from two places on the grounds. Plaques at its gates commemorate its history and honor alumni of the adjacent former Charlotte Hall School, such as Confederate rear admiral and brigadier general Raphael Semmes (1809–1877), born at Efton in Charles County.

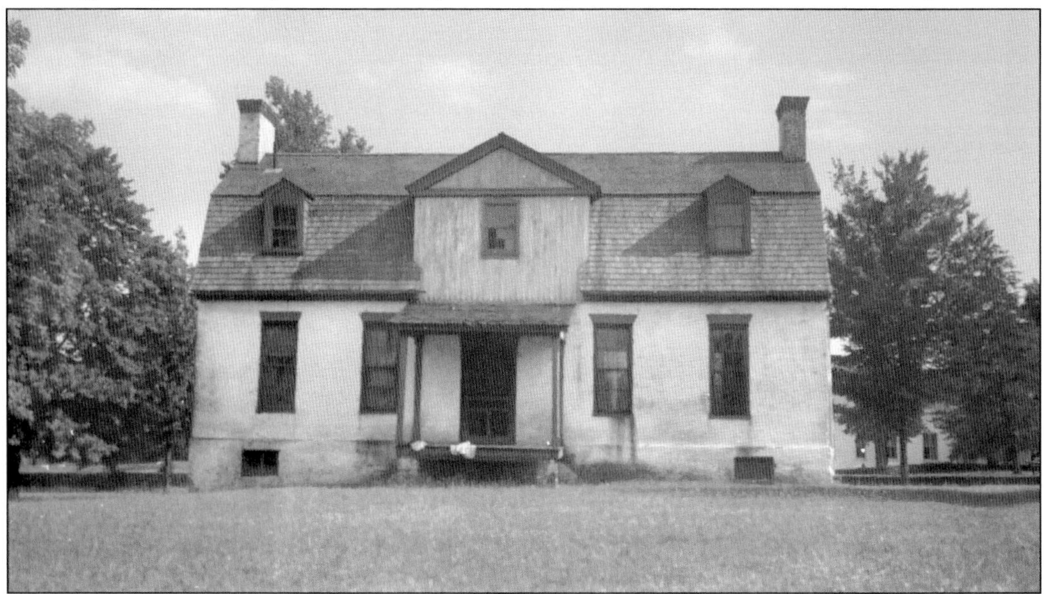

First contracted for construction in 1793, the White House at Charlotte Hall School was not completed until 1803. The one-and-a-half-story structure was built of brick with a gambrel roof, and it had a central hall flanked by two classrooms. Famous alumni include Adm. Raphael Semmes, Chief Justice Roger B. Taney, Lincoln's attorney Gen. Edward Bates, Episcopal bishop Thomas John Claggett, and many congressmen. (E.H. Pickering, HABS.)

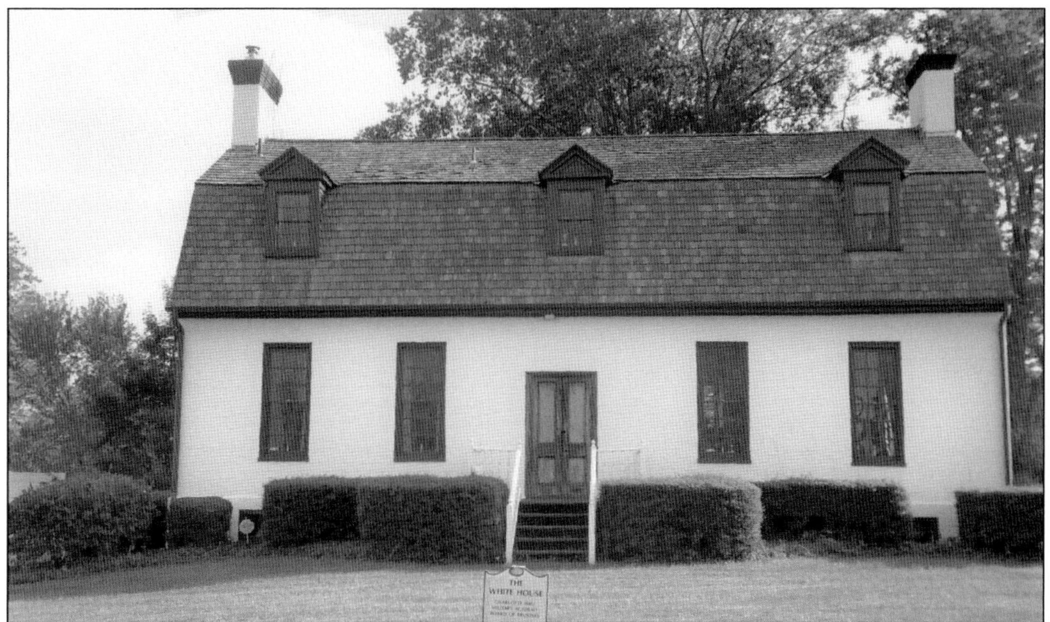

Charlotte Hall School, later called Charlotte Hall Military Academy, was established in 1774 and remained in continuous operation after 1796, until it was closed in 1976. As part of the efforts to maintain the former school's historic sites, the White House was restored and later alterations were removed. Today, it stands on the grounds of the Charlotte Hall Veterans Home, built within the former campus in 1982.

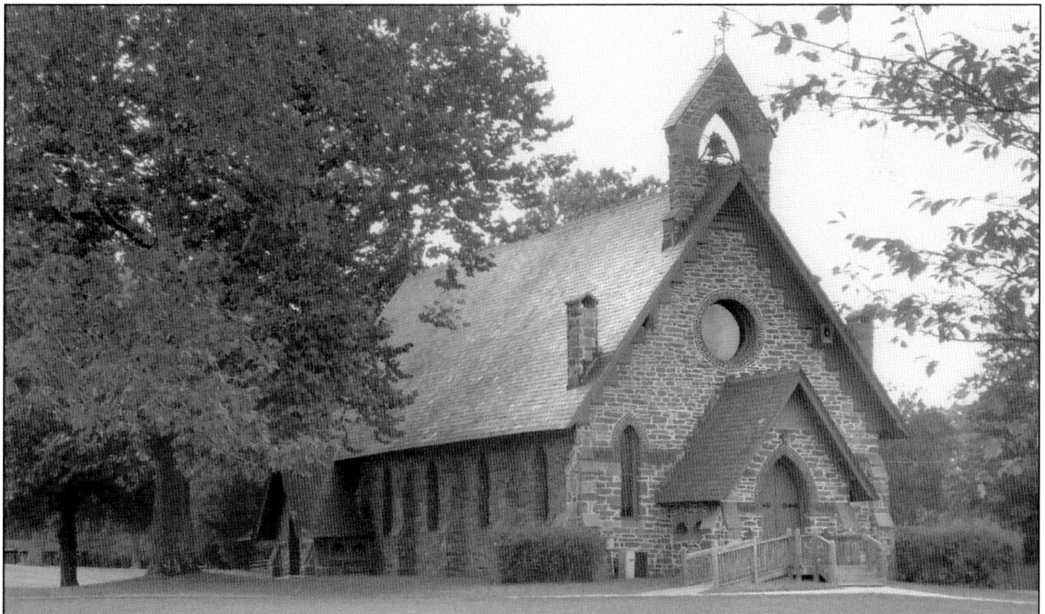

The granite Dent Memorial Chapel was built at the Charlotte Hall School in 1884. The Gothic Revival chapel was constructed to commemorate Rev. Hatch Dent Jr. (1751–1799), the first principal of the school (1796–1799). During the American Revolution, Dent served as an officer and was captured at the Battle of Brooklyn Heights in 1776, after which he returned to Maryland and entered the ministry in 1784.

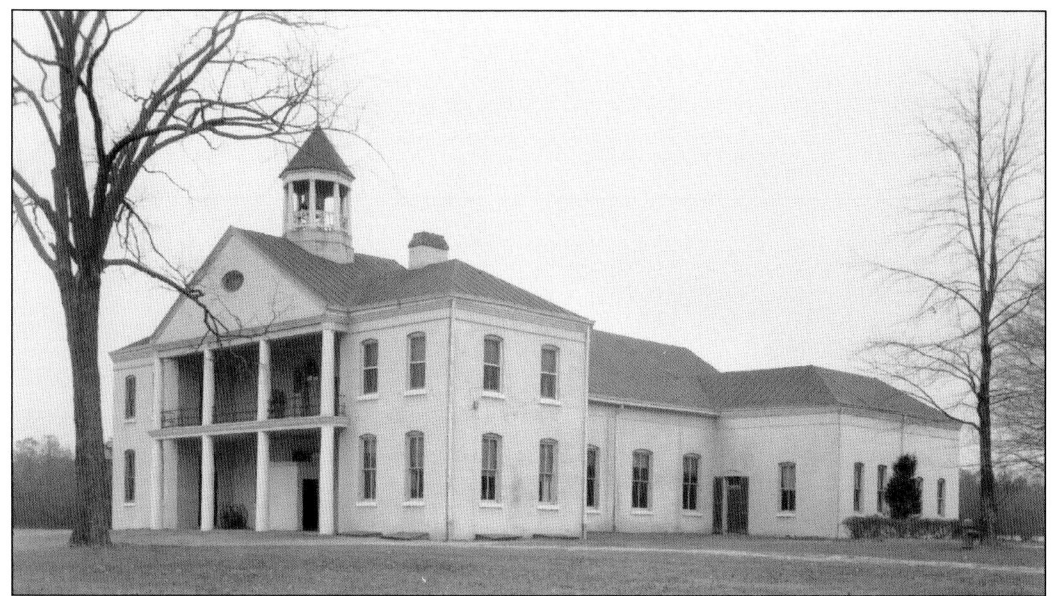

The two-story Charlotte Hall classroom building was constructed between 1896 and 1897 to replace two older structures that had been destroyed by fire. Originally built of brick on a T-shaped plan, the structure was expanded in 1931. The front of the building featured a two-story pedimented portico, and the roof supported an open octagonal belfry. The building was demolished in 1984 for the Charlotte Hall Veterans Home, but the bell remains there. (E.H. Pickering, HABS.)

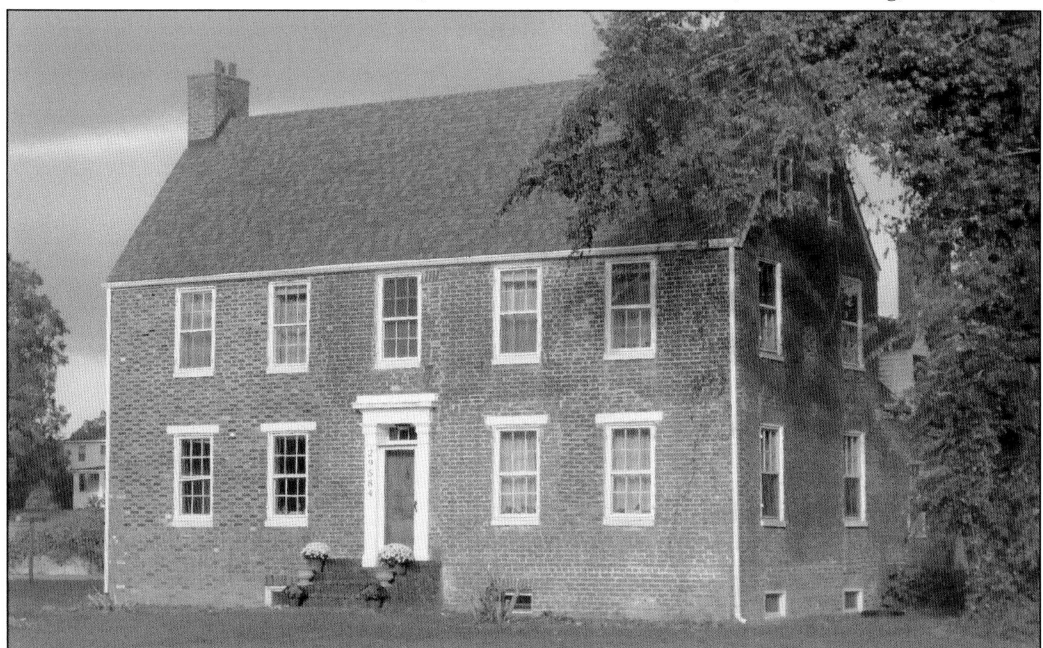

Known as Kilgour's Tavern, the Old Inn, or the William T. Briscoe House, this two-and-a-half-story Federal home stands prominently in the Charlotte Hall village. Built around 1797 and enlarged around 1820, the brick structure served as a tavern for people coming to Charlotte Hall School and Cool Springs. In 1855, William T. Briscoe, the school's principal, purchased it and lived there until his death in 1897.

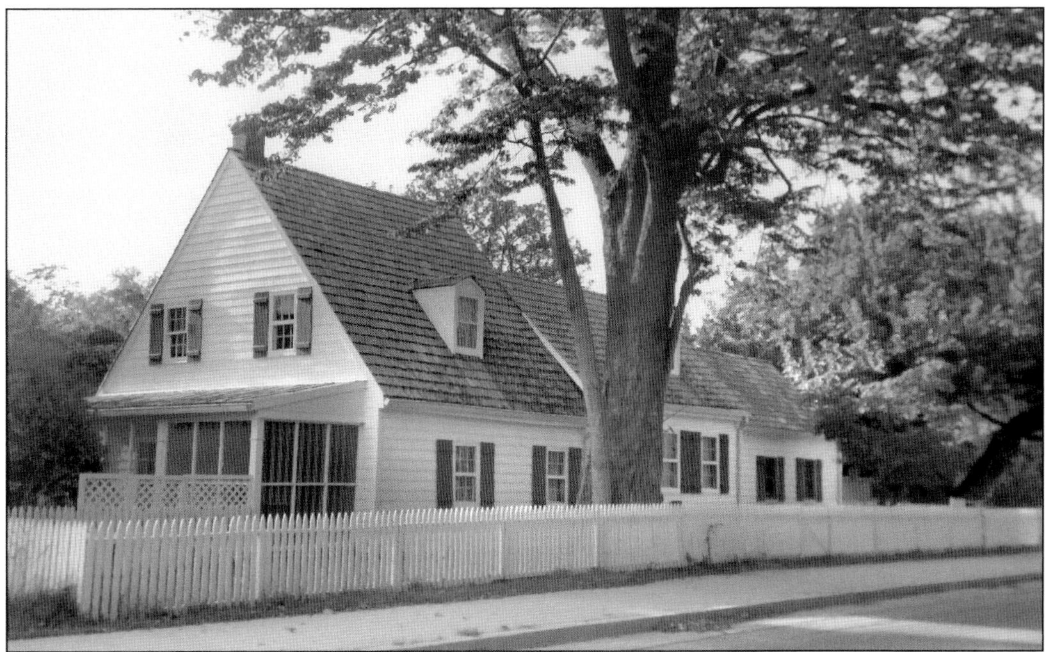

The oldest part of this one-and-a-half-story frame house was built shortly after 1803. The Reeves family occupied the home for much of the 19th century, during which time additions were made to the structure. Around 1914, John and Henrietta Chesley purchased the home, where they would operate the village post office and a candy shop, largely catering to students from the Charlotte Hall School.

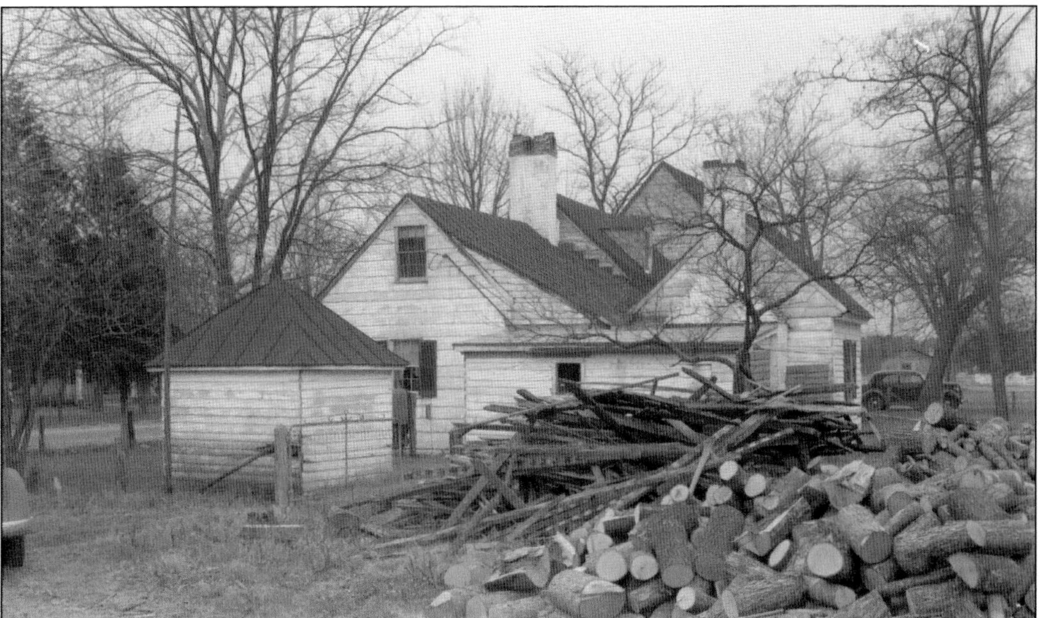

This 1936 photograph of the rear of the Chesley House in Charlotte Hall shows the variety of rooflines on the home, resulting from over a century of additions to the original structure. Currently covered in a cedar shake roof, the house is seen here with a standing seam metal roof. A pile of cut logs to be split for firewood remains as well. (E.H. Pickering, HABS.)

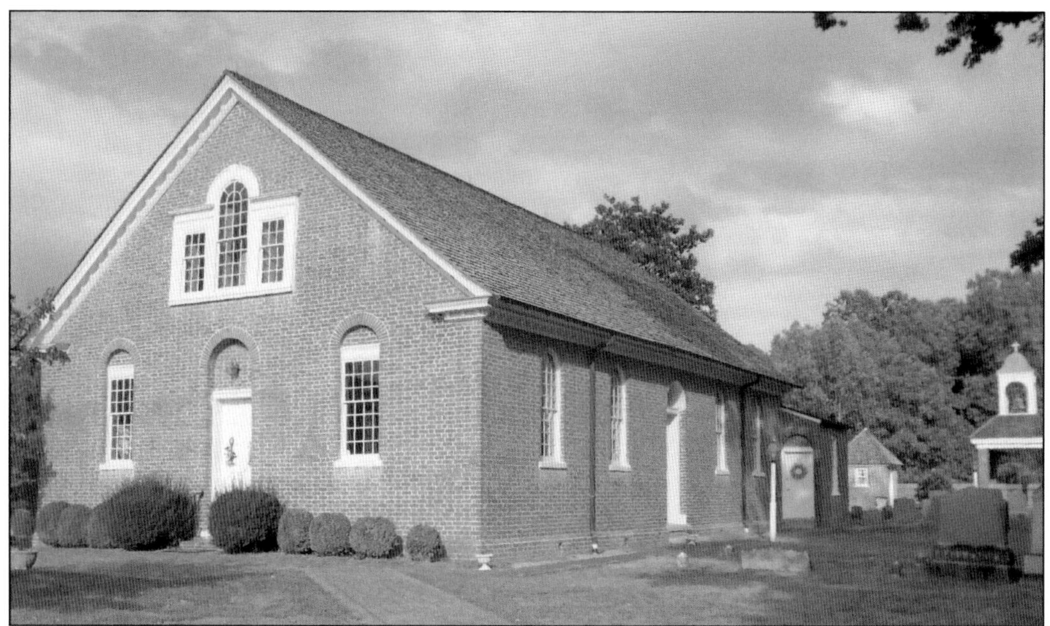

Master builders Samuel Abell Jr. and Richard Boulton constructed the reserved Georgian-style All Faith Episcopal Church in the Huntersville area of Charlotte Hall between 1766 and 1769. The gable-front, three-bay-wide, five-bay-deep church was built of brick with recessed arched windows and doorways. The distinctive three-part Palladian window above the west-facing front entry is original to the design.

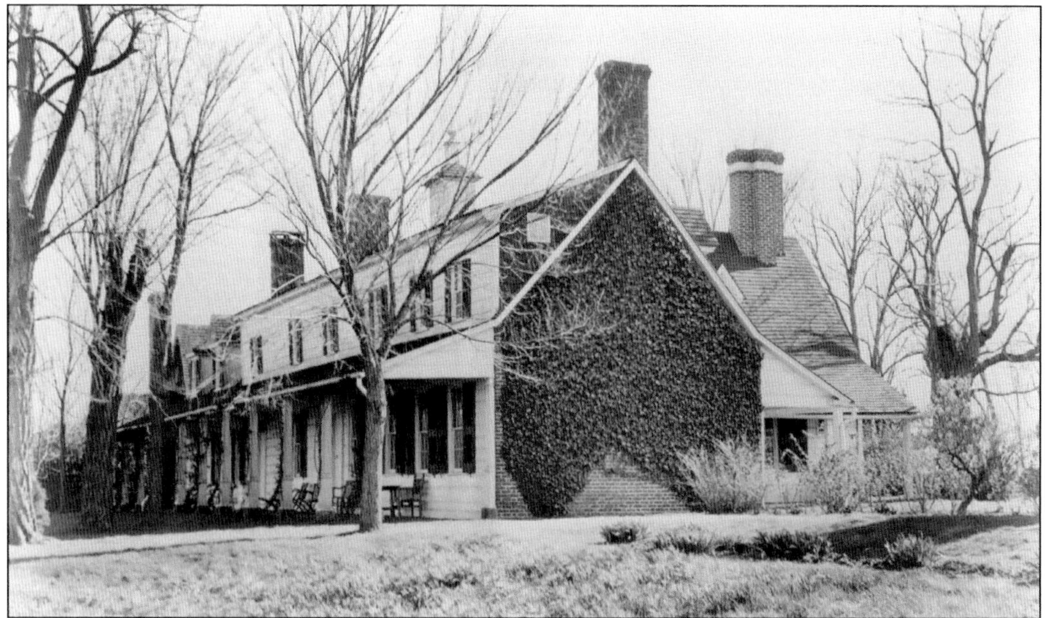

The construction of Sotterley mansion began around 1717. James Bowles, a member of the Maryland Council, had purchased the land in 1710 from what was once part of the Resurrection Manor grant to Thomas Cornwaleys in 1650. The one-and-a-half-story structure features more than 100 feet of wraparound porches. Master builders Samuel Abell Jr. and Richard Boulton added a Chinese Chippendale balustrade to the main stairway in 1767. (HABS.)

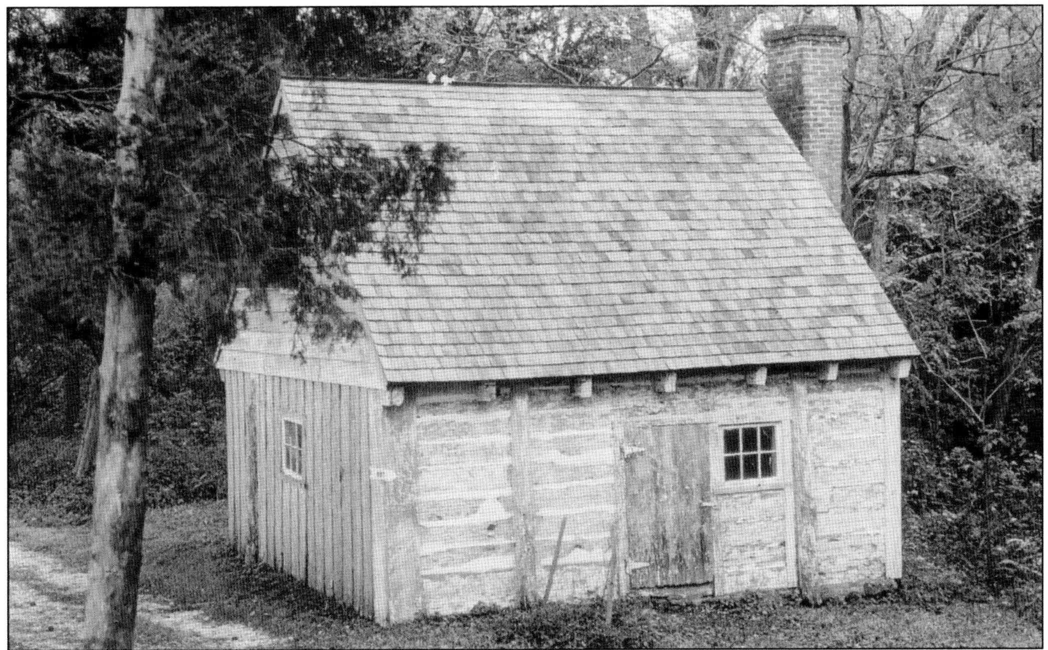

Managed by the Sotterley Mansion Foundation since 1961, this estate has well-preserved elements of its 300-year history for the public to discover and enjoy. Notable owners include Maryland governor George Plater III (1735–1792) and William Clarke Somerville of Mulberry Fields, who won the estate in a dice game. The lives of enslaved African Americans are also interpreted here through dwellings such as this slave cabin. (Douglas Barber, HABS.)

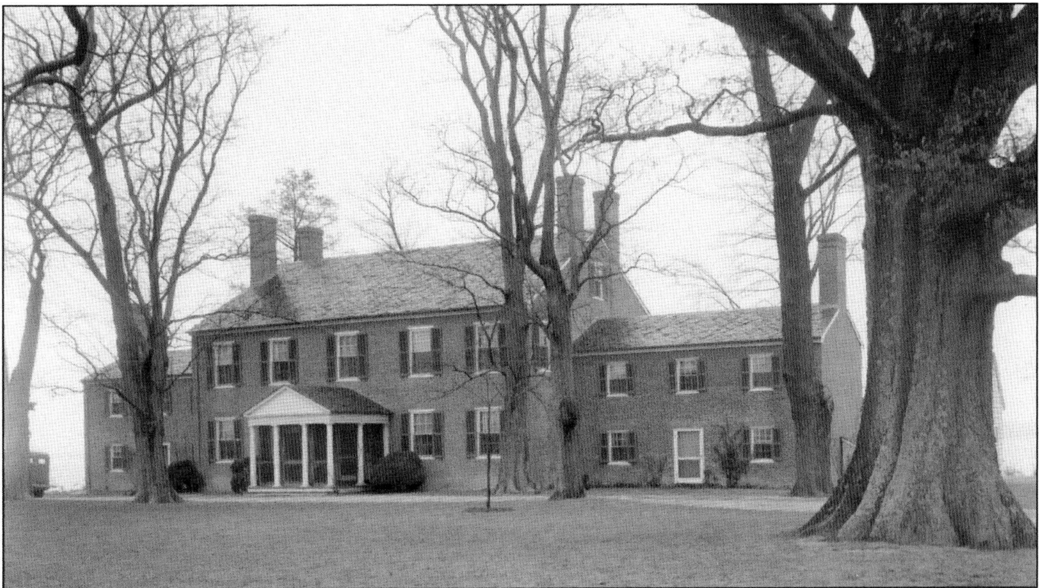

Dr. William Thomas built Cremona, a Federal-style home, east of Mechanicsville in 1819. The two-and-a-half-story brick structure is located along the Patuxent River on land first patented to John Ashcomb in 1658. In the 1930s, Maj. Gen. Howard C. Davidson (1890–1984), one of the country's first military aviators, owned the riverfront estate. During his ownership, the flanking two-story brick wings were added around 1930. (EH Pickering, HABS.)

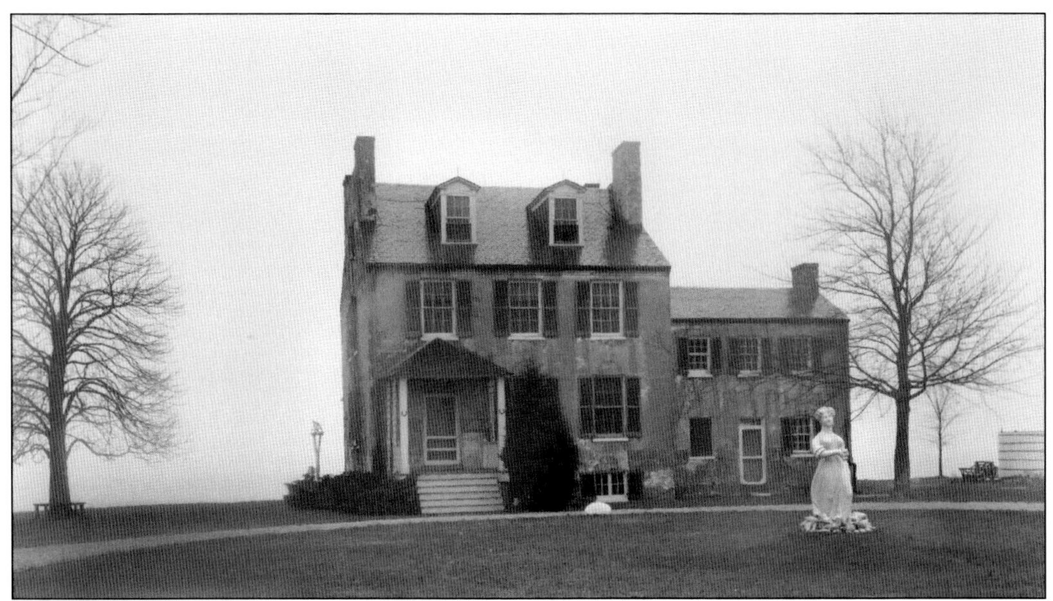

Near Cremona is De la Brooke Manor. George Thomas built the Federal-style manor house around 1835 after an earlier home on the site had been destroyed by fire. George Thomas, the brother of William Thomas of Cremona, named his estate in honor of their mother, Catherine Brooke Boarman. Built on a raised basement with scored stucco, the two-and-a-half-story, side-hall structure is a notable riverfront estate. (E.H. Pickering, HABS.)

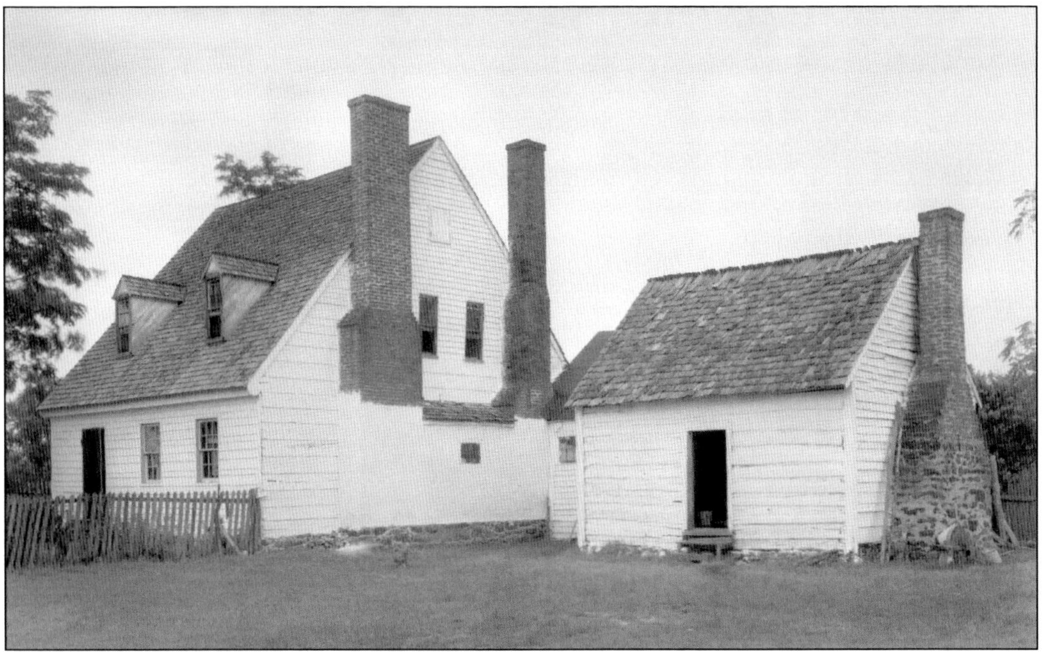

The 18th-century manor house of St. Cuthbert's Fortune and its adjacent slave cabin once stood near Hollywood. Owned by John H.T. Briscoe, a former state attorney, fire destroyed it in 1951. The St. Mary's County Historical Society built a pedestal from its bricks for a cannon from the *Ark* and the *Dove*—donated by the Jesuits of St. Inigoes—for placement at the historic jail in Leonardtown. (E.H. Pickering, HABS.)

Constructed between 1896 and 1898 in a parish established in 1691, St. Joseph's Catholic Church in Hollywood is the third church built for the congregation. Joseph Milburn of Leonardtown designed the Victorian Gothic church with a country style to replace an earlier frame church built there in 1824. The two-story wood structure is covered in weatherboard and shingles with an octagonal four-story belfry on its western gable-front entrance.

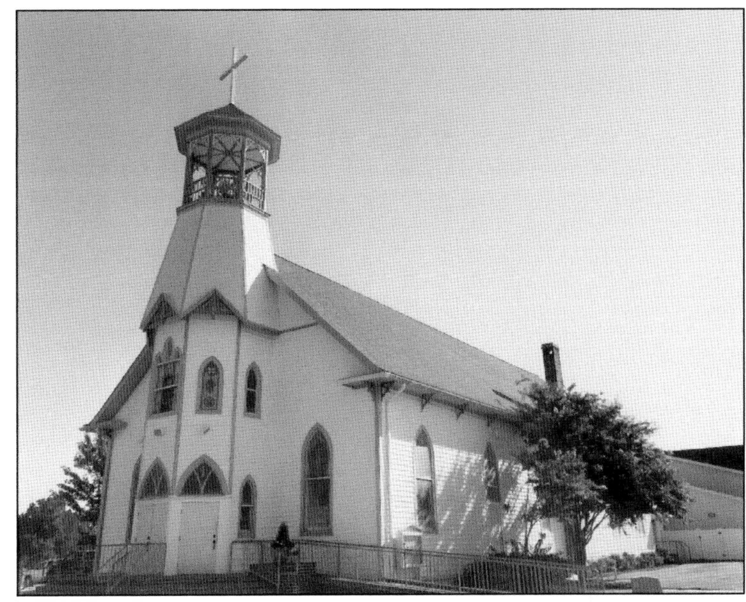

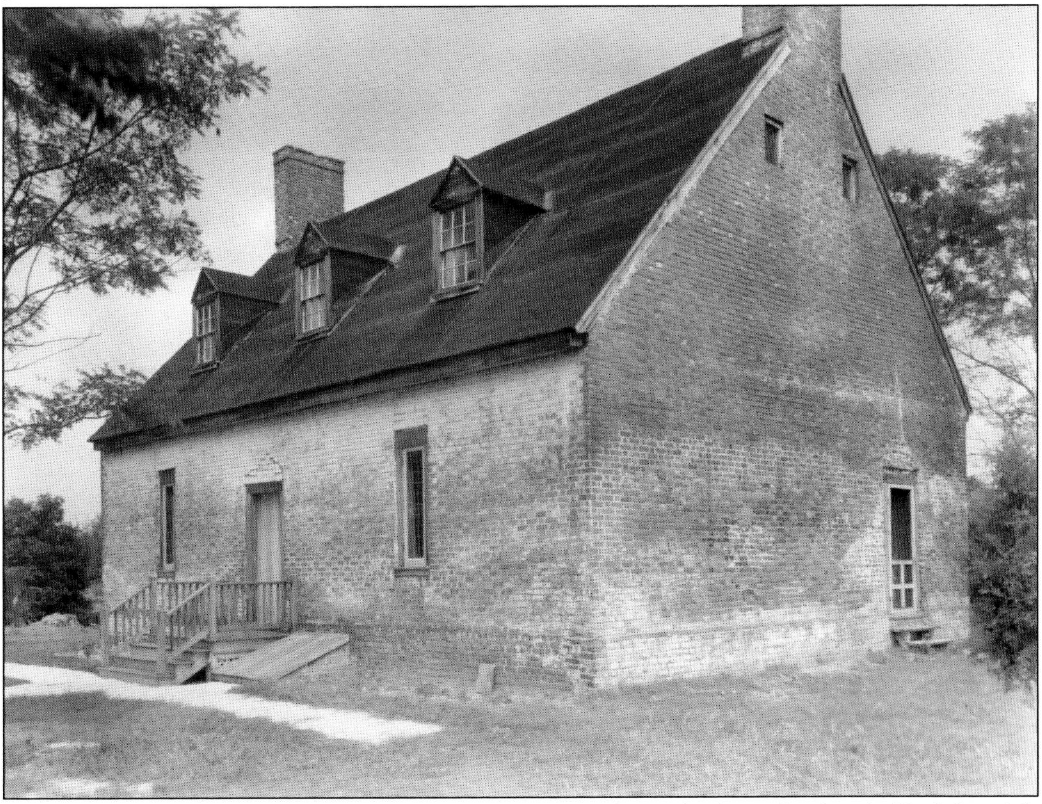

St. Richard's Manor is a one-and-a-half-story brick residence built in the first half of the 18th century with interior-set chimneys on each gable end. Maynard B. Barnes (1897–1970), a career diplomat, purchased the home in seriously dilapidated condition in 1930. He restored it between 1935 and 1945 with interior woodwork salvaged from period homes in the area that were being razed. (FBJPC, LOC.)

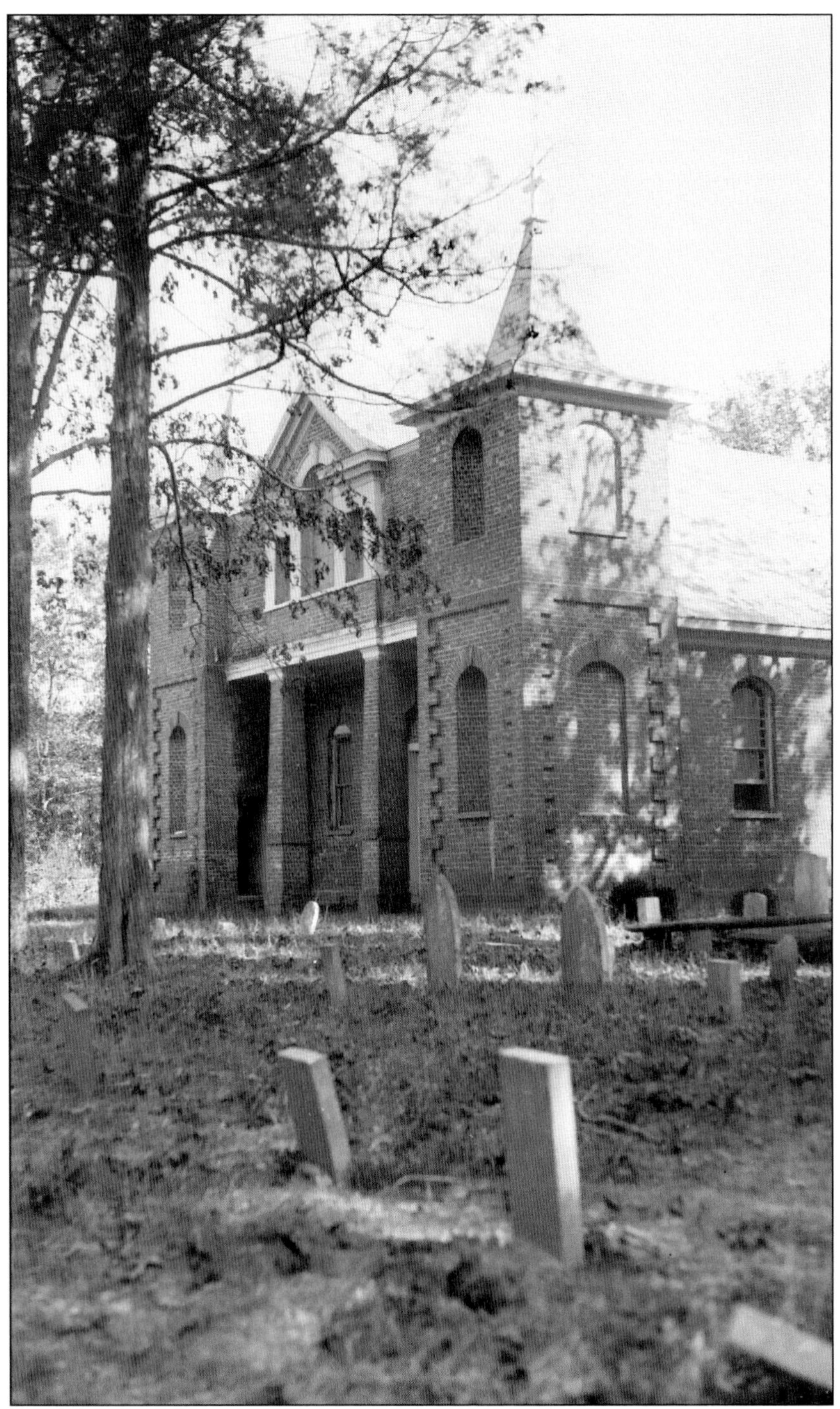

Established as a parish five miles east of Leonardtown in 1744, St. Andrew's Episcopal Church did not become an active congregation until 1753. Just like the All Faith Episcopal Church near Charlotte Hall, this church was designed and built by the team of Richard Boulton and Samuel Abell Jr. between 1766 and 1768 for a cost of 100 pounds sterling in currency and 160,000 pounds of tobacco. (Thomas T. Waterman, HABS.)

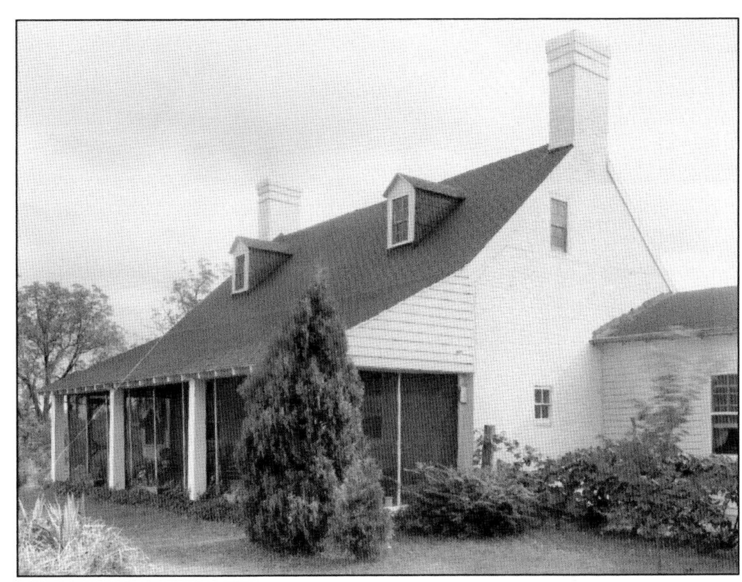

Built around 1775, Kingston is a one-and-a-half-story, three-bay brick house located along the bank where the mouth of Kingston Creek meets the Patuxent River in California. In 1789, John A. Thomas sold the Georgian-style house and its 150 acres to Col. Joseph Daffin, both of whom were veterans of the American Revolution. In recent years, the ancient house has had substantial wood-frame wings added. (FBJPC, LOC.)

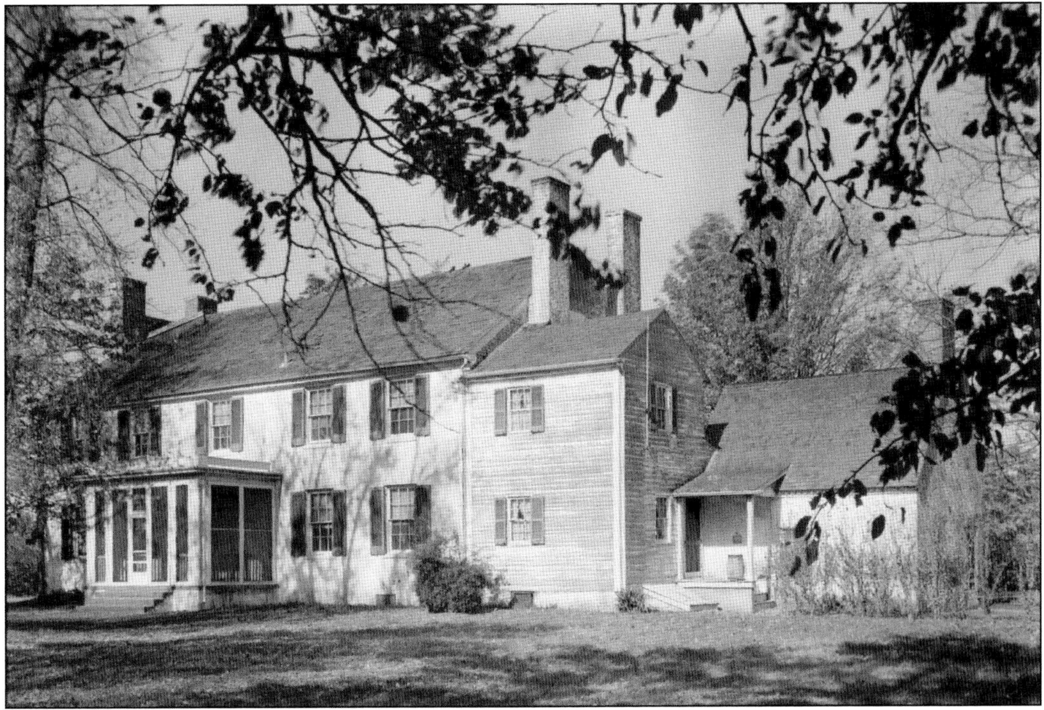

Built around 1745 as a side-hall, double-parlor residence by Nicholas Sewell, Mattapanny was extensively enlarged to its five-bay brick Federal appearance in the 1840s, with further additions and renovations in 1913 and between 1941 and 1943. Once a Calvert family holding and the site of a Jesuit mission in the 17th century, it became the Patuxent Naval Air Station commander's residence after the Navy acquired it in 1942. (E.H. Pickering, HABS.)

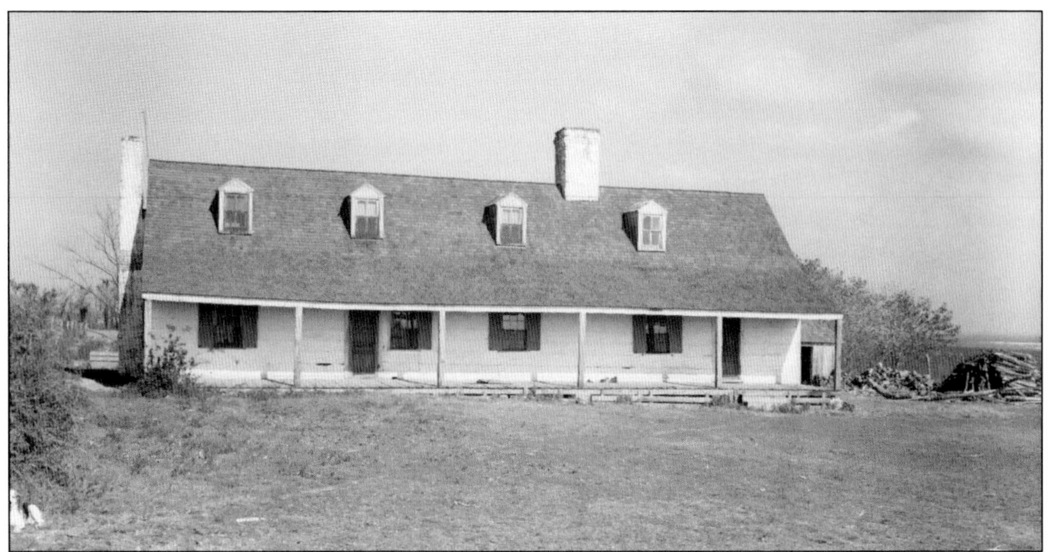

Around 1835, tobacco planter Henry J. Carroll built Susquehanna on a 1649 land grant. Capt. Henry Carroll and his wife, Araminta Thompson Carroll, purchased the property in 1767. The one-and-a-half-story home, with porches along the front and back, was dismantled in 1942 during construction of the Patuxent River Naval Air Station and reconstructed in Henry Ford's Greenfield Village in Michigan. (E.H. Pickering, HABS.)

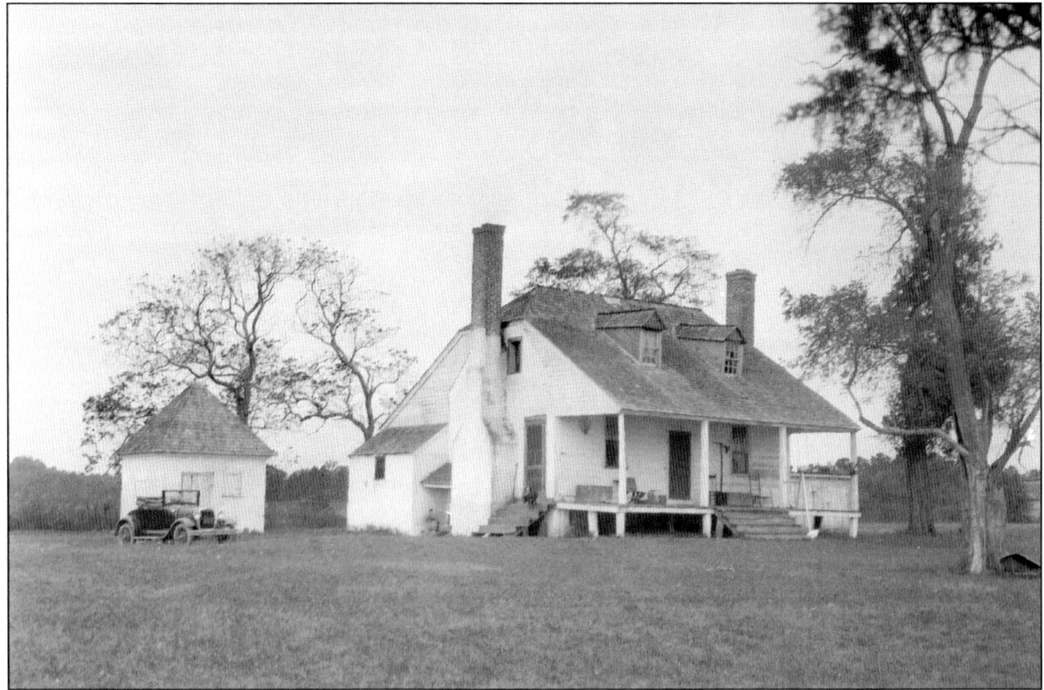

Long Lane Farm (Halfhead Folly) near Lexington Park was built as a small brick-ended hall and parlor home for Col. John Jarboe, who was born in France, then moved to Virginia, and finally came to Maryland in 1646 as a soldier for Gov. Leonard Calvert. Expanded in the 18th century and renovated in the 20th century, the home was damaged by fire in 1972, and it was demolished in 1984. (Delos H. Smith, HABS.)

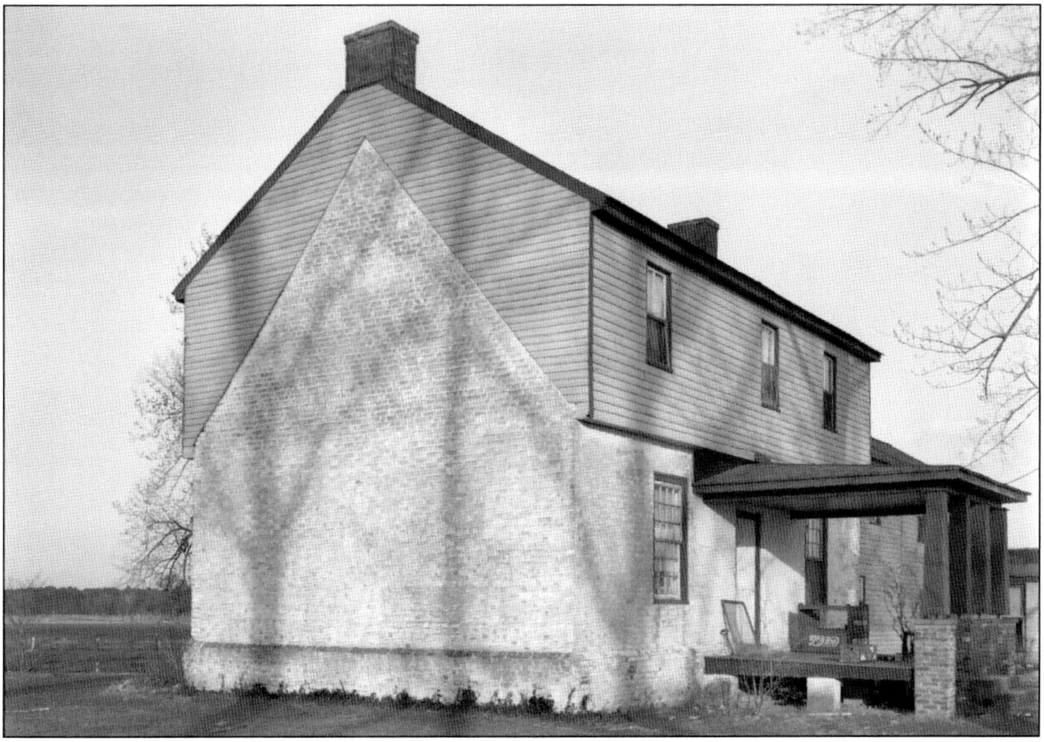

Overlooking Calvert's Bay on the Potomac, Calvert's Rest in Trinity Manor near Ridge was built after 1661 by William Calvert, Gov. Leonard Calvert's only son who drowned in 1681. Though the original shape of the one-and-a-half-story brick structure can be seen on the sides of the house, it was extensively expanded with a second floor and frame wing in the early 20th century. (Charles E. Peterson, HABS.)

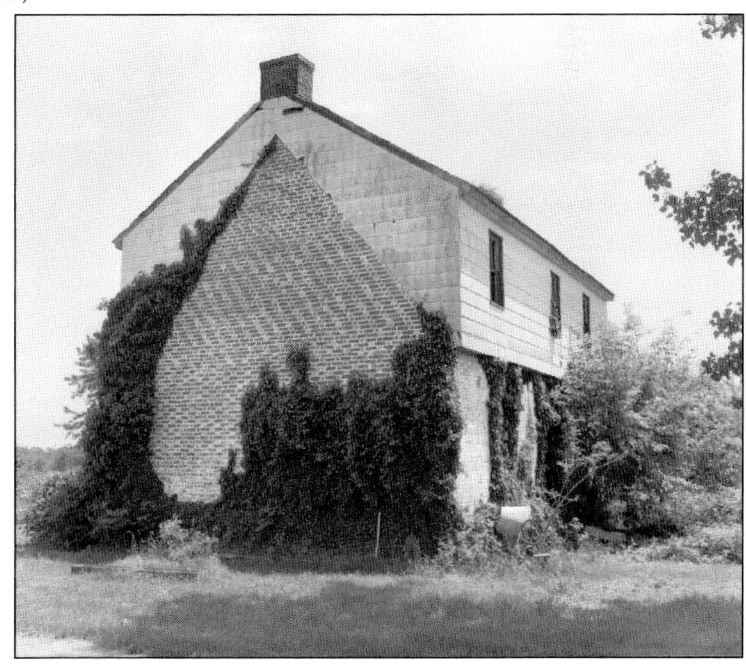

By 1972, Calvert's Rest had fallen into severe disrepair and the front porch had collapsed, following its service as a tourist hotel run by the Curley family early in the 1900s. Long the home of members of the Raleigh and Curley families, who sold it in the 1950s, the home's later additions were removed, and it was restored as a private residence in the 1990s. (Douglas Barber, HABS.)

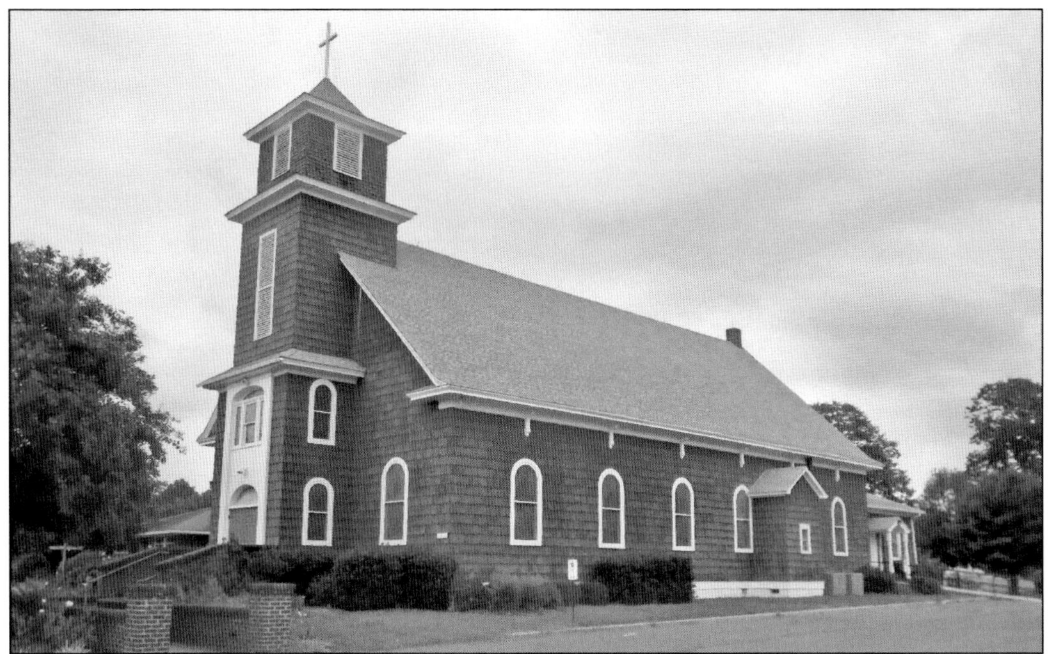

Begun as an 18th-century mission of St. Ignatius Church in St. Inigoes, St. Michael's Catholic Church had assembled 320 parishioners by 1823. Replacing a large frame church built in 1881, the current frame and shingle gable-front church was built in 1929. It is known for its dramatic use of decorative pressed tin on the walls and vaulted barrel ceiling, along with Gothic-arched, pressed-tin wainscoting.

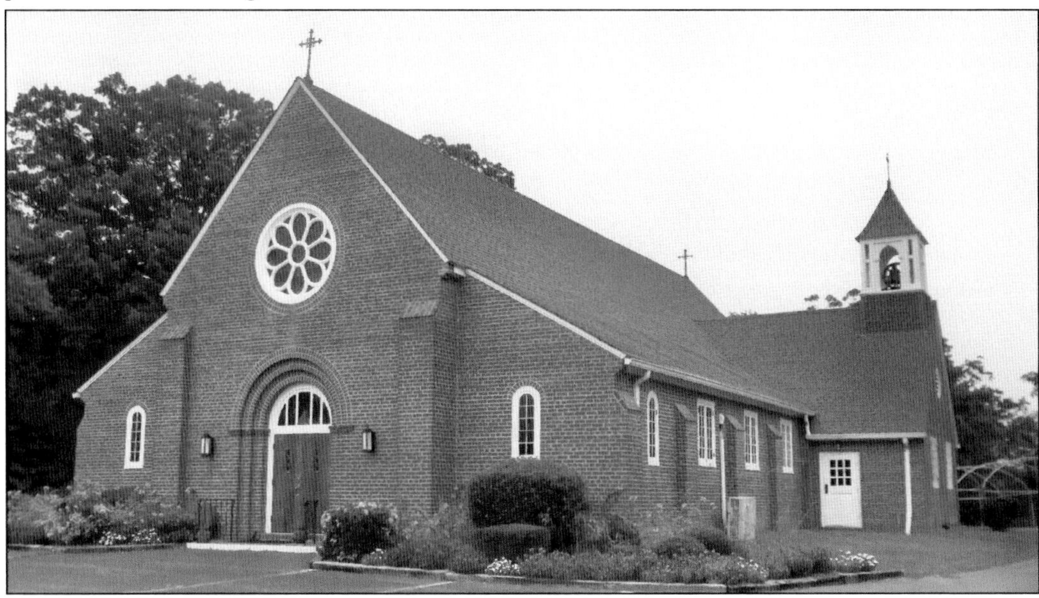

In 1937, renowned Washington architect Philip Hubert Frohman designed the St. Peter Claver Catholic Church in Ridge to replace an earlier frame sanctuary. In addition to its distinctive design, the church is significant for being the only predominately African American Roman Catholic parish in the county. It grew out of a sodality of the Blessed Virgin Mary for African American families at nearby St. Michael's Catholic Church on land given by the Biscoe family in 1901.

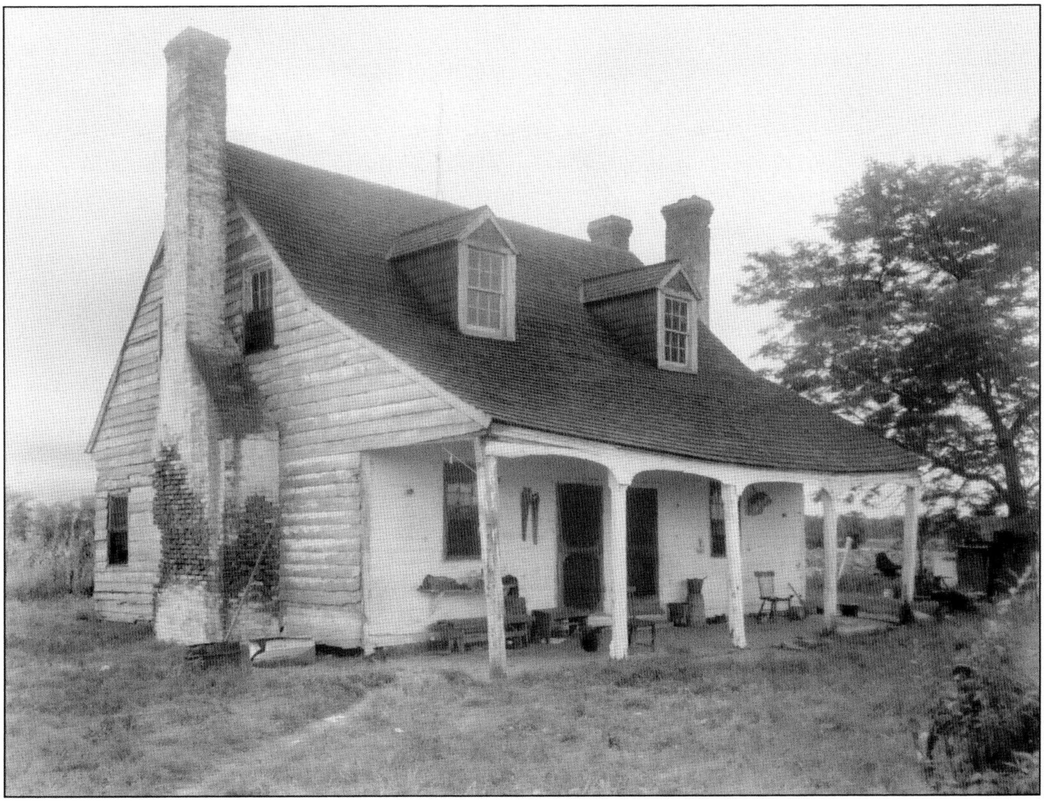

St. Jerome's Manor near Dameron is a one-and-a-half-story, coastal-style frame house with a generous porch running the length of its facade and brick chimneys at both ends. It was built on land first surveyed in 1648 for Capt. William Hawley, one of the first commissioners for the county. By the 1950s, the home had fallen into severe disrepair, until Elmer and Mona Olson restored it in 1976. (FBJPC, LOC.)

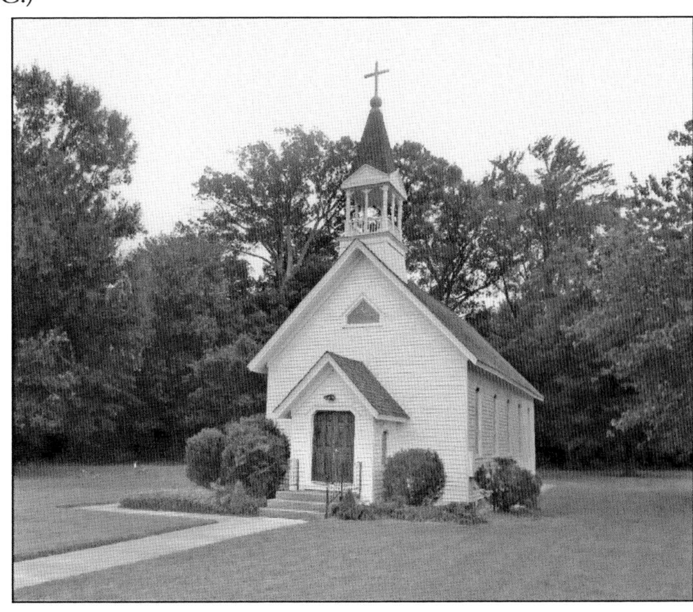

Built as a small chapel of ease for parishioners in southern St. Mary's County, the St. Mary's Episcopal Chapel in Ridge is a simple frame and clapboard Victorian sanctuary with a delicate open belfry above the entrance. It was constructed between 1883 and 1885 to replace an earlier chapel built in 1857 but was later sold and burned.

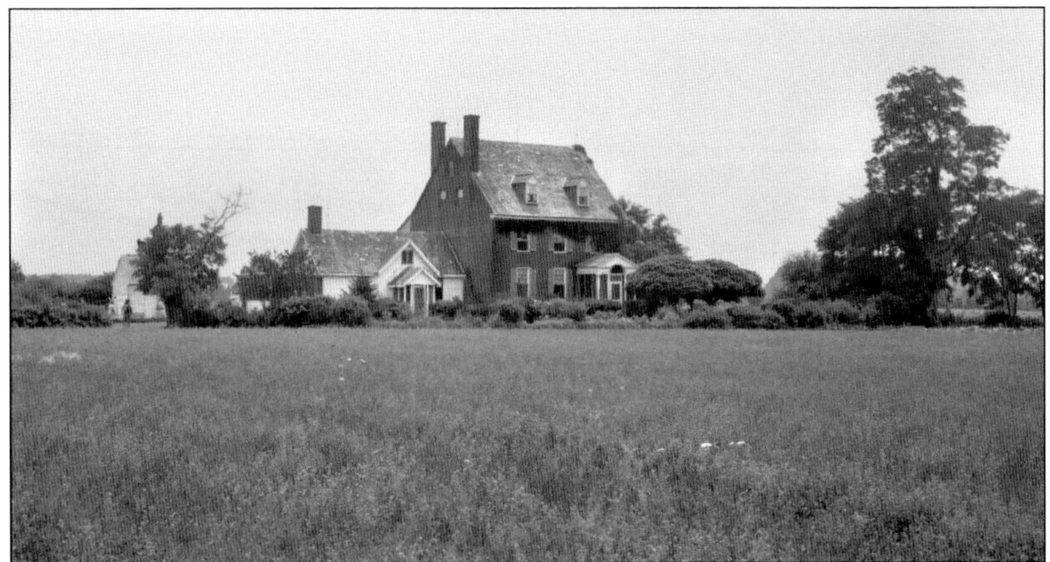

Located in Scotland along the road to Point Lookout, the Kirk Mansion was built in 1798 by James Kirk Jr., a planter and vestryman at William and Mary Parish. This imposing two-and-a-half-story, side-hall brick Federal residence was raided by the British during the War of 1812. From the 1940s to 1950s, owners Harry and Lila Beal operated a popular restaurant here. (John Collier, FSA, LOC.)

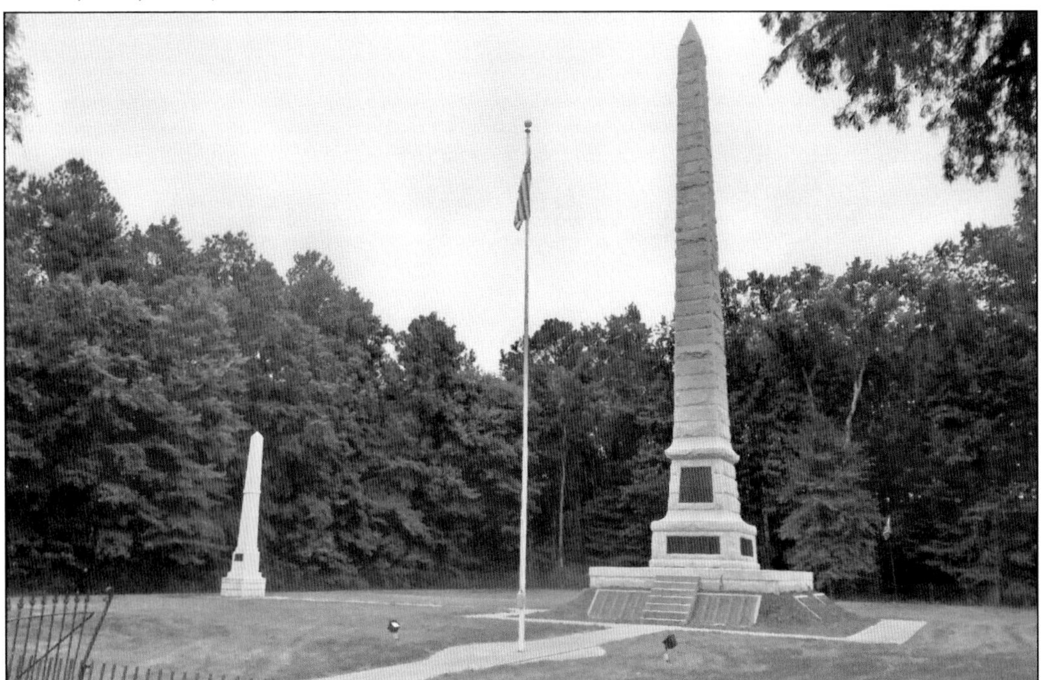

During the centennial of 1876, eleven years after the Civil War ended, St. Mary's County residents urged the state to erect a memorial to the Confederate prisoners of war once held at Point Lookout. The 25-foot marble obelisk commemorates the many soldiers buried in the cemetery. In 1911, the federal government placed a second, taller granite obelisk inscribed with more than 3,300 names of those interred there.

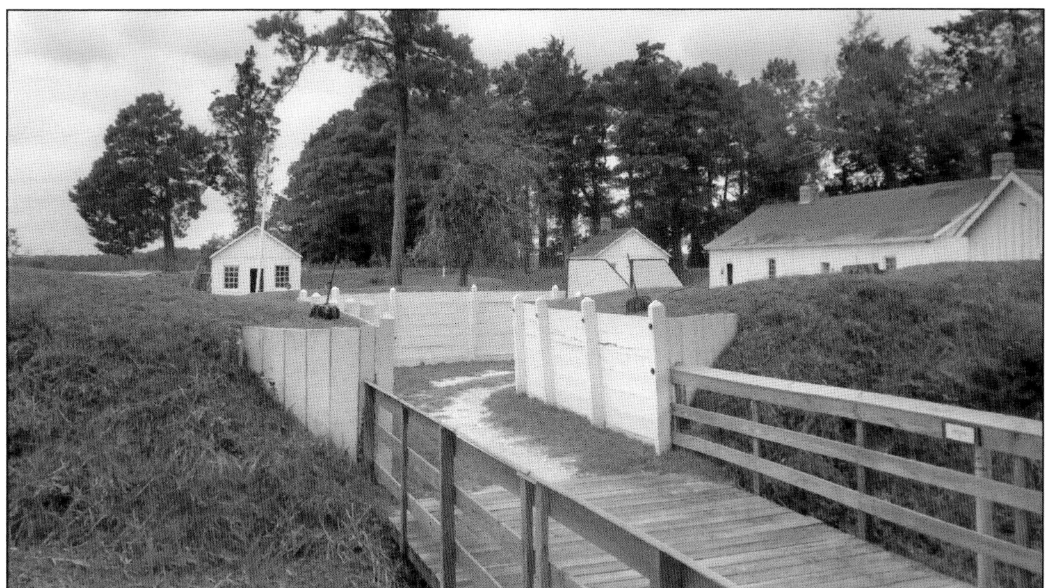

Built along the shore of Cornfield Harbor on the Potomac River, Fort Lincoln was the Point Lookout Prison Camp's main line of defense during the Civil War. The central parade ground was contained within a low yet thick square earthen embankment surrounded by a dry moat and defended by cannons placed at each corner. It was never attacked during the war.

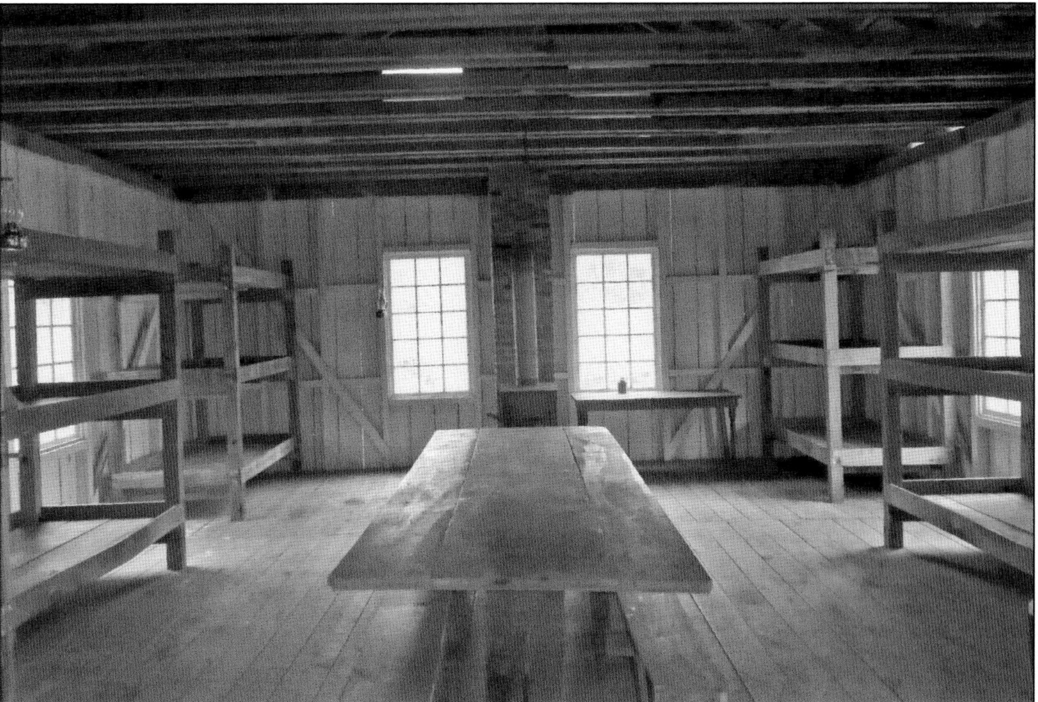

Using original architectural plans and historical photographs, Point Lookout State Park and the Friends of Point Lookout volunteer organization have reconstructed replicas of the barracks and other buildings within the walls of Fort Lincoln. Visitors to the compound can enter the faithfully reconstructed barracks to better understand the life of the Union troops stationed there.

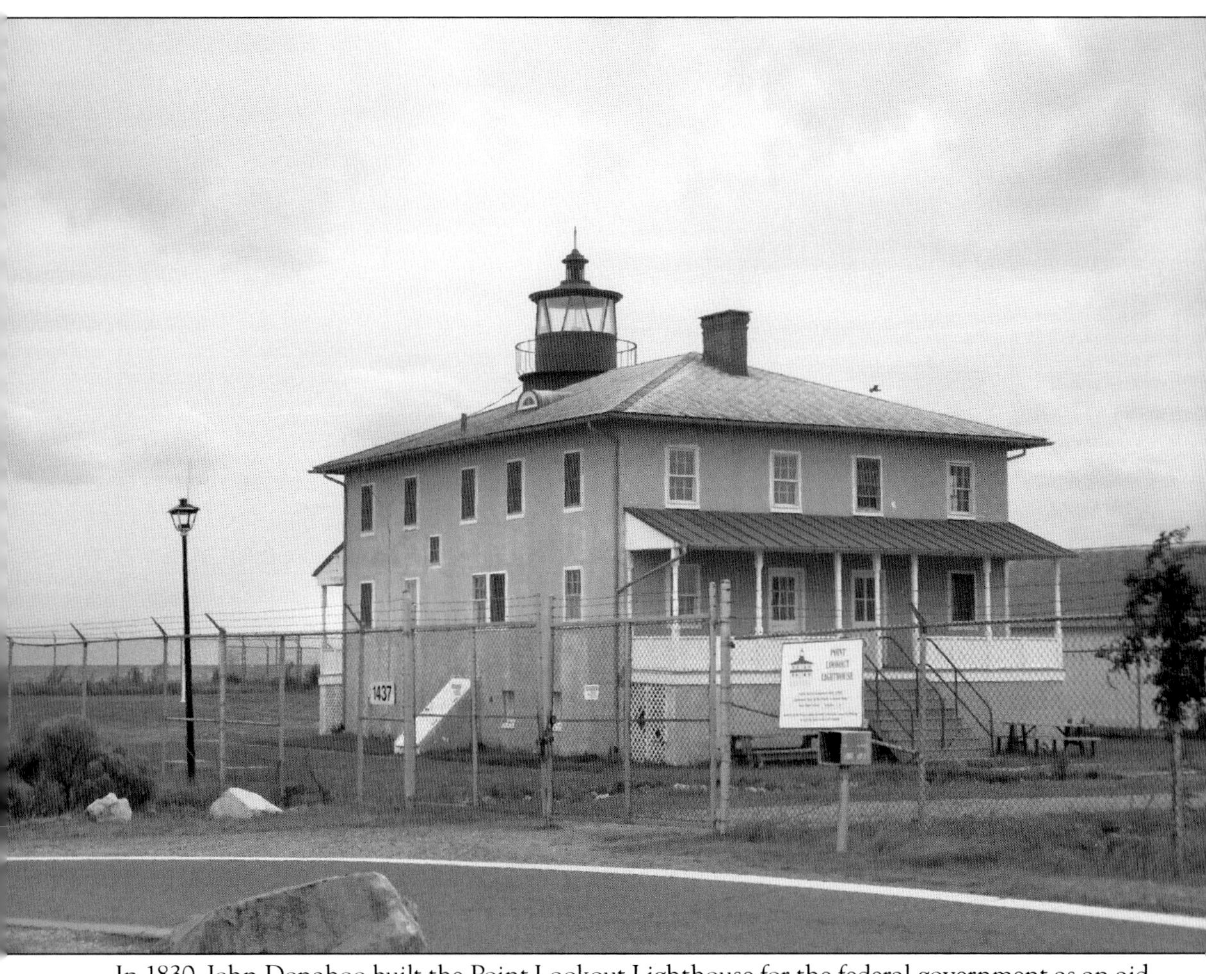

In 1830, John Donahoo built the Point Lookout Lighthouse for the federal government as an aid to navigation. Greatly expanded in both 1883 and 1927, the lighthouse and keeper's quarters are located on the southernmost point of the county at the confluence of the Potomac River and Chesapeake Bay in Point Lookout State Park. The light was extinguished in 1966 and is in need of extensive repair.

Two

Calvert County

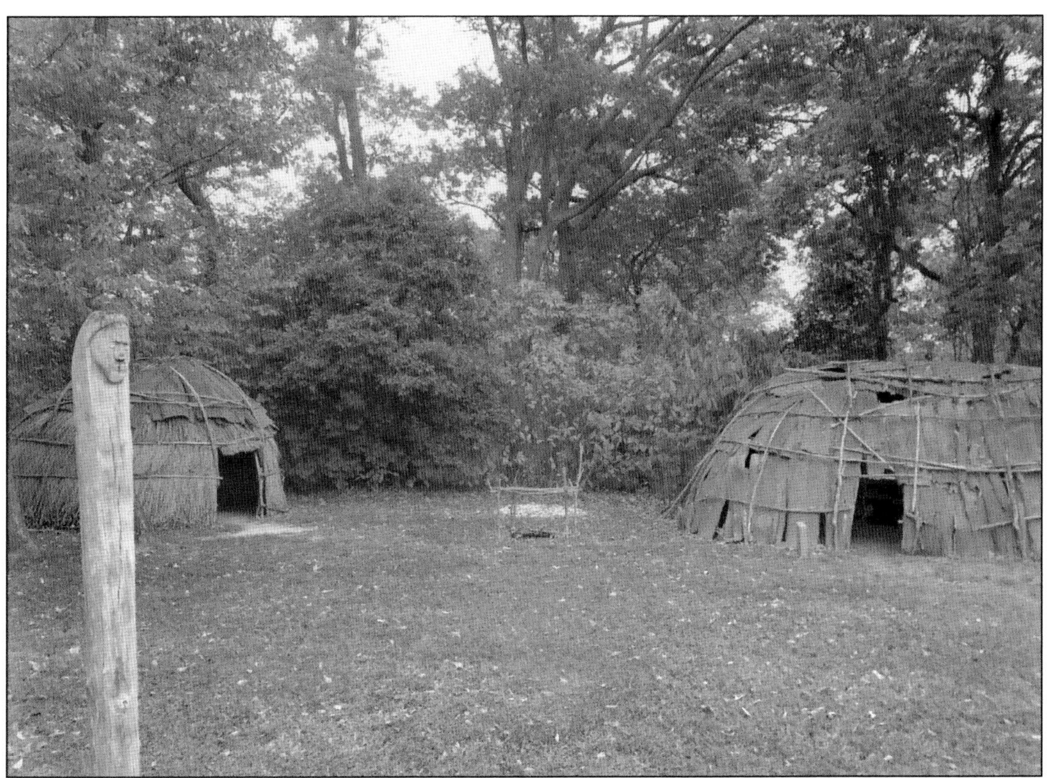

Before the coming of European colonists, Southern Maryland had been occupied by several Algonquian-speaking tribes, including the Patuxent and the nearby Piscataway-Conoy. Within Jefferson Patterson Park & Museum is a re-created Patuxent Indian village, similar to the palisaded settlement that Capt. John Smith would have seen on his visit to the area in 1608, prior to the founding of the Maryland colony.

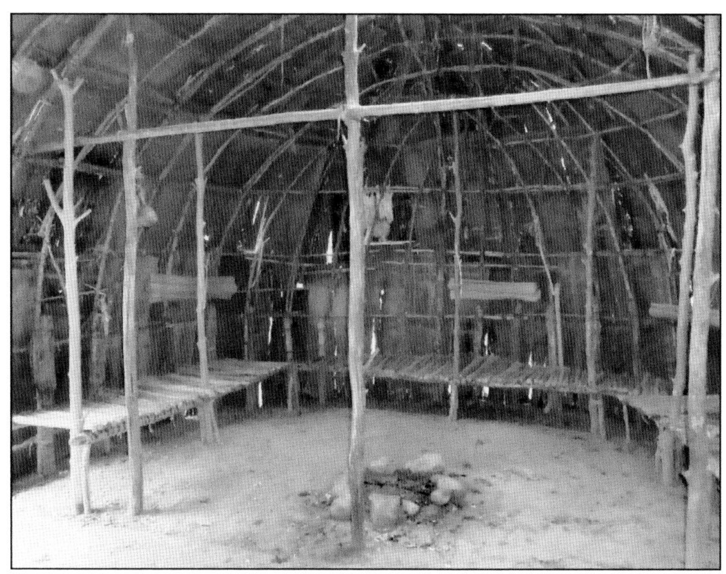

Using information gleaned from archaeological excavations, architectural studies, colonial records and artwork, and other sources, park professionals have reconstructed several dwellings typical of Indian tribes from Maryland and eastern North America. The homes were made of bent saplings tied together to form a strong but flexible structure that would be covered in tree bark, woven mats, or animal skins, with built-in benches for sitting or sleeping.

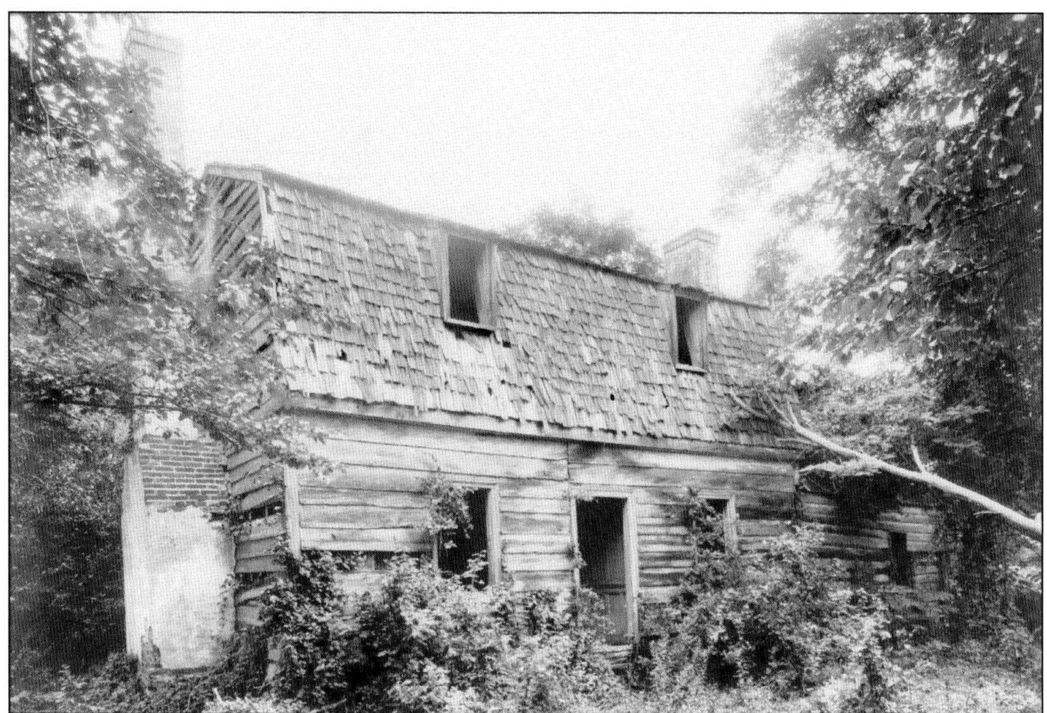

Great Eltonhead Manor was built on a 5,603-acre estate first claimed by Edward Eltonhead in 1651 and granted by Lord Calvert in 1658. By the time of this 1925 photograph, the ancient manor house had been abandoned and fallen into disrepair. All that exists today of the site, which is situated on private property, are the ruins of the chimneys that flanked either end of the home. (Harry B. Leopold, HABS.)

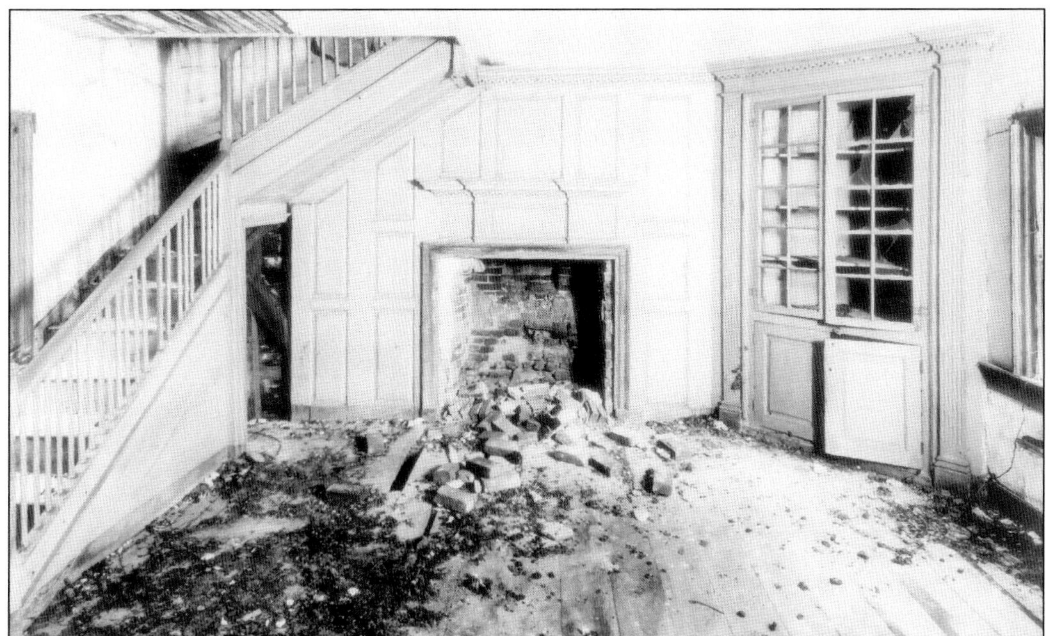

The house known as the Old Eltonhead Manor was built in the mid-18th century on an estate patented in the prior century. Given the home's deteriorated condition in 1925, Hamilton Owens, the owner at the time, presented the exquisite wood paneling shown in this photograph to the Baltimore Museum of Art, where it has been preserved in the Eltonhead Manor Room. (Harry B. Leopold, HABS.)

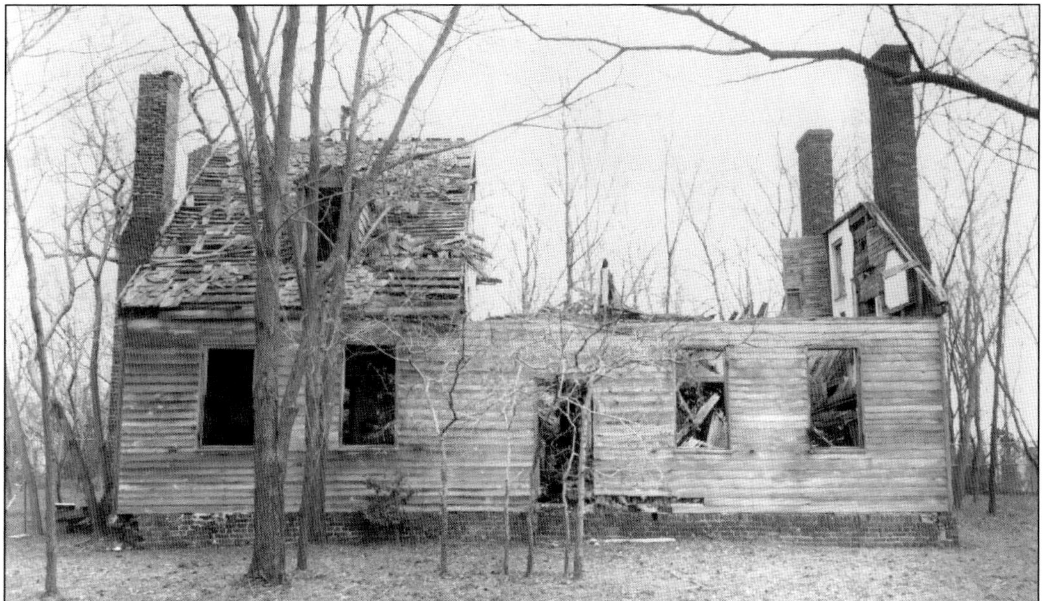

Appointed as a member of the Governor's Council in 1652, Richard Preston was granted this land in 1658. The property changed hands and names over time, first known as Charles's Gift in 1676 and then as Wilson's Farm after 1691, when this house, originally called Preston's Cliffs, was built on the site. It was in ruins when this photograph was taken for a historic survey in 1972. (Douglas Barber, HABS.)

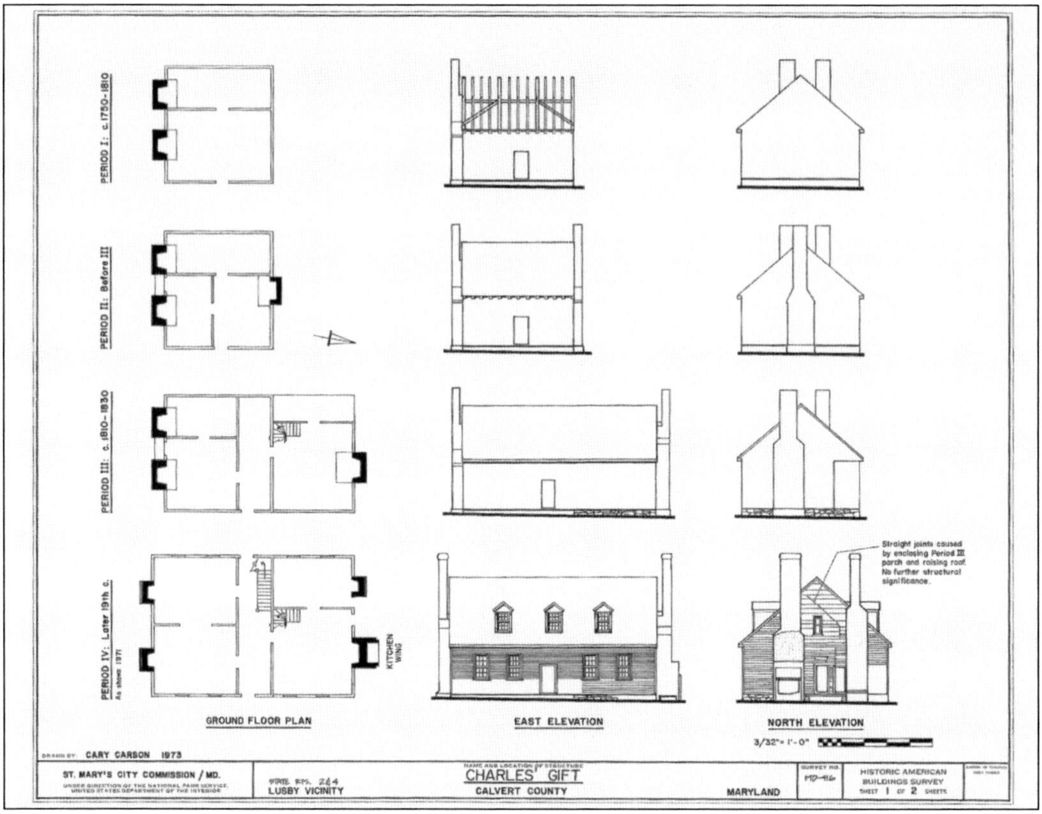

PERIOD I: c.1750–1810

PERIOD II: Before III

PERIOD III: c.1810–1830

PERIOD IV: Later 19th c.
As shown 1971

KITCHEN WING

Straight joints caused by enclosing Period III porch and raising roof. No further structural significance.

GROUND FLOOR PLAN

EAST ELEVATION

NORTH ELEVATION

3/32" = 1'-0"

DRAWN BY: CARY CARSON 1973

ST. MARY'S CITY COMMISSION / MD.

LUSBY VICINITY

CHARLES' GIFT

CALVERT COUNTY

MARYLAND

HISTORIC AMERICAN BUILDINGS SURVEY

SHEET 1 OF 2 SHEETS

This 1973 Historic American Buildings Survey drawing prepared by the St. Mary's City Commission presents the physical changes to the home at Preston's Cliffs, from the late 17th century through the early 19th century. Having evolved from a simple two-room colonial cottage to a typical Southern Maryland manor house, the structure now stands in ruins on private property in the area of Calvert Cliffs. (Cary Carson, HABS.)

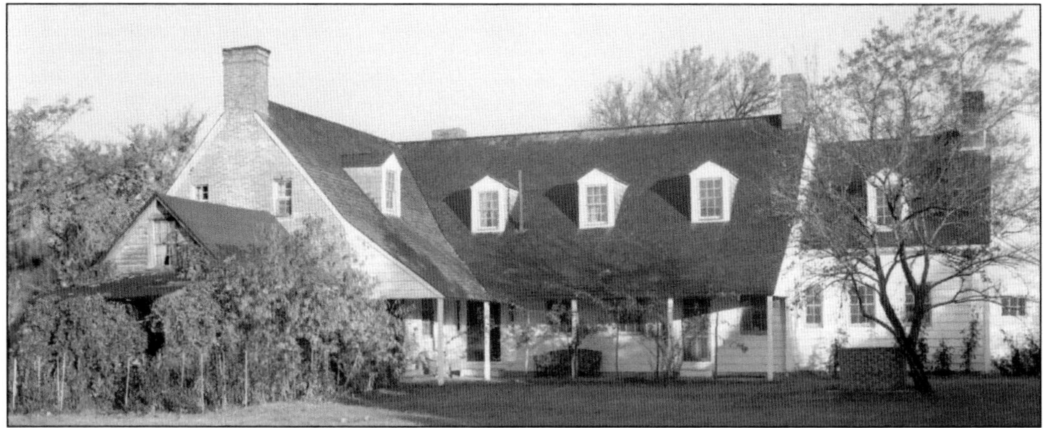

Preston-on-the-Patuxent is considered a fine representative of the tobacco plantations that characterized the region, with extensive landholdings and ready access to the water for shipment of the prepared leaves. Taken by famed photographer Frances Benjamin Johnston in 1936, this image shows the rear of the restored home and the additions made to it over two centuries of occupation. (FBJPC, LOC.)

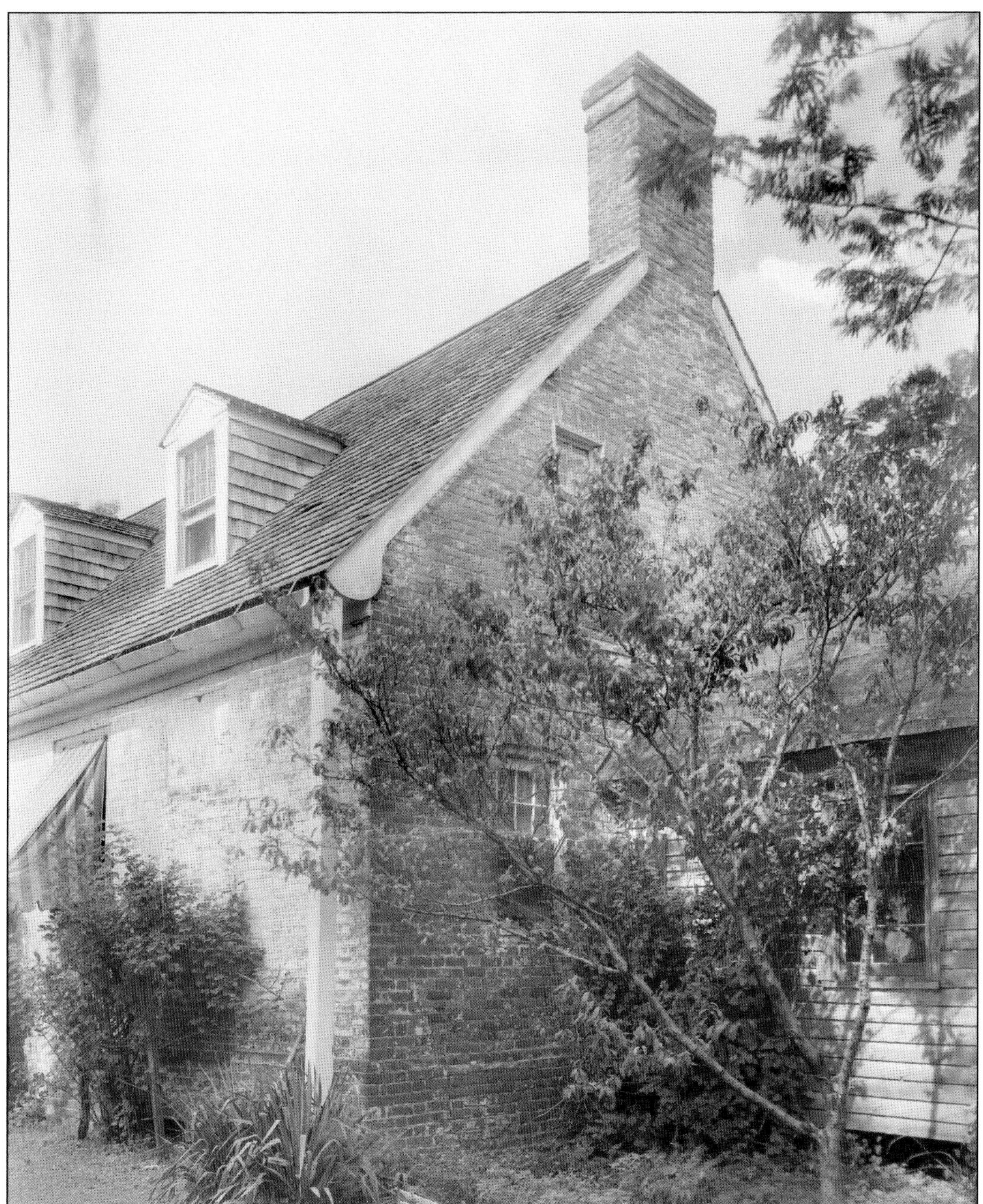

Preston-on-the-Patuxent is a one-and-a-half-story brick Colonial home built on one of Richard Preston's other land holdings. Though it was once believed to date from the second half of the 17th century, more accurate assessments of the oldest parts of this home seem to indicate a date from the 1720s, with other changes taking place through the 19th century and an early-20th-century restoration. (FBJPC, LOC.)

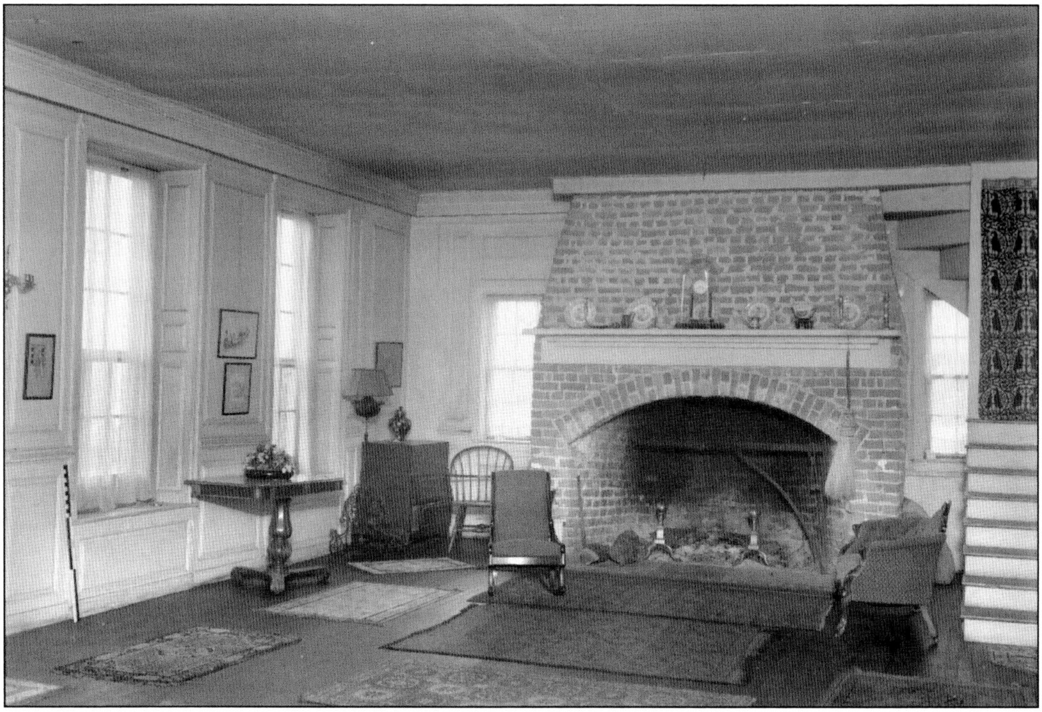

The simplicity of the exterior of many Colonial Southern Maryland homes belies a reserved but elegant interior. The finely made wood paneling and generous brick fireplace and hearth in Preston-on-the-Patuxent would have witnessed generations of family and social gatherings throughout the years. (E.H. Pickering, HABS.)

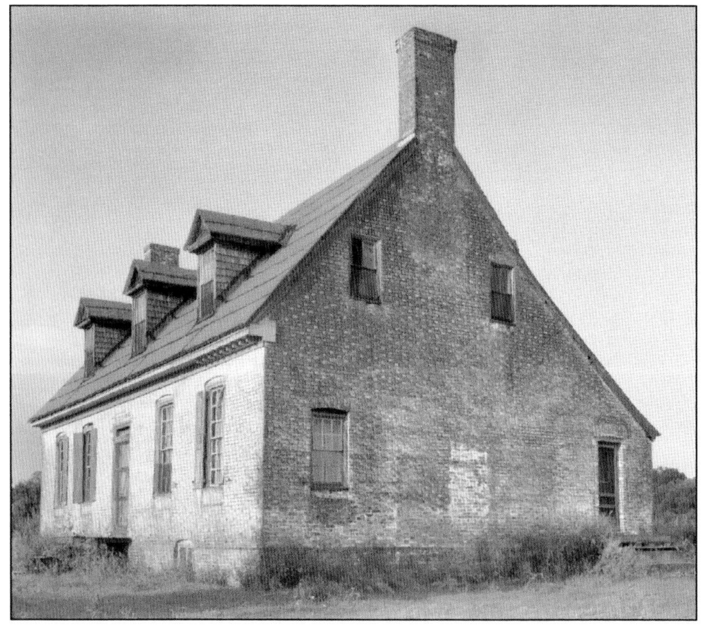

Patuxent Manor, also known as the Grahame or Graeme House, is a one-and-a-half-story mid-18th-century brick home located in the village of Lower Marlboro, near the Patuxent River. Built about 1743, the home's fine interior woodwork was so admired that it was removed and sold to the Henry Francis du Pont Winterthur Museum in the 1930s. (FBJPC, LOC.)

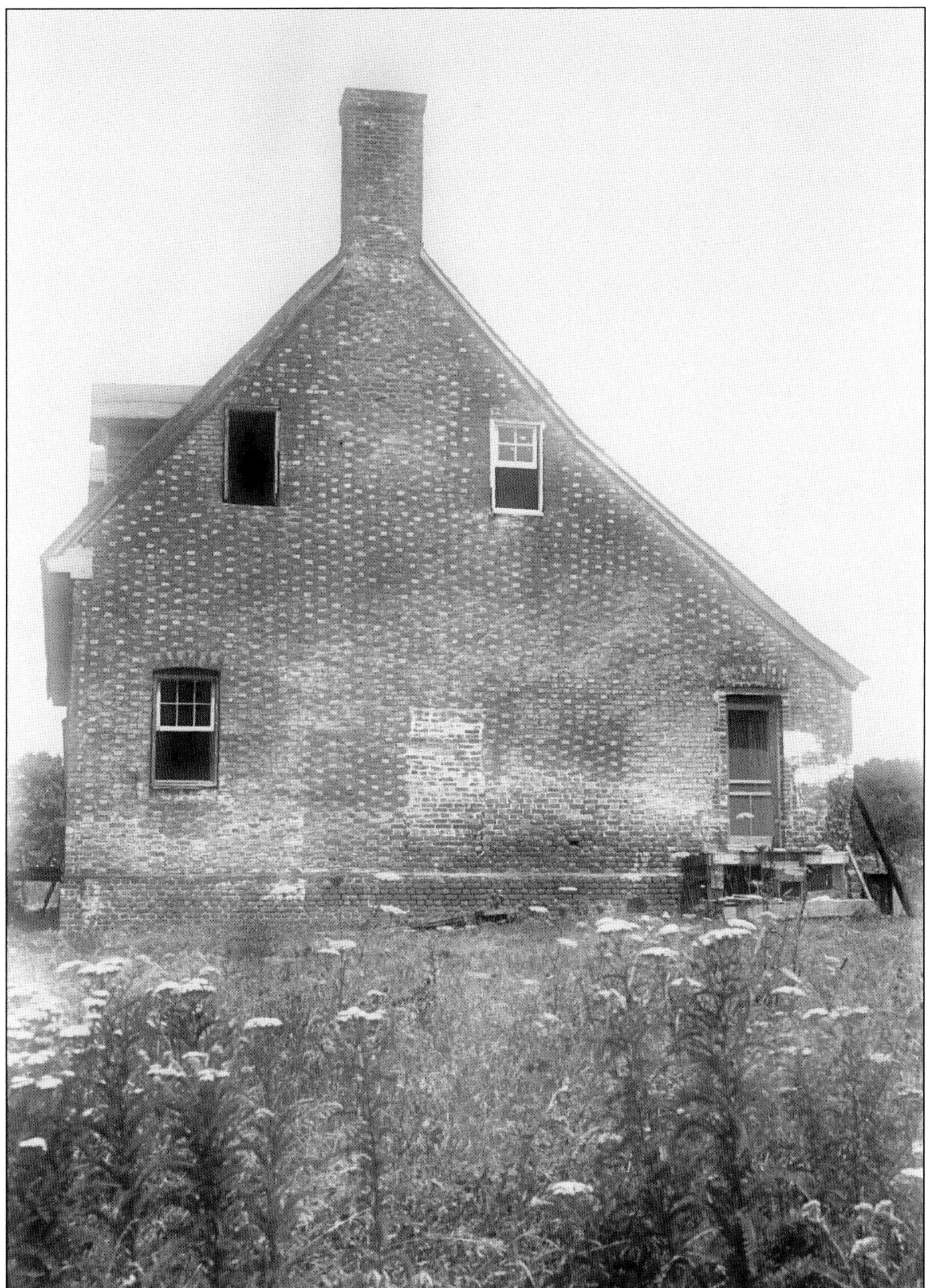

The rear of Patuxent Manor shows the steeply pitched and elongated back half of the roof, which is not uncommon on Southern Maryland homes of the period. This type of roofline is typically called a catslide in Maryland and known as a saltbox in New England. (FBJPC, LOC.)

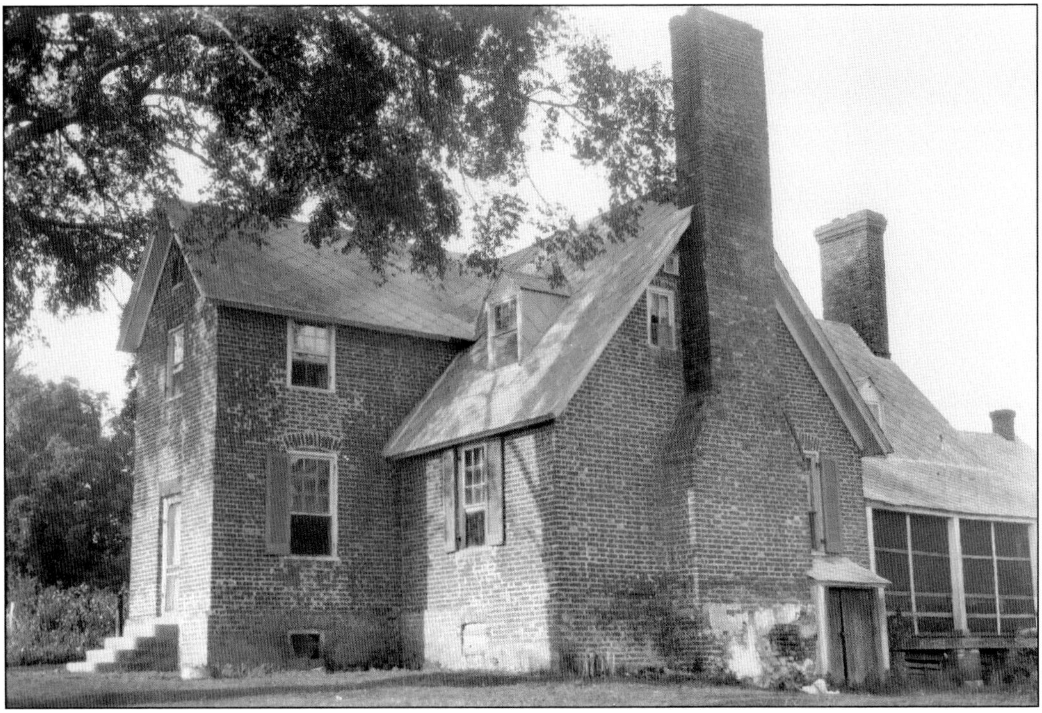

Cedar Hill, also called the Gantt House, in Barstow is the only remaining example of a two-and-a-half-story brick Colonial home built on a cruciform foundation plan in Southern Maryland. Though most of the present house dates from the mid- to late 18th century, the earliest part may date from before 1714, at which time it was under the ownership of merchant-planter John Bigger, who served in the Colonial militia and assembly in Annapolis. (HABS.)

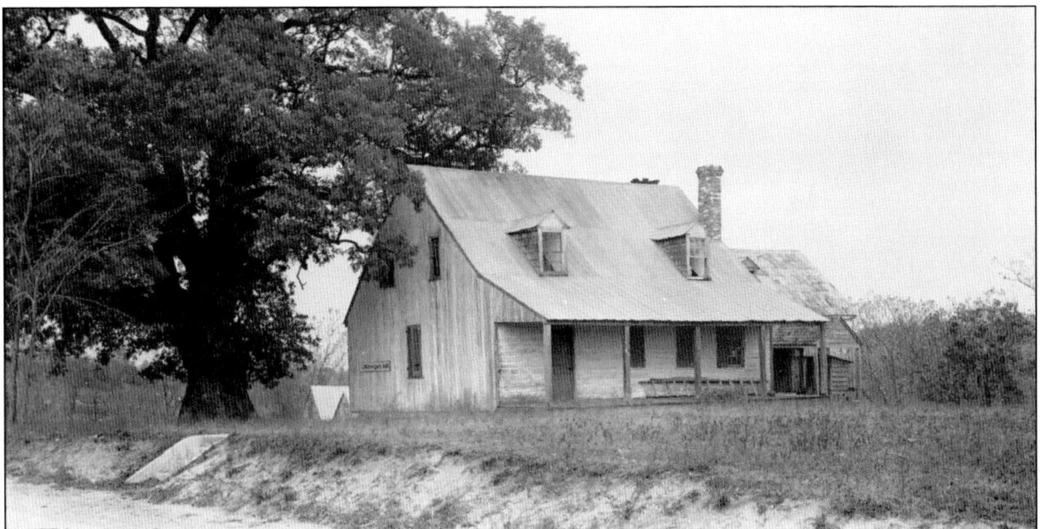

During the Great Depression, drivers would stop for a drink in Huntingtown at J.W. Armiger's Bar in the basement of his house. The family of John Walter Armiger, a World War I veteran and farmer, acquired the c. 1790 John Norfolk House in 1908. The house later had to be moved back several hundred yards to prevent it from being demolished for road widening in 1968. (Delos H. Smith, HABS.)

Built between 1670 and 1700, the house at Morgan Hill Farm, also called the Day-Breedon House, near Morgan's Fresh is a one-and-a-half-story wood farmhouse on a stone foundation that was originally constructed as a hall and parlor house with a large central chimney. Like many historic homes, the structure has undergone numerous changes over the last 300 years, but it retains great integrity. (R. Randolph Langenbach, HABS.)

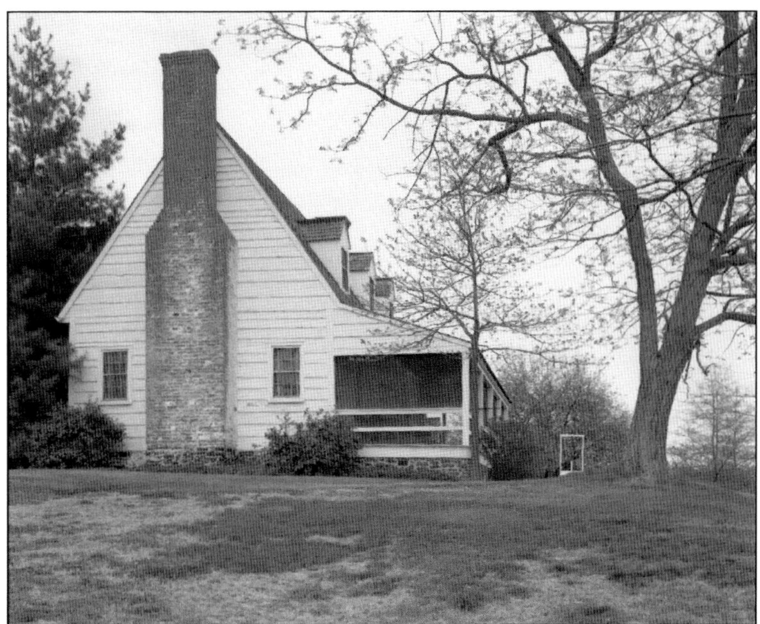

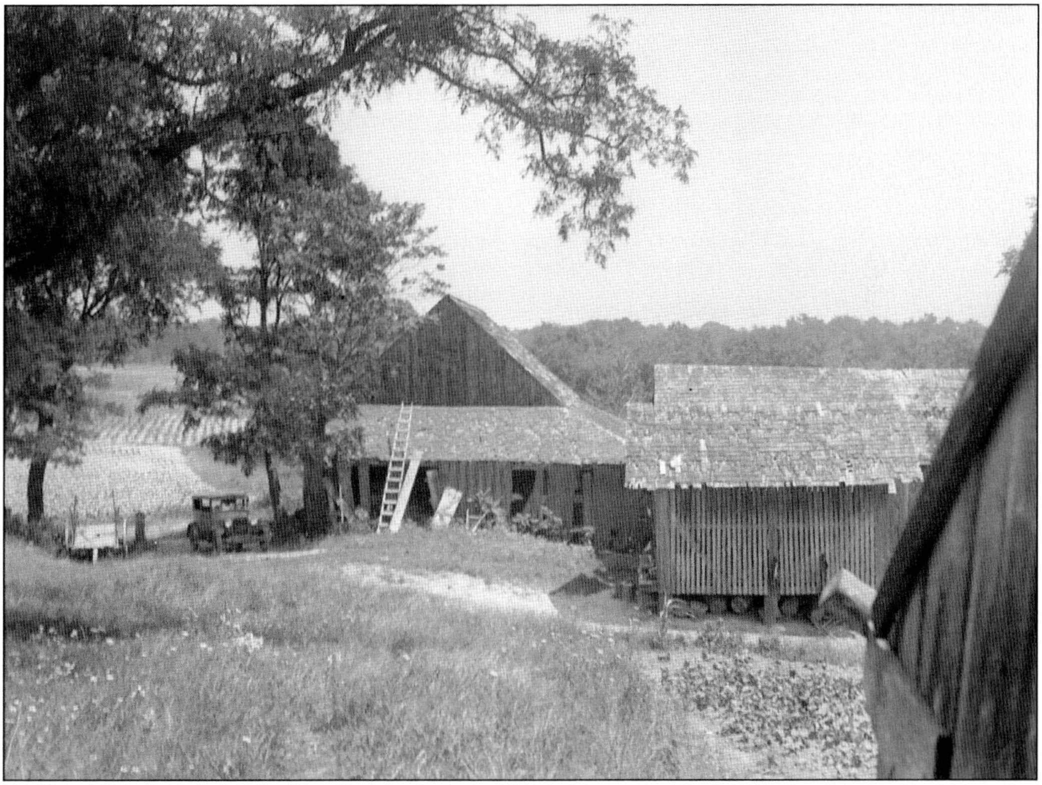

Located west of Lusby near St. Leonard Creek, Morgan Hill Farm was built on land granted to Capt. Phillip Morgan in 1651. The farm has a remarkably well-preserved historic landscape, with its barn, corncrib, and smokehouse surviving into recent years. This photograph of the farm was taken in 1934. (Delos H. Smith, HABS.)

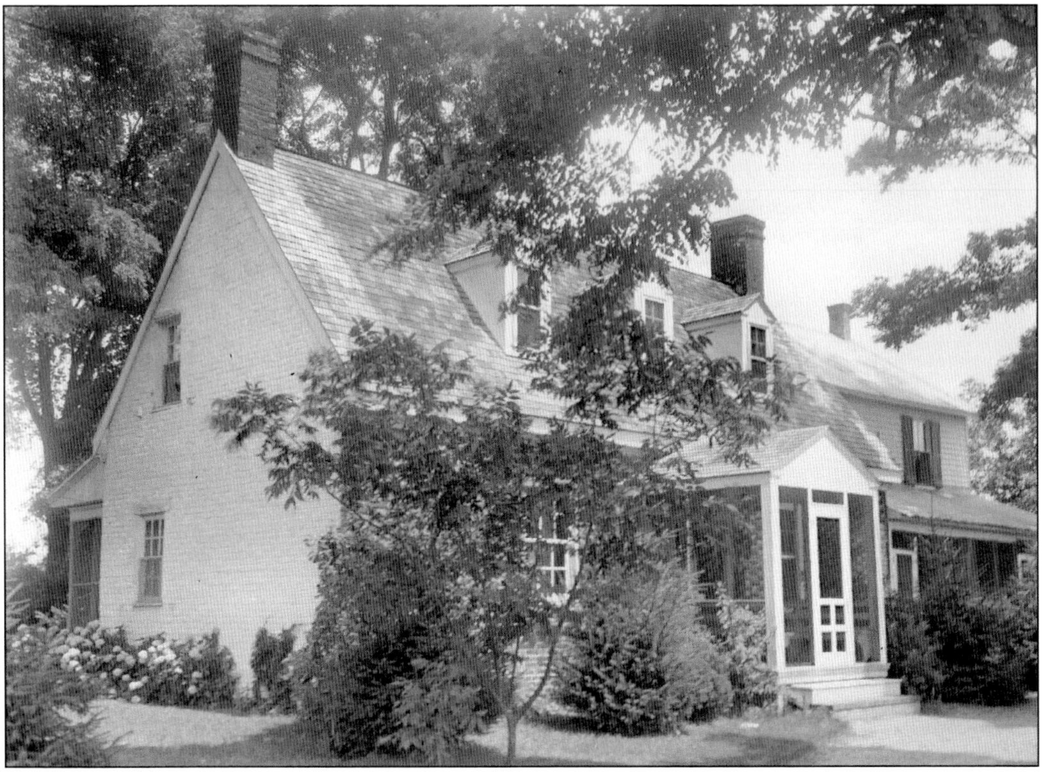

Parrott's Cage, a one-and-a-half-story, three-bay brick home, was built around 1652, making it one of Southern Maryland's oldest manor houses. Located near Wallville, the land was granted to William Parrott by Lord Calvert in 1649. Through Parrott's wife, Elizabeth Parran, the property has remained in the Parran family since that time. One of its notable residents was Revolutionary War surgeon Thomas Parran. (Delos H. Smith, HABS.)

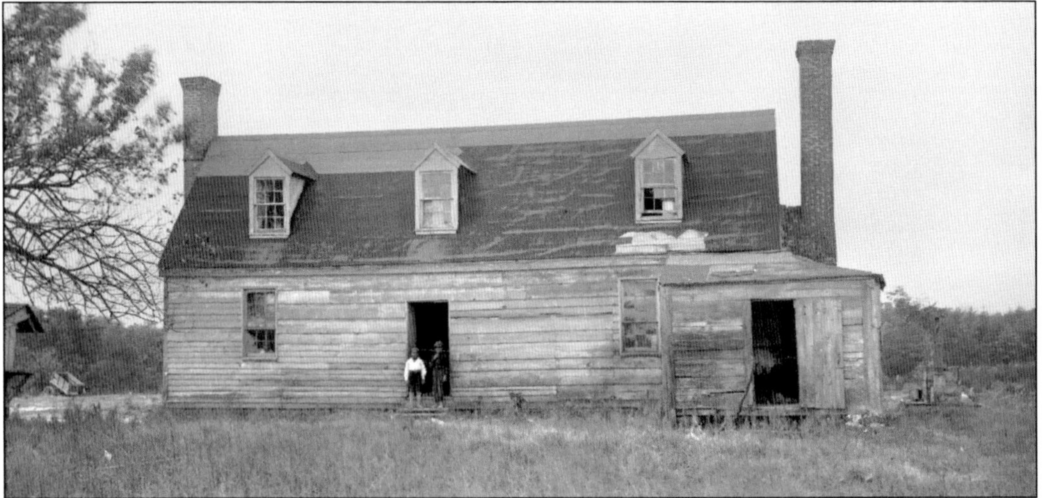

Built around 1750, Parran's Park in Lusby was a one-and-a-half-story, three-bay farmhouse with three pedimented dormers, random-width wood sheathing, and both an all-brick fireplace and a stone-and-brick fireplace on each gable end. The house began as a one-room structure and appears to have been expanded around 1825 to the form seen here in 1934. (E.H. Pickering, HABS.)

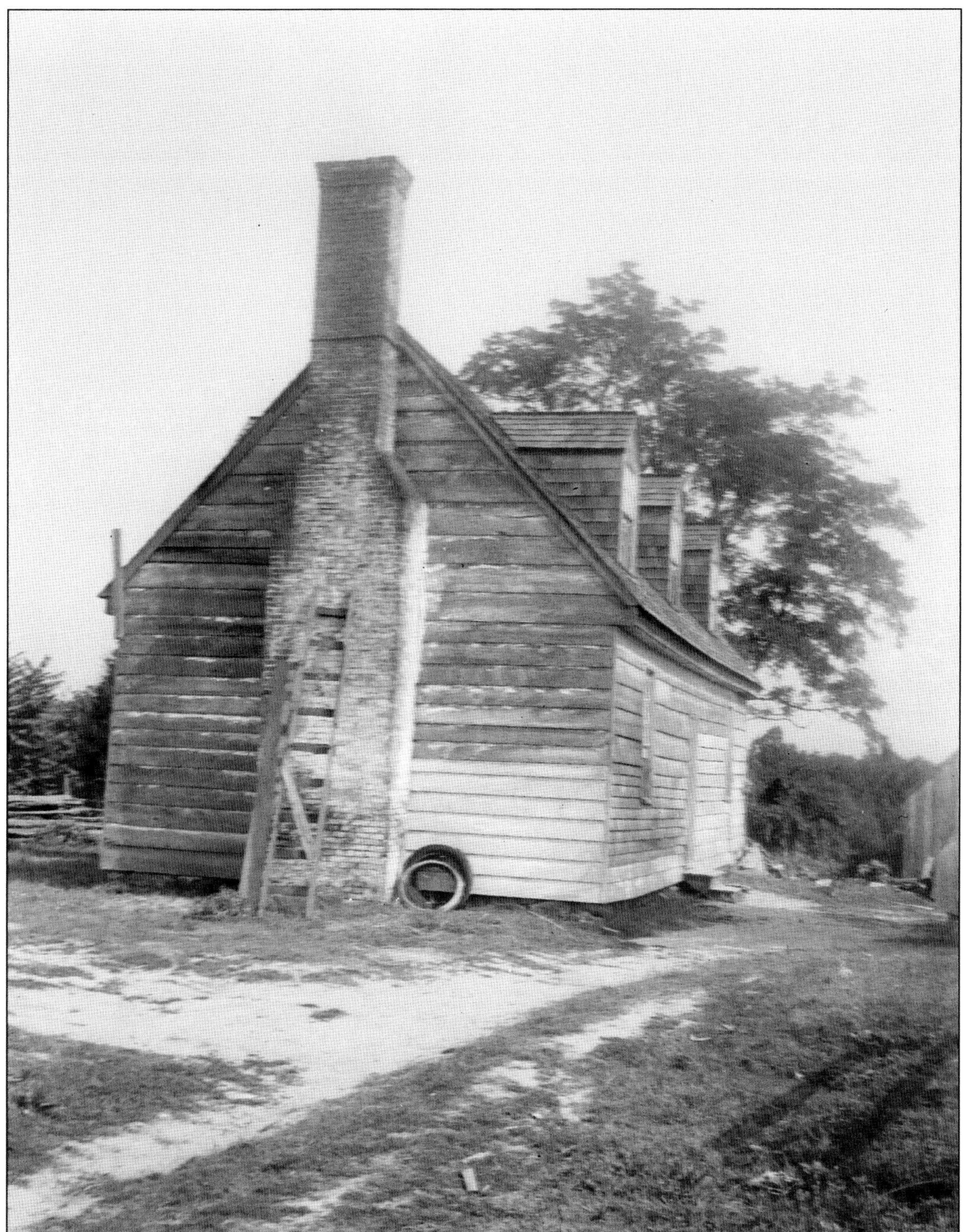

Parran's Park, also called the Goldstein House, was once owned by the late Maryland comptroller Louis L. Goldstein (1913–1998), who hailed from nearby Prince Frederick. Later used as a rental property, the home was severely damaged by fire in 1955 and then abandoned. By 1972, it had been left in ruins and was demolished. Several of the farm's former barns survive on the grounds of the Calvert Cliffs Nuclear Power Plant. (Delos H. Smith, HABS.)

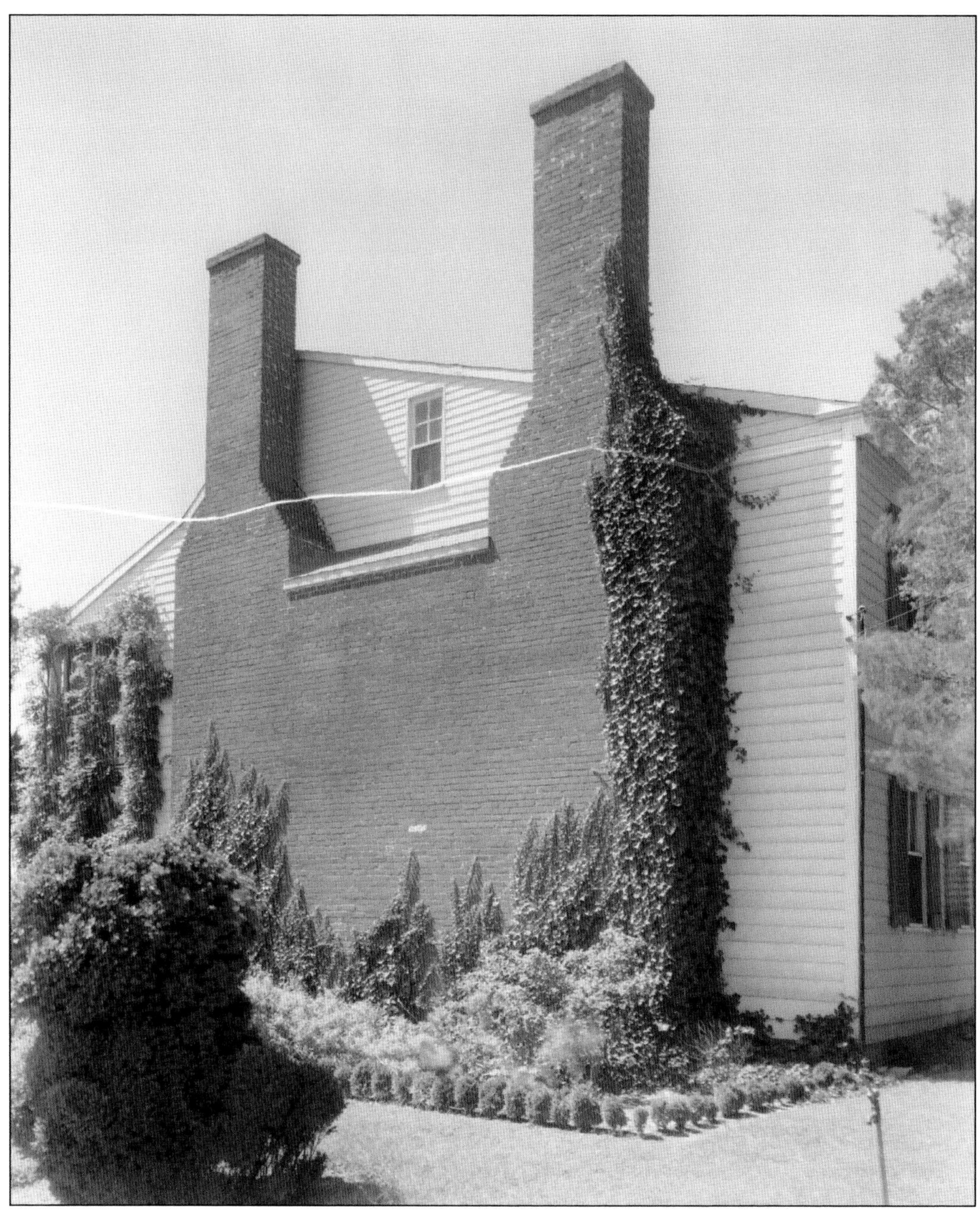

Spout Farm is named for the "spout," or spring, flowing from the bluff where it was built overlooking the mouth of St. Leonard's Creek and the Patuxent River. Incorporating a 17th-century kitchen as its dining room, the home had taken shape by 1780. Its most unusual feature is a pair of massive brick end chimneys connected by two-story brick pents and covered by sloping roofs on the exterior. (FBJPC, LOC.)

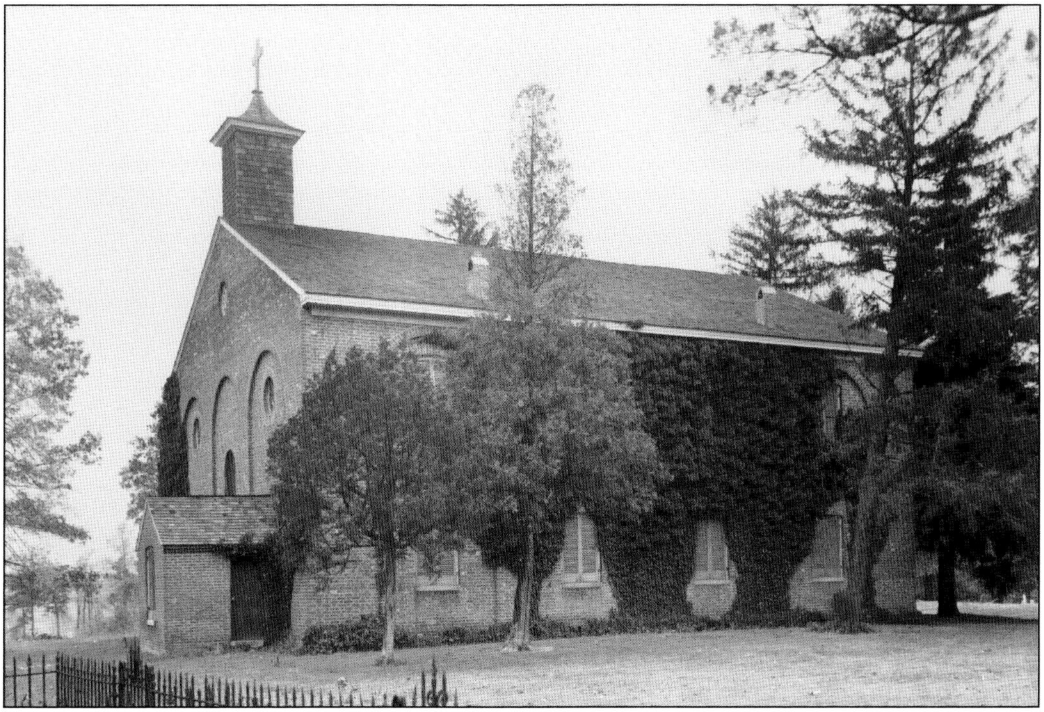

In 1692, an act of the Maryland Legislature established the Anglican (Episcopal) parish in which the existing All Saints Church of Sunderland in northern Calvert County was built between 1774 and 1777. The Georgian-style church was constructed of bricks to replace the first church built of logs at the site in 1695. (E.H. Pickering, HABS.)

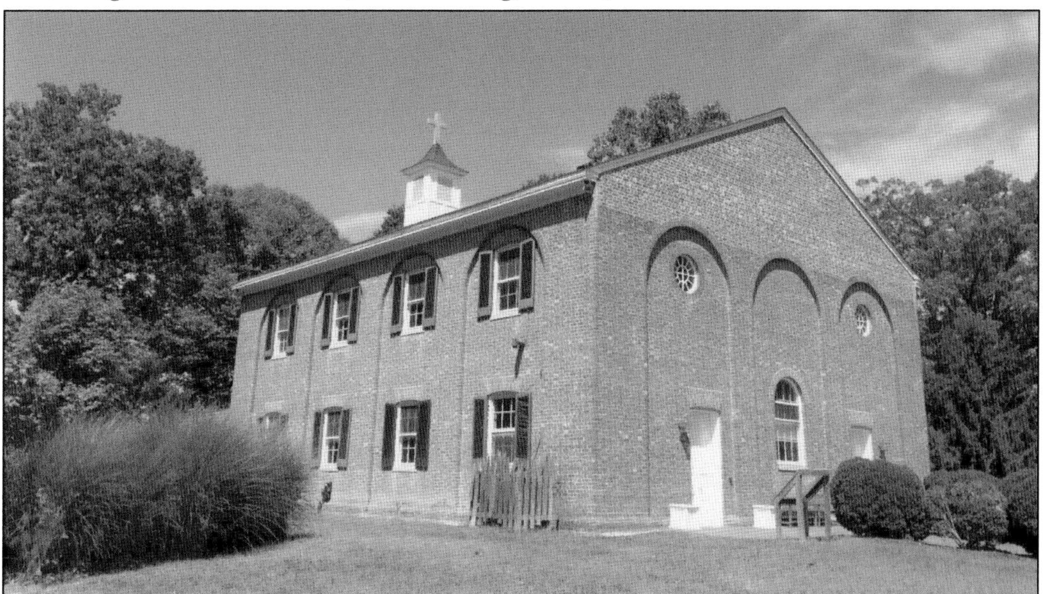

The construction of All Saints Church, built with decorative two-story recessed arches on each side, occurred during the tenure of Rev. Thomas John Claggett (1743–1816) as its rector. In 1792, Claggett, a graduate of Princeton and later Washington College in Chestertown, became the first American-born Episcopal Church bishop to be elected and consecrated in the United States.

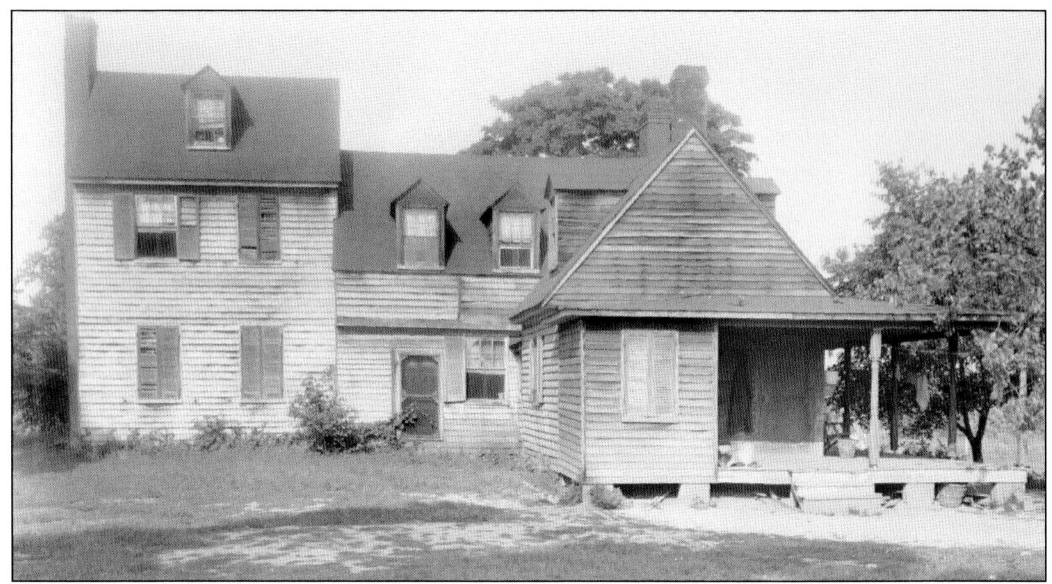

The oldest part of the John Stanforth House, or Huntingfields, in Huntingtown is the two-and-a-half-story north end, which was built between 1697 and 1722, when Stanforth purchased the property from Rev. Thomas Cockshalt. Both men were affiliated with the nearby All Saints Church, where Cockshalt was the rector and Stanforth was a warden. At one time in shambles, the home was completely restored in the 1960s. (Delos H. Smith, HABS.)

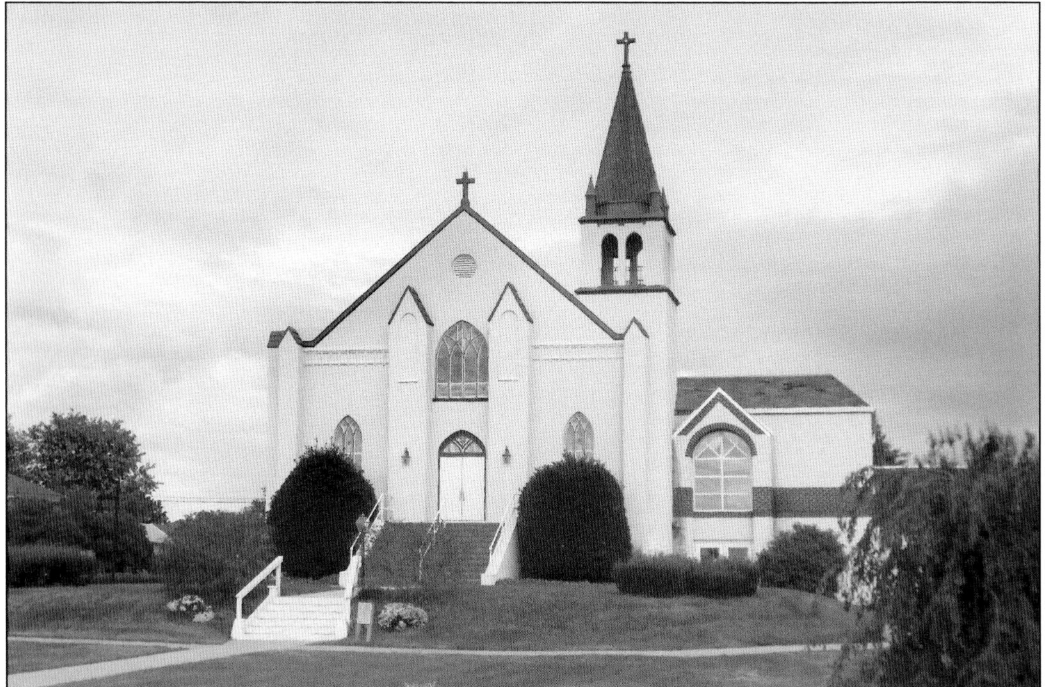

Located on the north side of the Narrows inlet across from Solomon's Island proper, Our Lady Star of the Sea Catholic Church was first established as a parish in 1888. The present Gothic Revival church was built of stuccoed masonry 40 years later and has been serving the local community ever since.

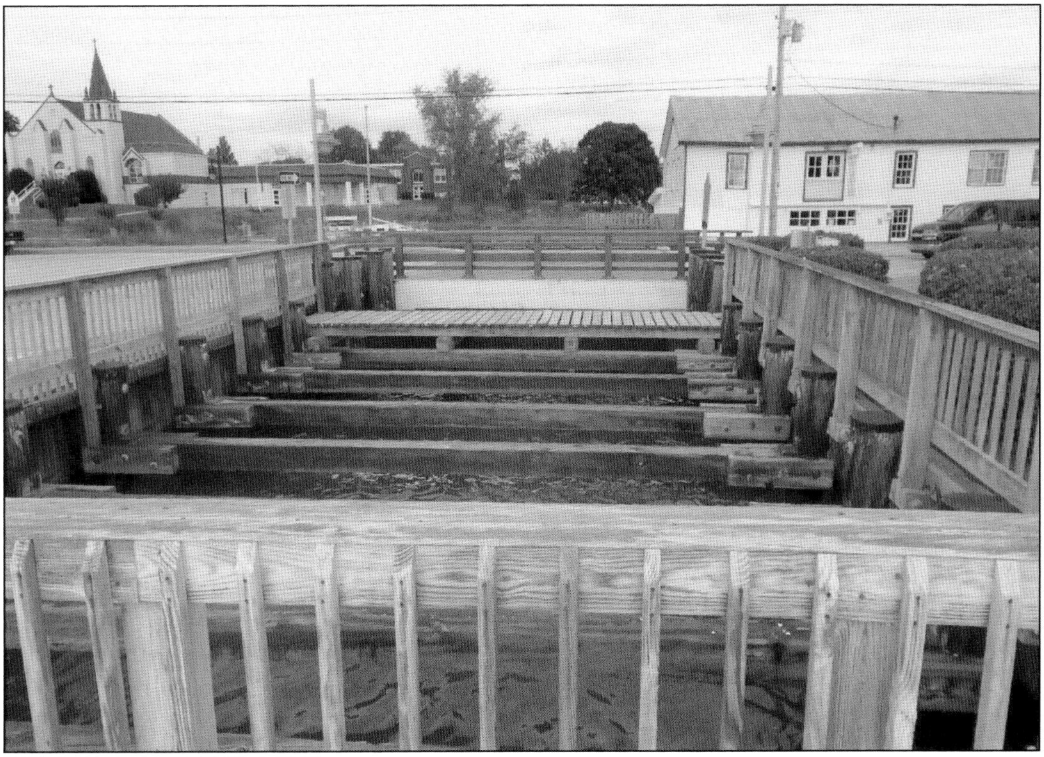

Separating the Calvert County peninsula from Solomon's Island is a small channel known as the Tide Box that connects the Patuxent River with the Narrows inlet. The channel was much wider in the past, but it was narrowed to close to its present size as a result of bridge, causeway, and seawall construction from 1895 to 1915.

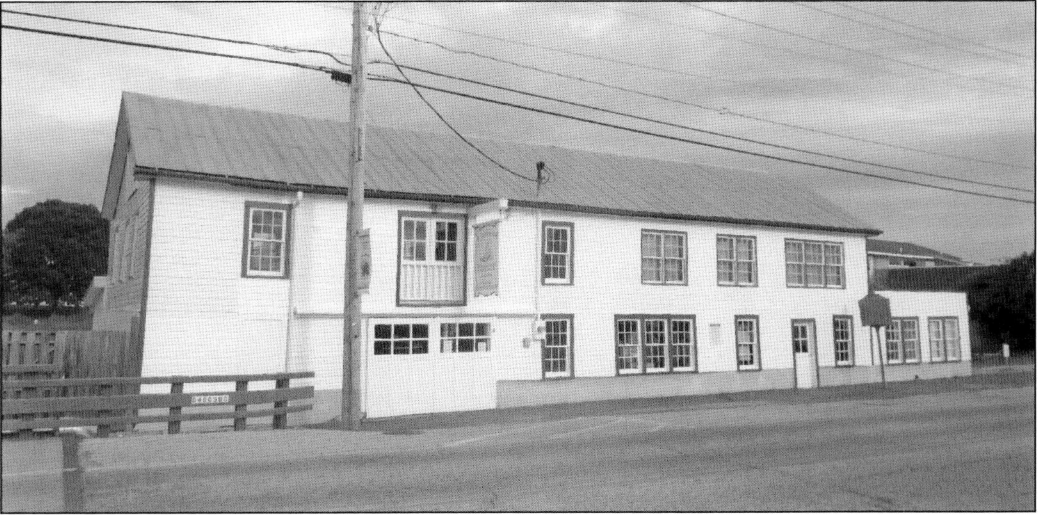

Adjacent to the Tide Box and across the Narrows from Our Lady Star of the Sea Catholic Church is the J.C. Lore Oyster House. Built in 1934 to replace an earlier structure damaged in a 1933 hurricane, the oyster house is an extant example of an early-20th-century seafood packinghouse that represents the region's historic tie to the once extensive seafood industry and its economic importance to the state.

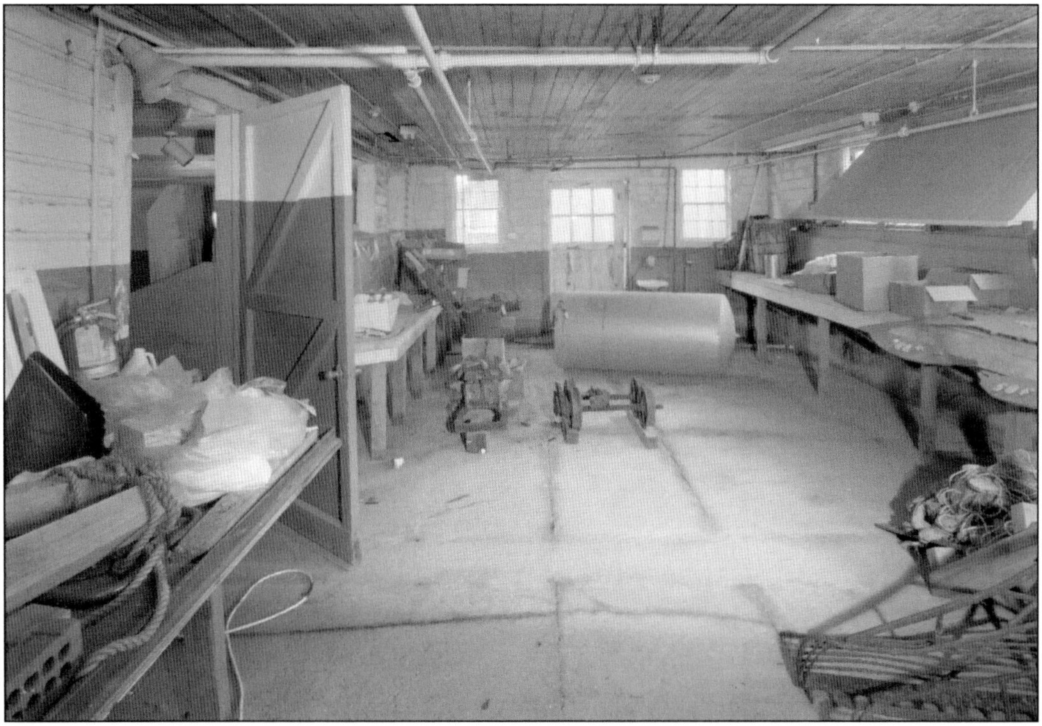

Designated as a National Historic Landmark because of its integrity and significance, the J.C. Lore Oyster House retains much of its original layout and equipment. Today, the building is operated as a facility of the nearby Calvert Marine Museum. During the summer, it is open for tours discussing the natural ecology of the oyster and the history of the oyster-packing industry. (Justine Christianson, HABS.)

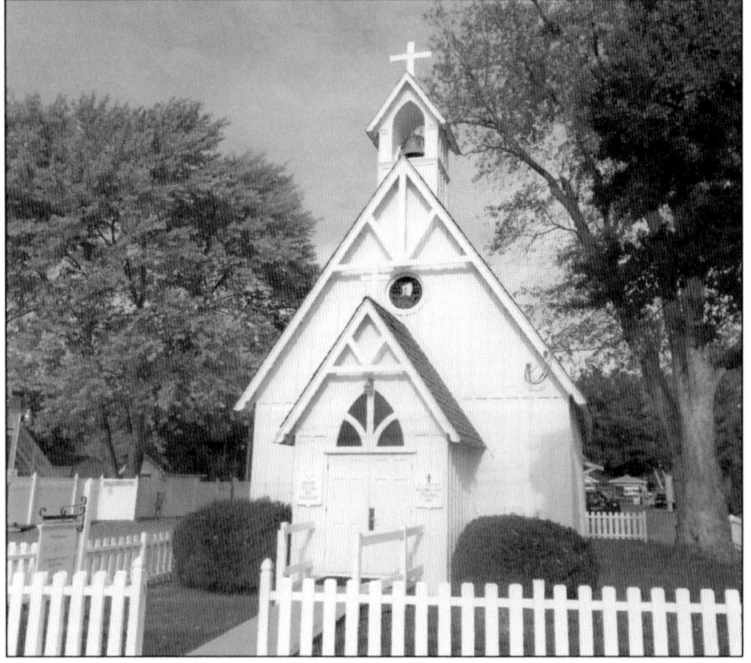

Maryland's Episcopal bishop William Paret consecrated St. Peter's Chapel for parish use in 1890. Topped by a small belfry and adorned by stained-glass rose and lancet windows, the tiny Carpenter Gothic structure is one of the few board-and-batten churches standing in Southern Maryland.

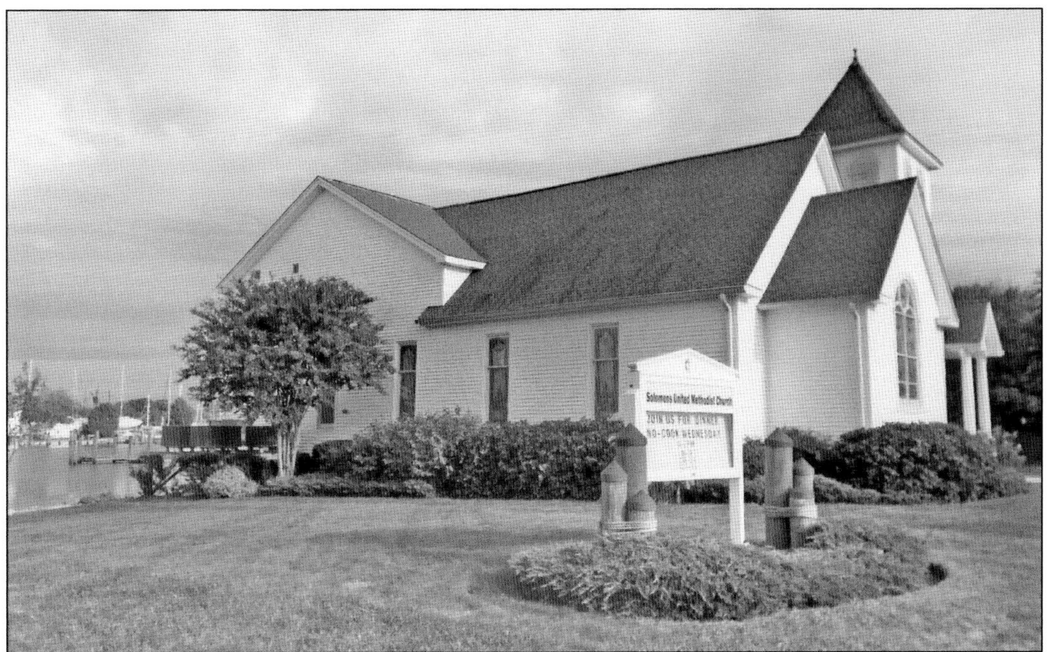

Organized as a congregation in 1866 and built in 1870, the frame and weatherboarded Solomon's United Methodist Church backs onto waterfront land donated by Isaac Solomon, for whom the island was renamed in 1867 due to his oyster-packing operations here. The island had been known as Somervell's Island since 1740 and, prior to that, as Bourne's Island in 1680.

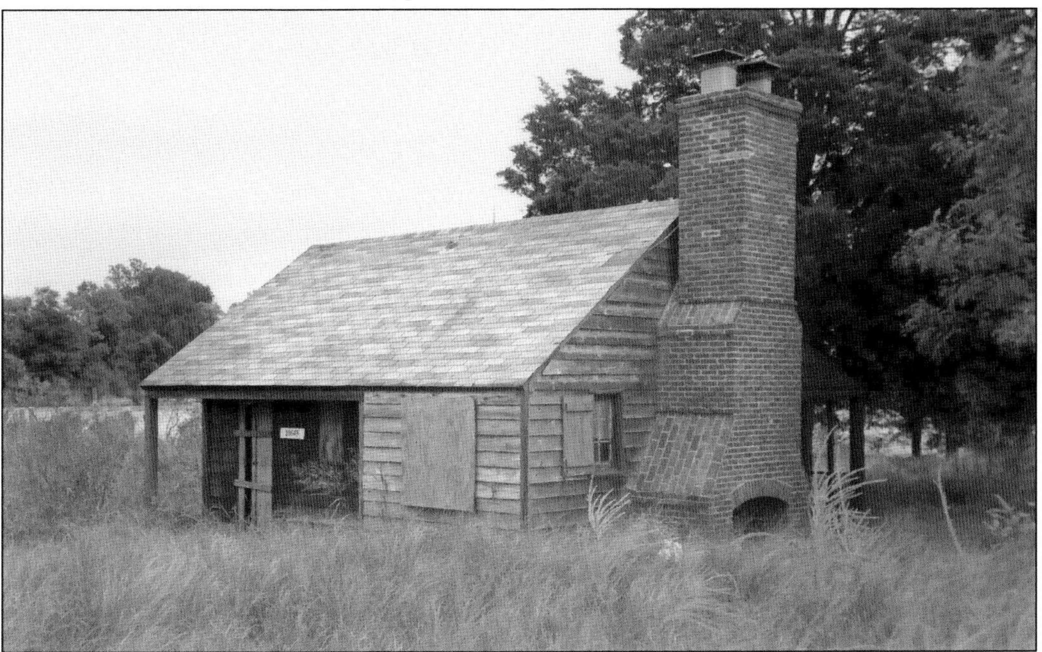

Situated on a small, sandy spit that juts into the confluence of St. Leonard's Creek and the Patuxent River, this small beach cottage with the region's traditional shouldered brick chimney was the first structure built for Washington socialites Jefferson and Mary Marvin Breckenridge Patterson on the property that they had acquired as their country estate, Point Farm, in 1932.

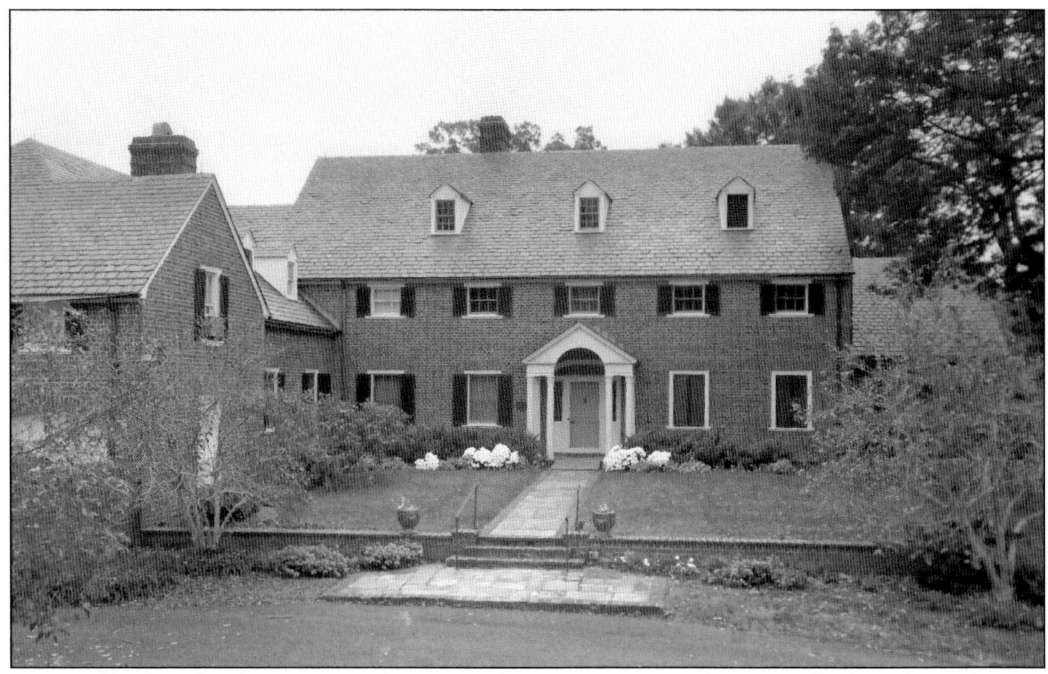

Designed by famed architect Gertrude Sawyer, the Pattersons' main house was built in the traditional Colonial Revival style of Southern Maryland and the Chesapeake Tidewater between 1932 and 1934. Both Jefferson and Mary had inherited fortunes. He served as a career diplomat while she was a foreign news correspondent during World War II. The 10,400-square-foot mansion hosted many visiting foreign officials, diplomats, and business leaders.

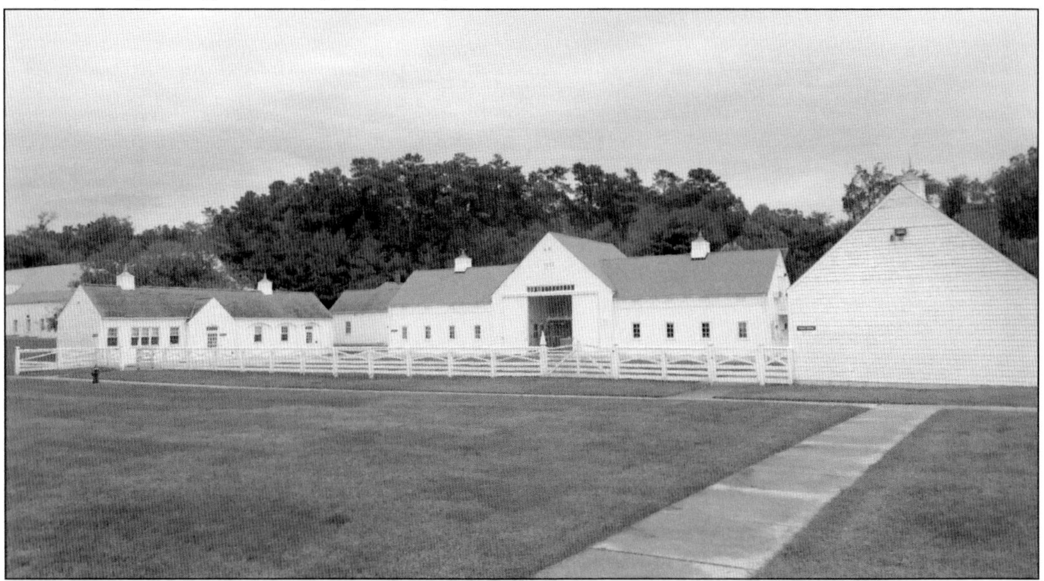

Following the death of her husband in 1977, Mary Marvin Patterson donated Point Farm to the State of Maryland in 1983. Many of the property's estate buildings have become important elements of the Jefferson Patterson Park and its programs. The dairy barn, one of the first structures that Gertrude Sawyer designed and built for the Pattersons in 1932, now serves as the facility used for the preparation of museum exhibits.

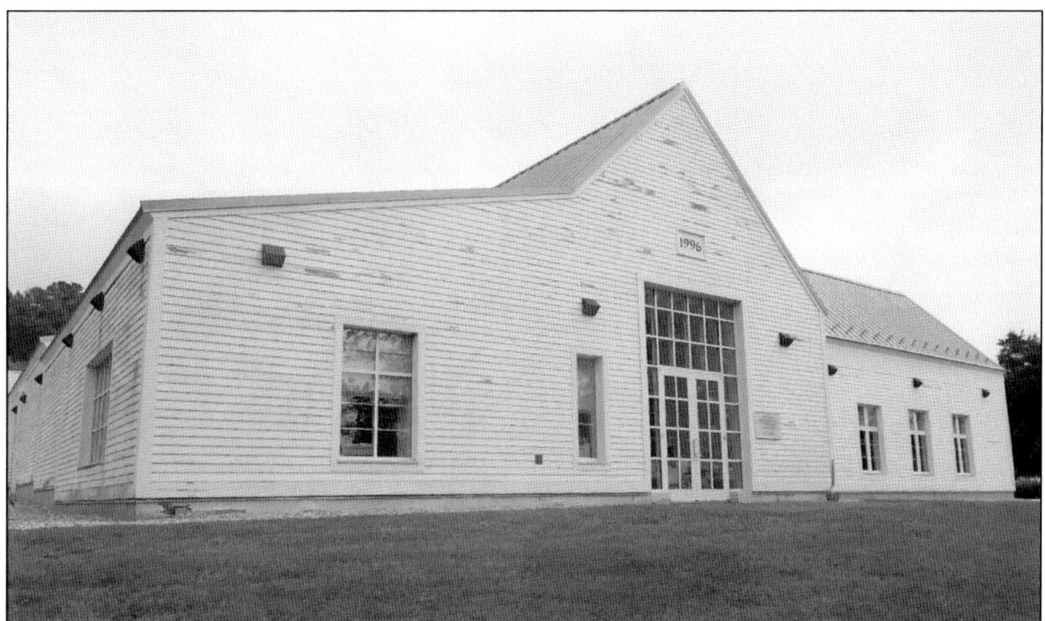

Adjacent to the 1932 dairy barn is the Maryland Archaeological Conservation Laboratory (or MAC Lab) building, erected in 1996 and opened in 1998. The MAC Lab holds the archaeological collections of the State of Maryland. Here, they are cleaned, conserved, catalogued, stabilized, and stored. Researchers come to the lab to study its collections and use its large research library to better understand the rich heritage of Southern Maryland and the state.

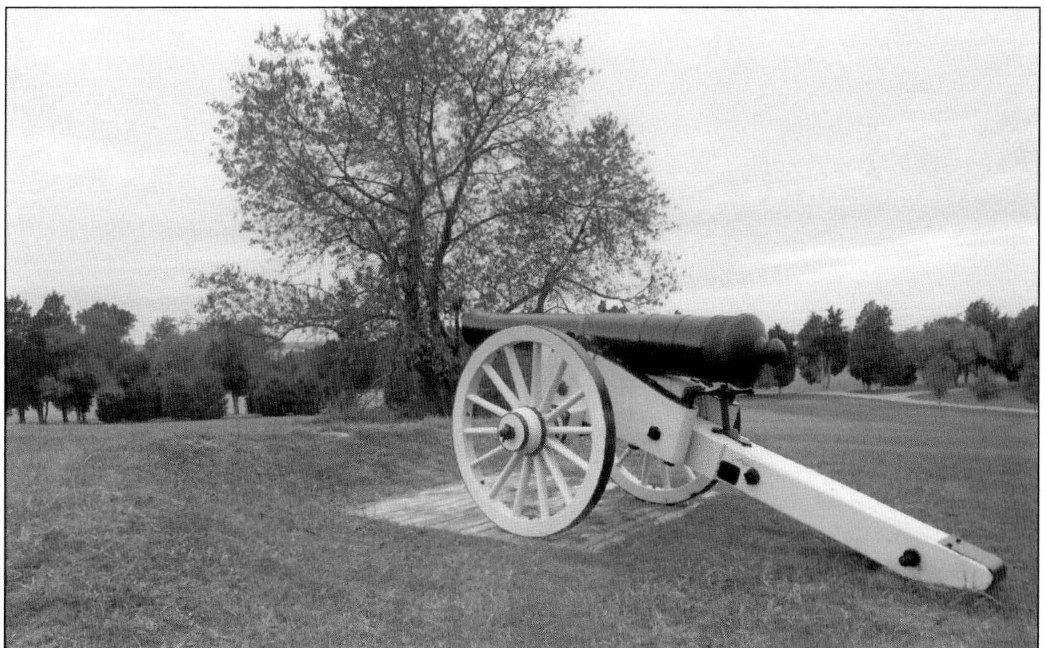

It was also here, along the waters of Jefferson Patterson Park's 560 acres, that land and sea forces under the command of American commodore Joshua Barney twice battled to a draw the much larger British naval force in the first and second Battles of St. Leonard's Creek in June 1814 in an attempt to slow the enemy's advance to the city of Washington.

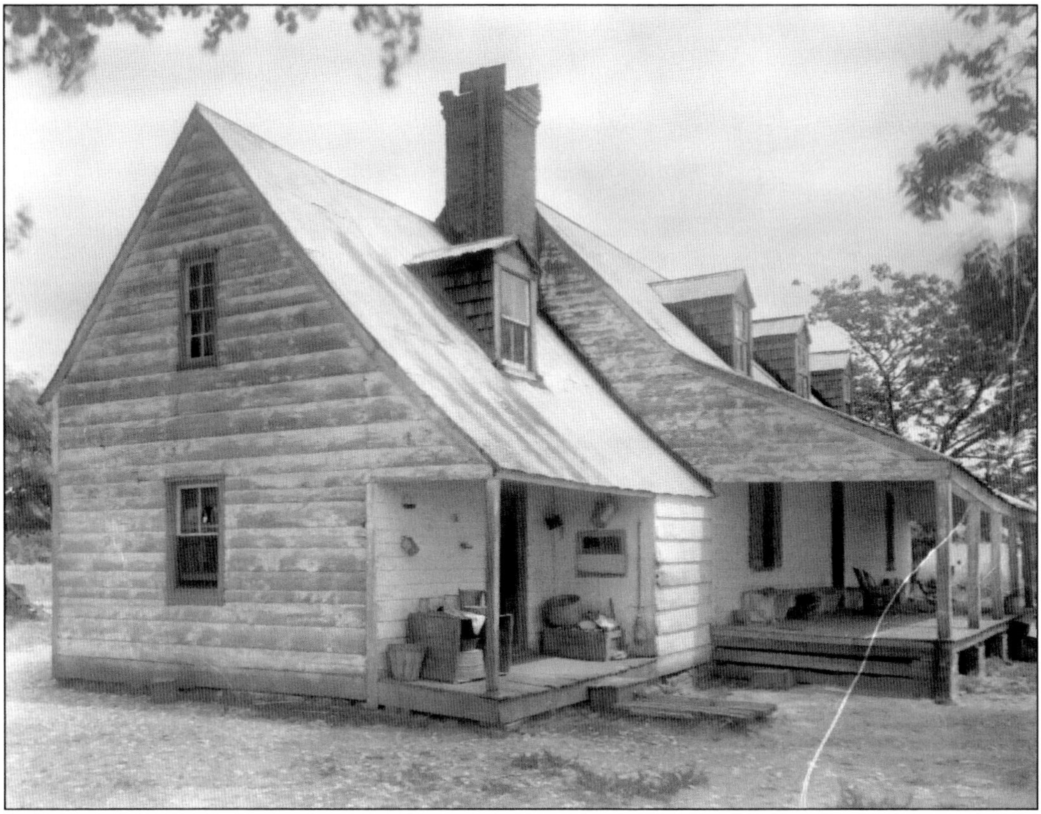

Built on part of the Eltonhead Manor grant to John Rousby in 1667, the one-and-a-half-story Rousby Hall is the third house on the site since the 17th century. Earlier homes were destroyed by the British during the American Revolution (1780) and the War of 1812 (1814). The present house at Drum Point across from Solomon's Island may incorporate elements of the earlier structures. (FBJPC, LOC.)

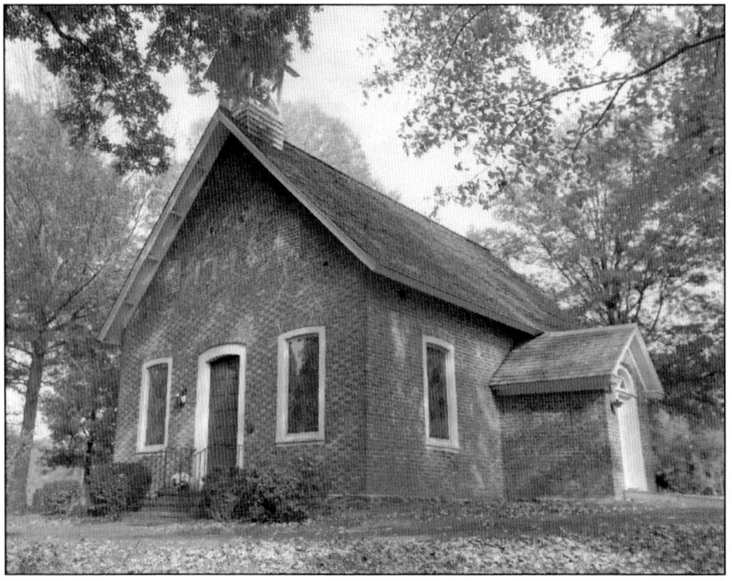

Built in 1748 to replace a wooden chapel from around 1684, Middleham Chapel near Calvert Cliffs is the oldest religious building in Calvert County. Repaired and remodeled in both 1792 and 1893, the brick cruciform-plan structure operated as a chapel of ease for the larger Christ Church (Episcopal) parish in Port Republic and retains the use of a bell that settler John Holdsworth provided to the chapel in 1699.

In November 2014, members of Middleham and St. Peter's Parishes established a memorial to the slaves once owned by parishioners before the Civil War and whose remains are interred in unmarked graves in the churchyard surrounding Middleham Chapel.

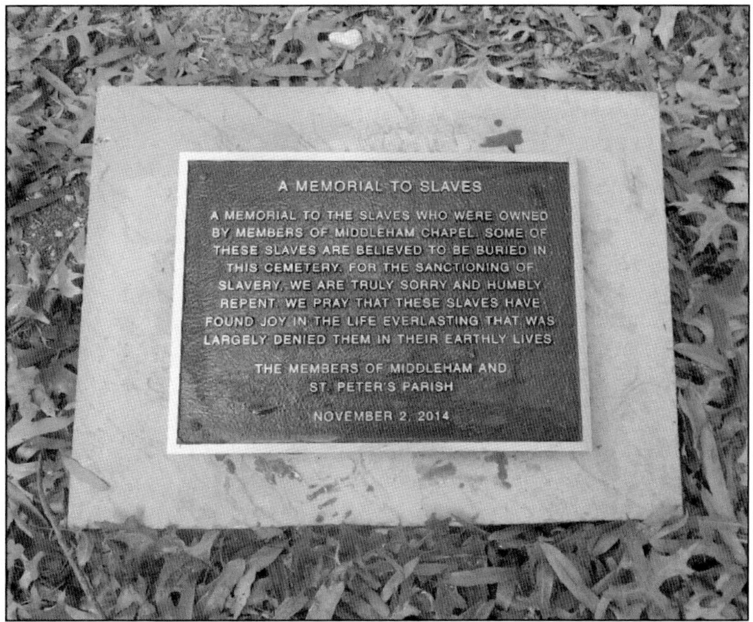

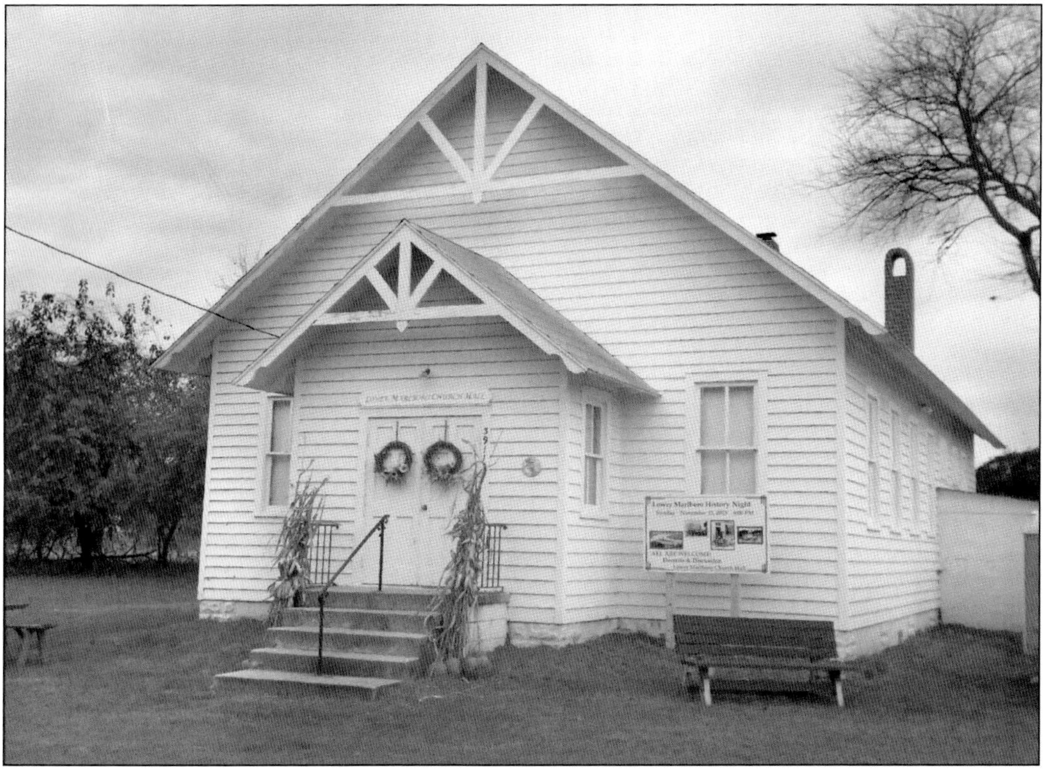

The Lower Marlboro Church Hall was built in 1930 to serve as the meeting place of the Patuxent Council No. 192 of the Junior Order United American Mechanics. The wood-frame and weatherboard-sided lodge was constructed in a Craftsman style with some Queen Anne detailing. The group met in the lodge until 1964, when it was conveyed to the Lower Marlboro United Methodist Church, which uses it as a community meeting facility.

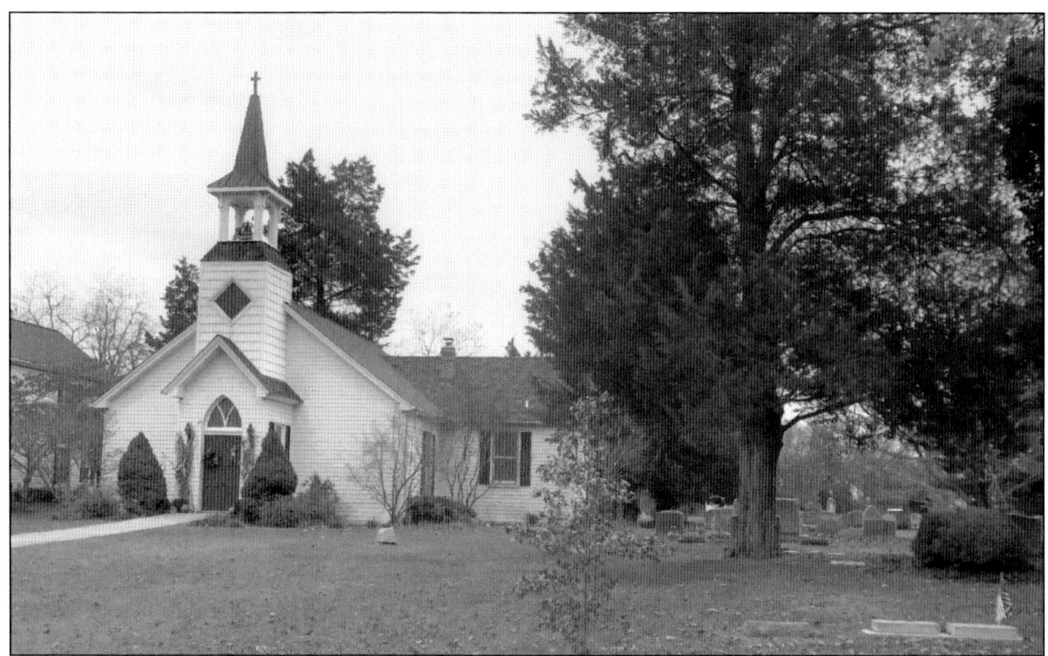

The wood-frame and clapboard-sided Lower Marlboro United Methodist Church, also known as Largent's Chapel after its builder Rev. J.J. Largent, was erected in a vernacular interpretation of the Gothic Revival style in 1868. Its present appearance was largely achieved after a renovation in 1889 and with the addition of the bell tower in 1905.

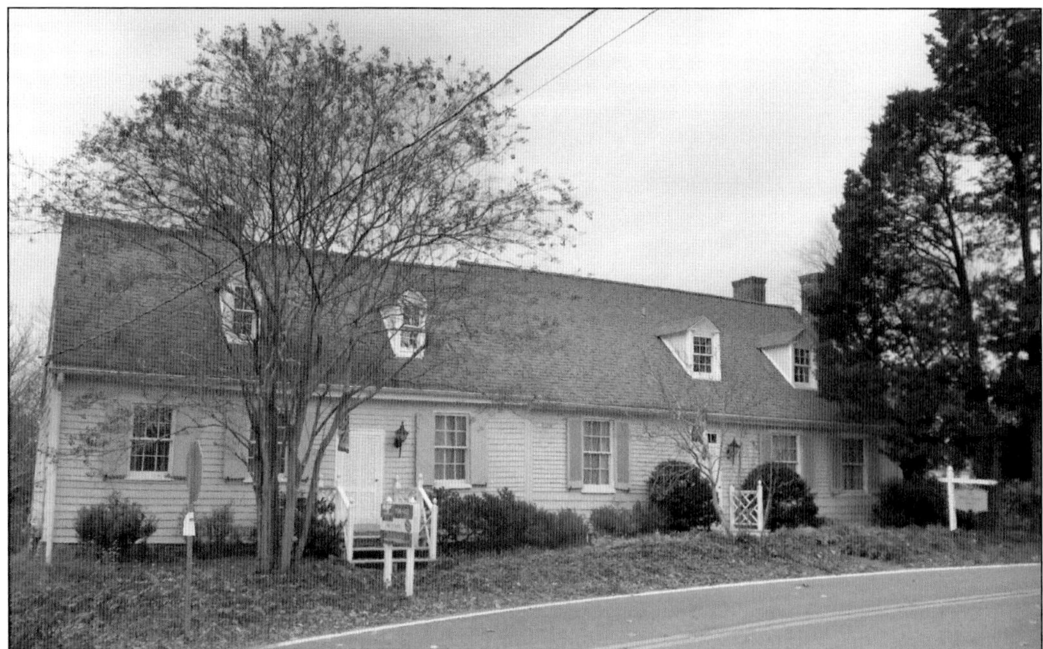

The oldest building in Lower Marlboro is the Harbour Master's House, or Hinman's Store (after a family who ran a business there), which overlooks the Patuxent River and the town dock. The building is actually comprised of two adjacent structures: the northern half built around 1670 and the southern half built in the 19th century. It survived a British raid of the town in June 1814.

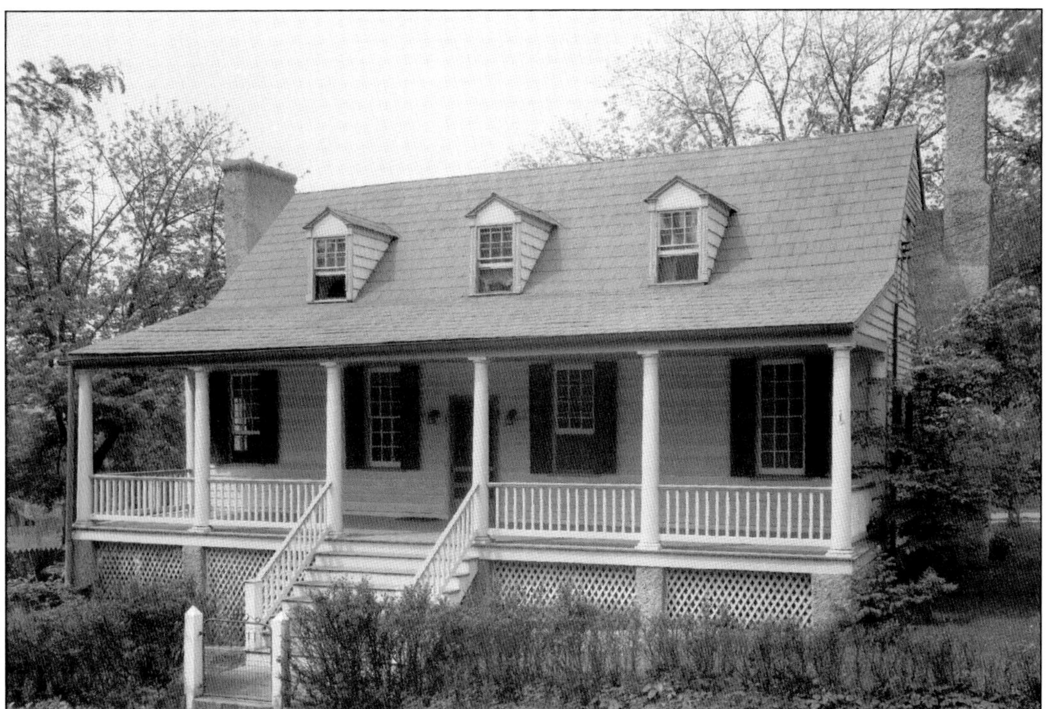

The Wilson-Diggs House is located just north of the Lower Marlboro village center, along the north bank of Graham Creek. Originally built in Upper Marlboro in Prince George's County around 1704, the house was moved to this area in the early 20th century, when it was photographed by the Historic American Buildings Survey in 1936. (John O. Bostrup, HABS.)

The Wilson-Diggs House (left) is one of several historic residences overlooking the marshes along Graham Creek in the Over the Creek on the Patuxent historic district. This collection of historic houses was saved from demolition elsewhere by Montgomery County home builder Perry Van Vleck and then restored in Lower Marlboro in the 1970s. The county designated them as historic structures in 1985.

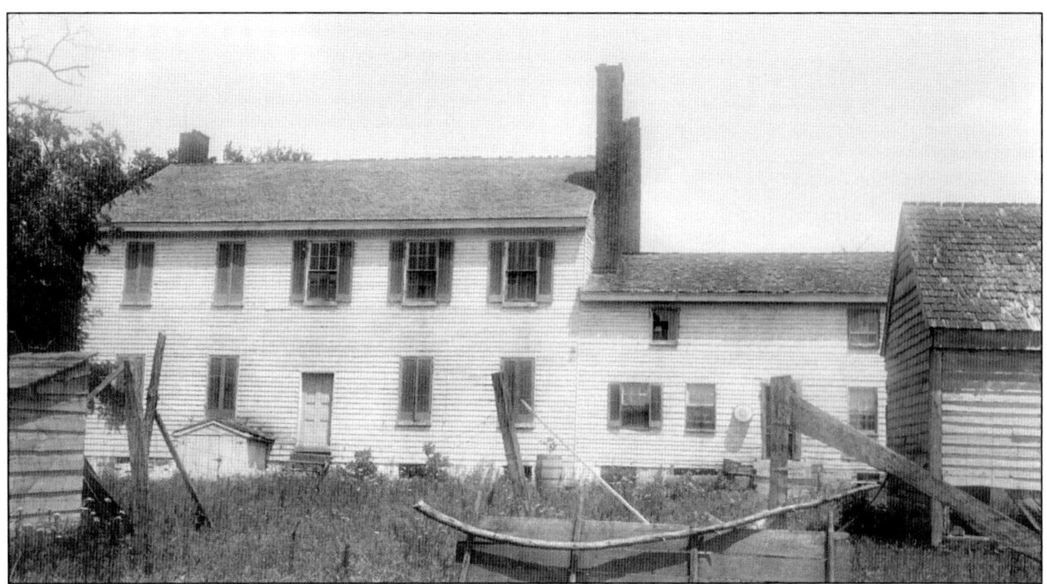

Also called the Dr. David Russell Talbot House, Hampton is a Federal-style home built in 1830 by David Carcaud, who was Dr. Talbot's grandfather and whose family suffered as Loyalists during the American Revolution. Situated atop the second-highest hill in the county in Chaneyville, the two-story frame house was enlarged in 1844, and a two-story columned porch was later added in 1946. (Delos H. Smith, HABS.)

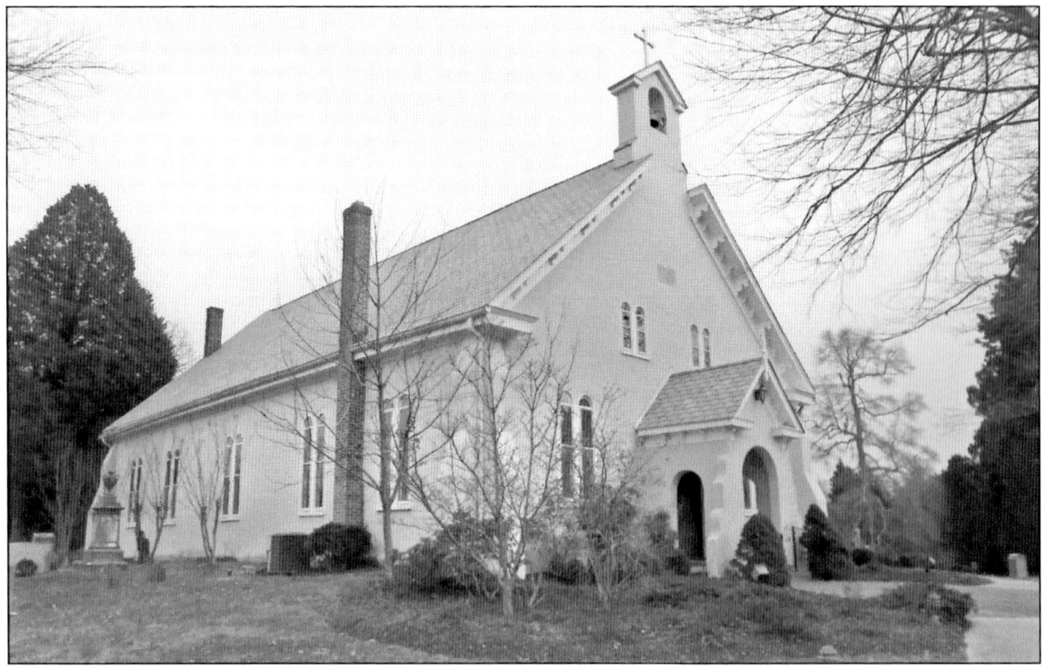

At this site in Port Republic, a log structure was established as one of the original Anglican churches of the Maryland colony in 1672. The current Christ Episcopal Church incorporates remnants of a brick church constructed here in 1772, but it was essentially rebuilt in its present Victorian Romanesque form in 1906, with the reconstruction of all major walls and 20,000 new bricks to complete the project.

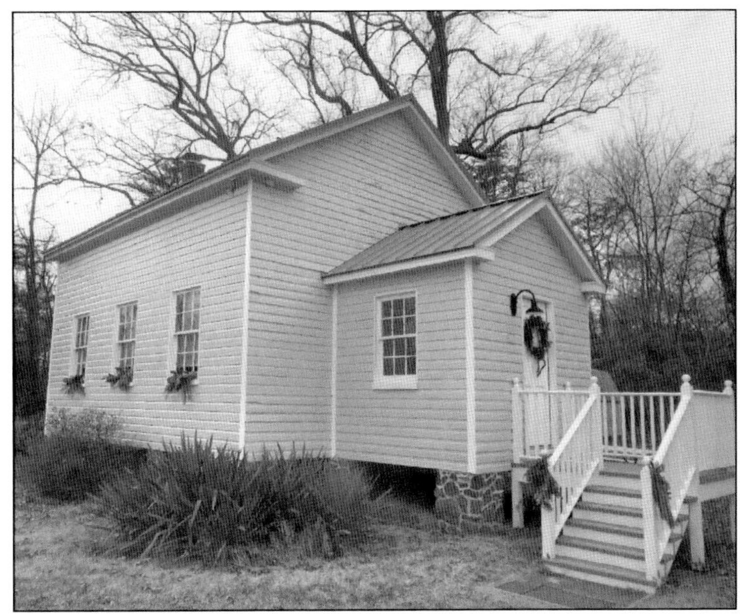

Built in 1870 and closed in 1932, Port Republic School No. 7 is one of Calvert County's last remaining one-room schoolhouses for white children. It was located in a place where no student would have to walk more than three miles to attend. Grades one through seven were all taught in the same room, usually by a single teacher for all subjects. The school was restored during the US bicentennial.

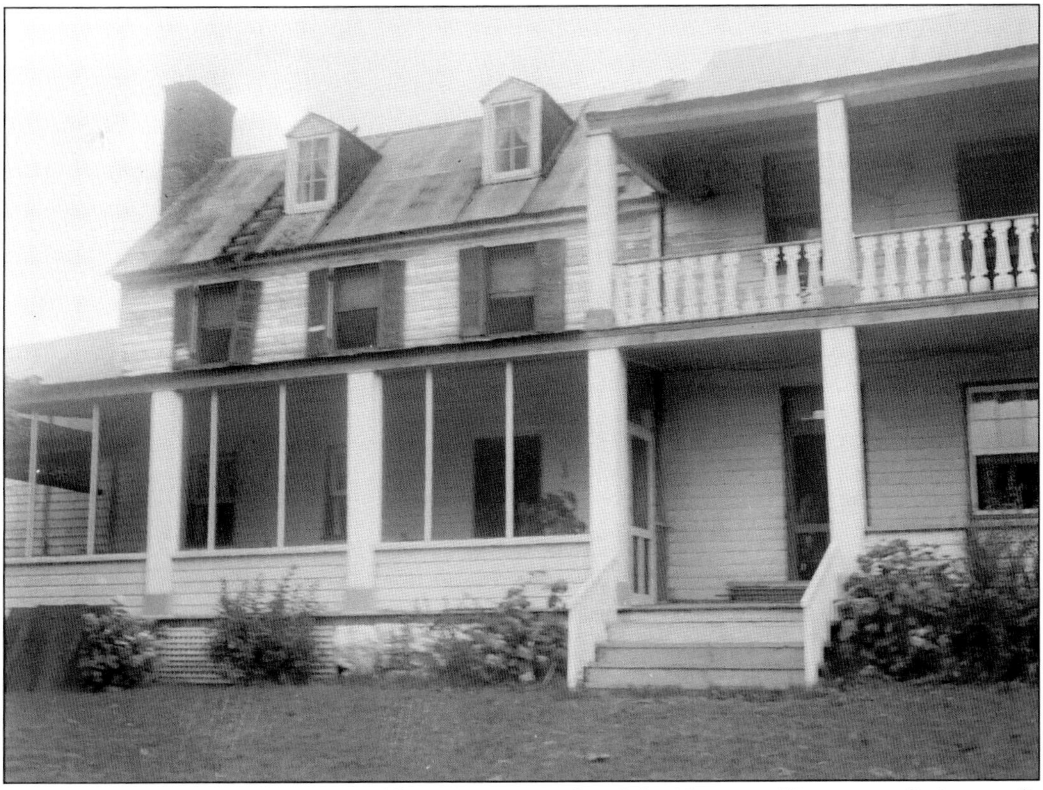

In 1940, the Historic American Buildings Survey confused the Horsmon House near St. Leonard's Creek with the nearby Mackall House, or Brewhouse, which is the birthplace of Maryland governor Thomas Johnson (1732–1819) and Louisa Johnson (1775–1852), wife of Pres. John Quincy Adams. The Horsmon House is a telescoping farmhouse typical of Southern Maryland in the early 19th century. The second-story porch was removed in the 1960s. (Delos H. Smith, HABS.)

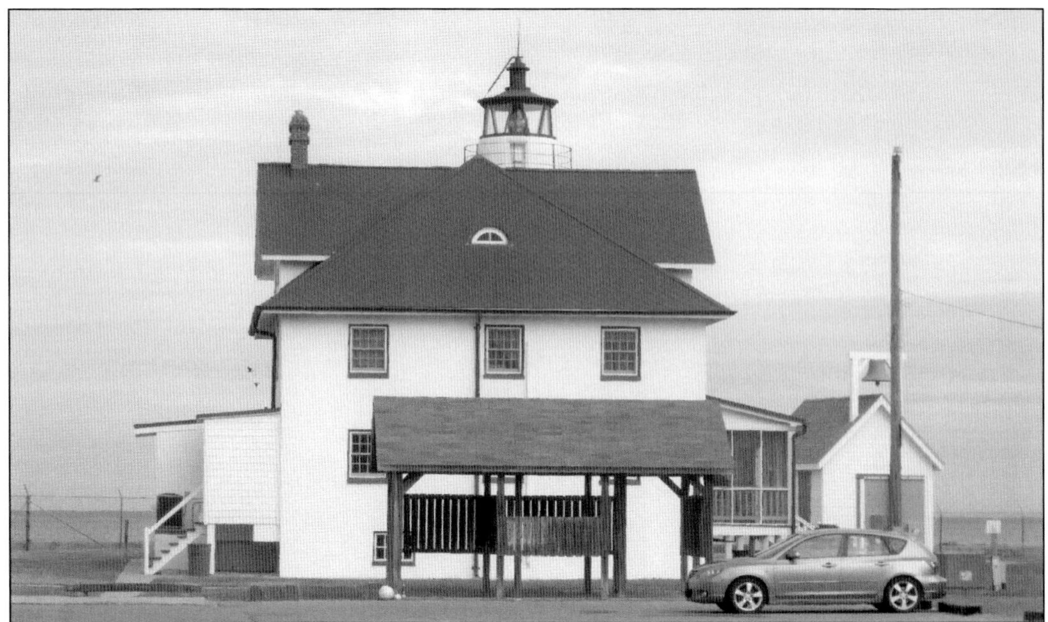

The Cove Point Lighthouse near Calvert Cliffs is one of a dozen lighthouses constructed by master builder John Donahoo of Havre de Grave, Maryland, between 1825 and 1853. Of the seven still standing in Maryland and Virginia, the Cove Point Lighthouse, built in 1828, was his fifth lighthouse for the government, and it is the oldest one left in Southern Maryland. The light keeper's house was expanded in 1883.

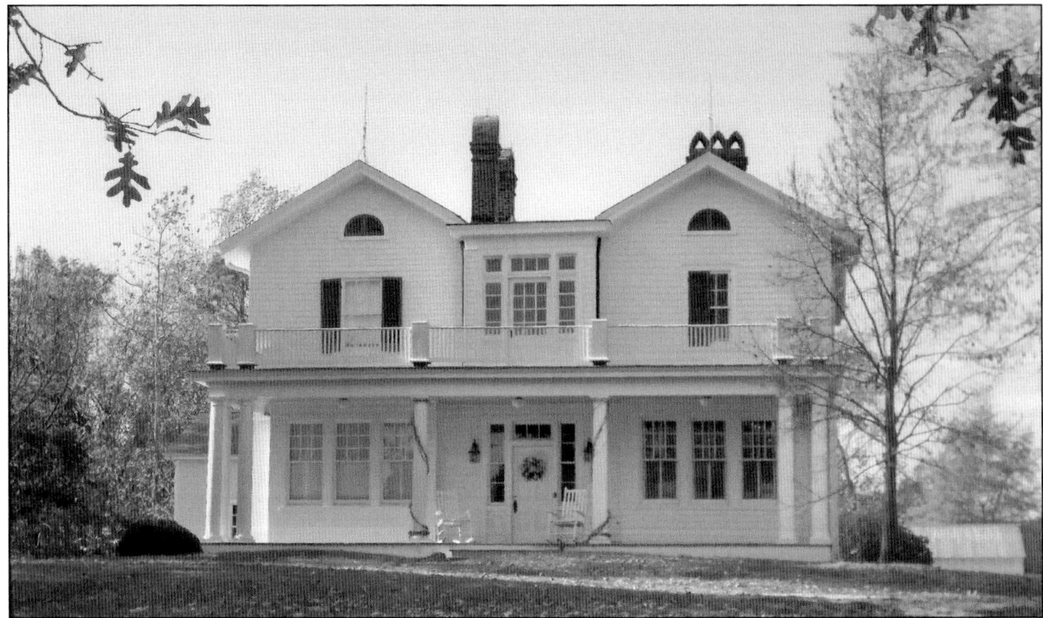

Located in Prince Frederick, Linden is a two-story frame home built in the Italianate style in 1868 and significantly remodeled with Colonial Revival elements in 1907. The family of attorney Henry Williams had acquired the land in 1747, and the home was built the year he married Georgeanna Weems. Williams was a member of the Maryland House of Delegates during the Civil War and was later elected to the state senate.

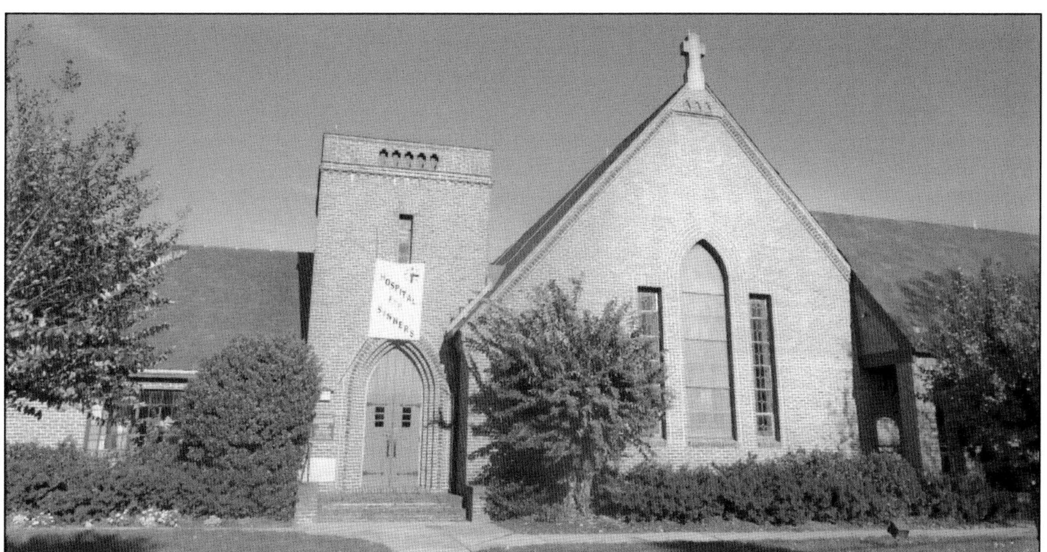

Designed by prominent Washington architect and Catholic congregant Donald S. Johnson (1907–1974), AIA, St. John Vianney was intended to resemble an English country church. Archbishop Michael J. Curley of Baltimore laid the cornerstone in 1937 and dedicated it in 1939. Begun as a mission of Our Lady Star of the Sea on Solomon's Island, it became its own parish in 1965 and has greatly expanded in recent years.

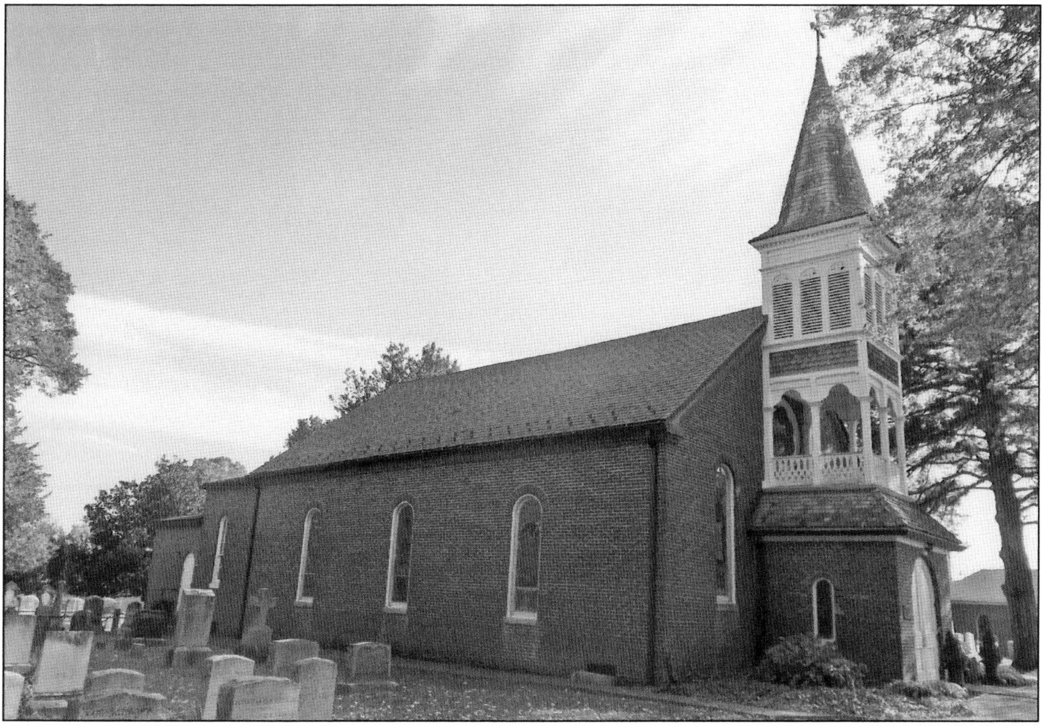

Built between 1841 and 1842, the St. Paul's Episcopal Church stands in the center of Prince Frederick. Originally three bays long, the brick church's nave plan was expanded with a fourth bay to the rear in 1981. The ornate bell tower was added to the facade in 1885 through a donation from Charles S. Parran, and the churchyard was enclosed by a decorative iron fence in the 1890s.

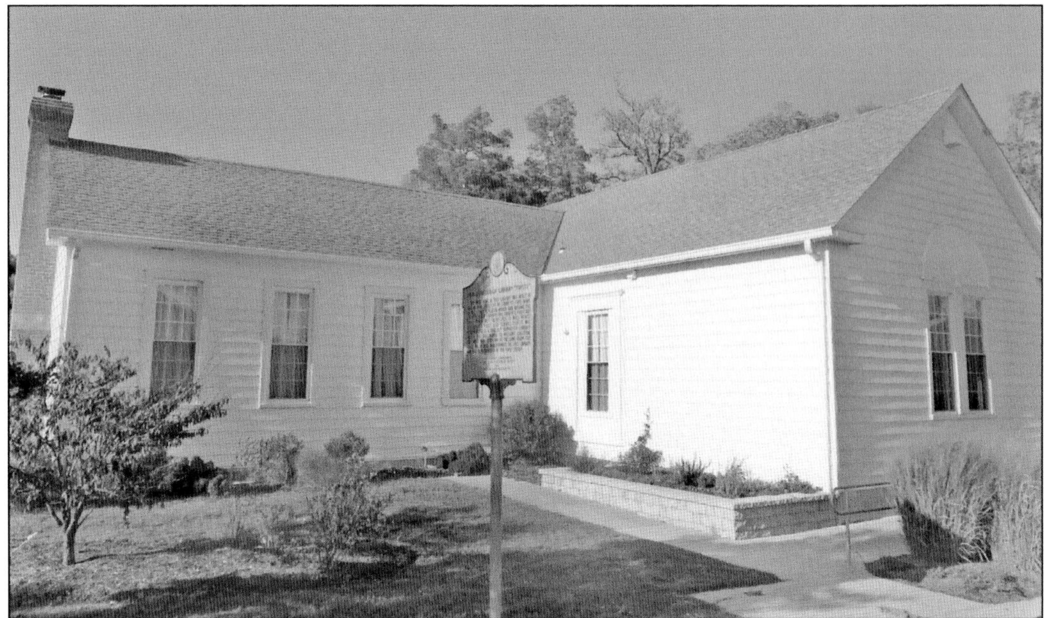

The west wing of the Prince Frederick Public Library was constructed as Calvert County's first bank in 1903. The building was acquired as the county's first library in 1913 and was used for meetings of the area's first Boy Scout troop in 1916. It also served as the community's first high school before being moved to its present location in 1961.

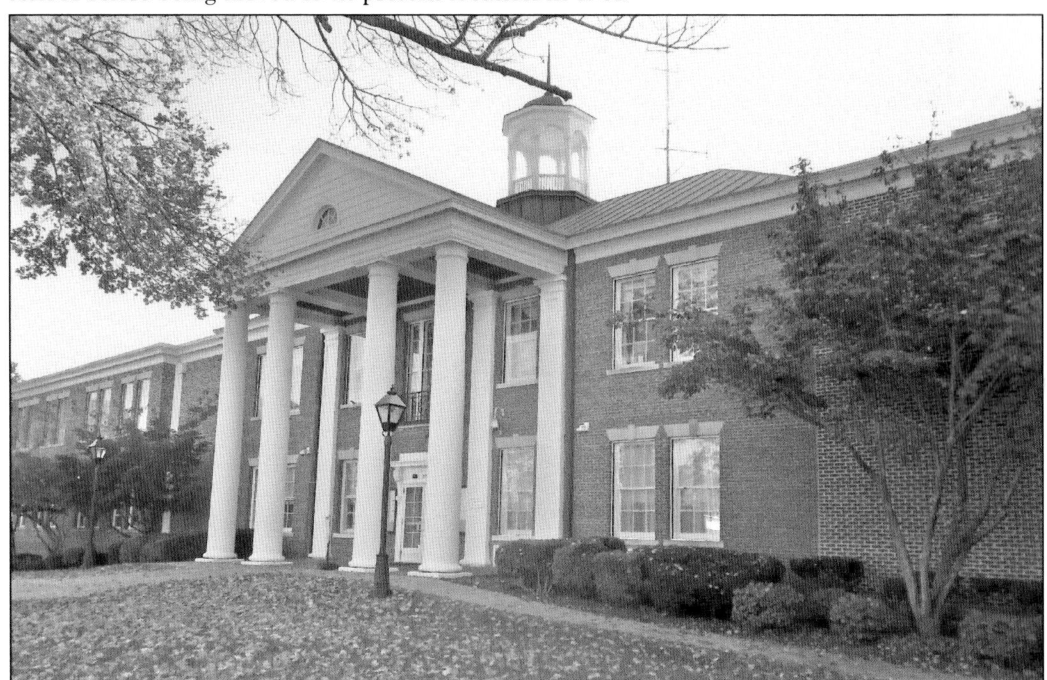

Begun in 1915 and designed in a Federal Revival style, the two-story, hip-roofed brick Calvert County Courthouse is one of the largest public institutions in Southern Maryland. Memorials to Calvert Countians who served in both World War I and II, Korea, and Vietnam stand on the grounds, which were dedicated as Veterans Green on Memorial Day 1999.

Among the memorials in front of the courthouse is a monumental, allegorical bronze sculpture of a female warrior dedicated in 1920 to local residents who served during World War I. It was created by famed Maryland sculptor Edward Berge (1876–1924) of Baltimore, who studied under renowned sculptor Auguste Rodin in Paris.

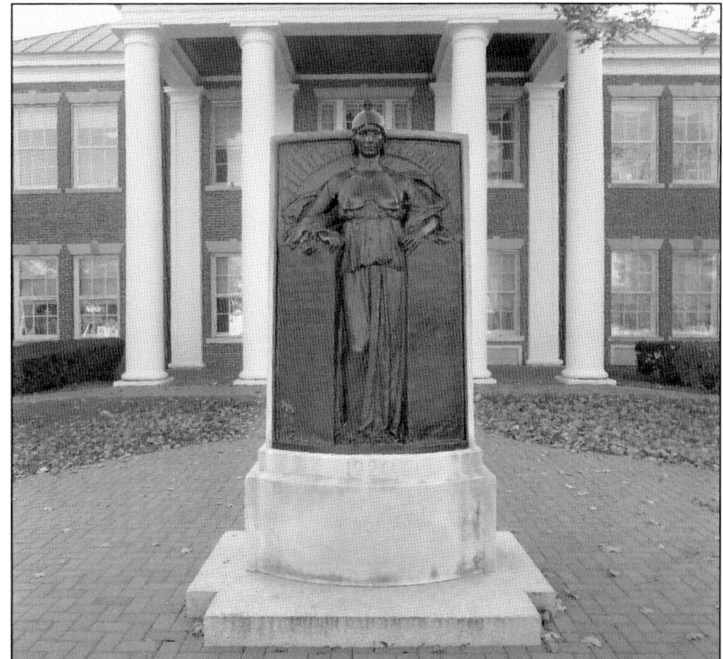

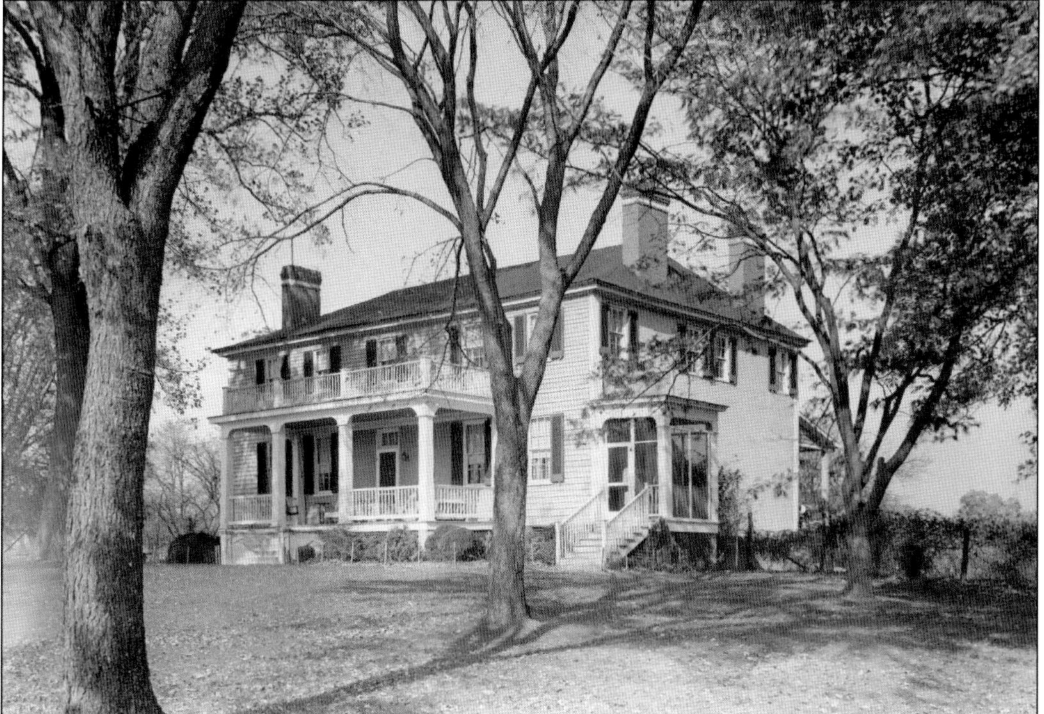

Taney Place is a c. 1700 Georgian house situated on a 1658 land grant to James Berry. The Taney family purchased the property in 1685 and built the five-bay, two-story home of brick and wood. The fifth chief justice of the United States, Roger Brooke Taney (1777–1864), grew up on this property. A religious man, Taney freed his own slaves but became infamous for his 1857 *Dred Scott v. Sandford* decision. (E.H. Pickering, HABS.)

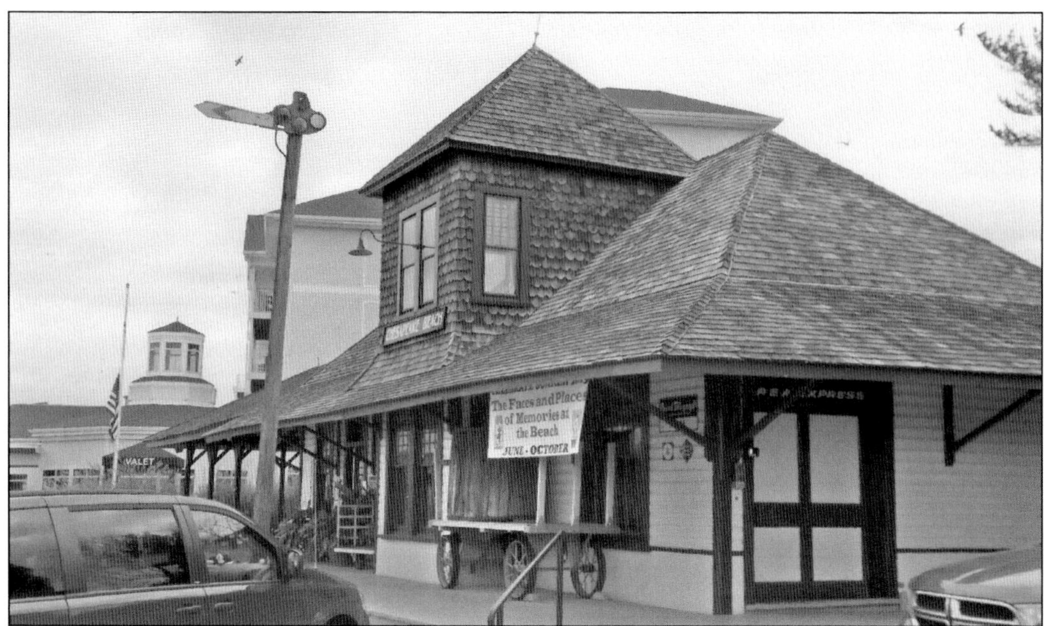

Located on the south bank of Fishing Creek as it enters the bay, the Washington & Chesapeake Railway Company station (now the Chesapeake Beach Railway Museum) was built in 1898 to service Washington-area tourist passengers seeking amusement and diversion from life in the city. The station was restored and listed in the National Register of Historic Places in 1980.

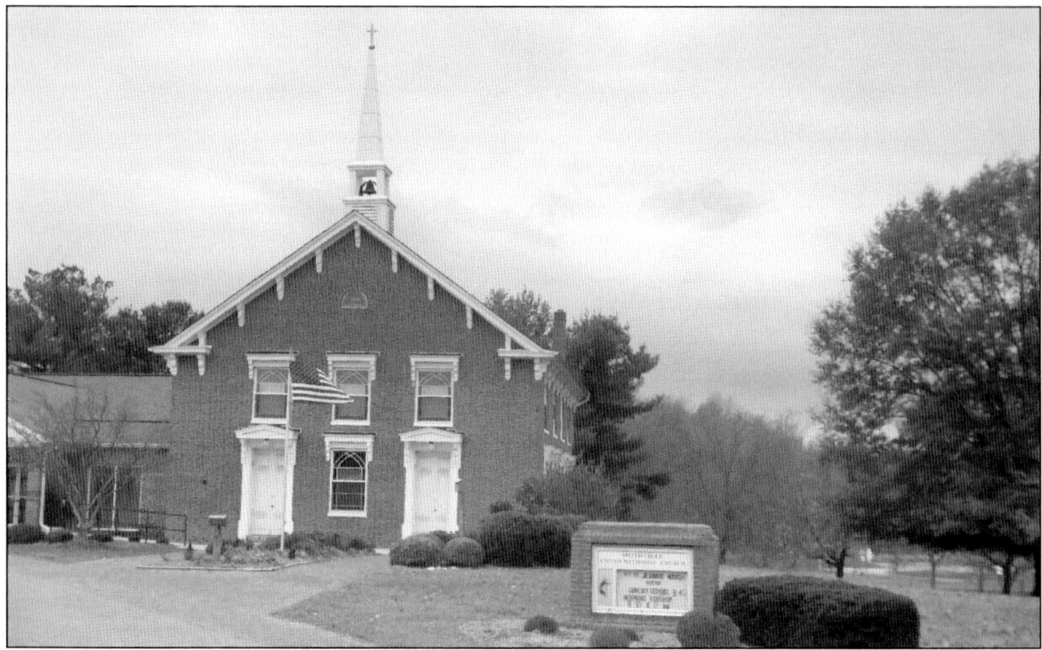

Once covered by ministers riding a circuit started in 1781, northern Calvert County had amassed the largest Methodist congregation in the newly independent United States by 1789. Smithville United Methodist Church is a two-and-a-half-story Greek Revival structure with Italianate cornice details. It was built between 1840 and 1843 on land donated by member Fielder B. Smith, with donations of bricks and wood from other members.

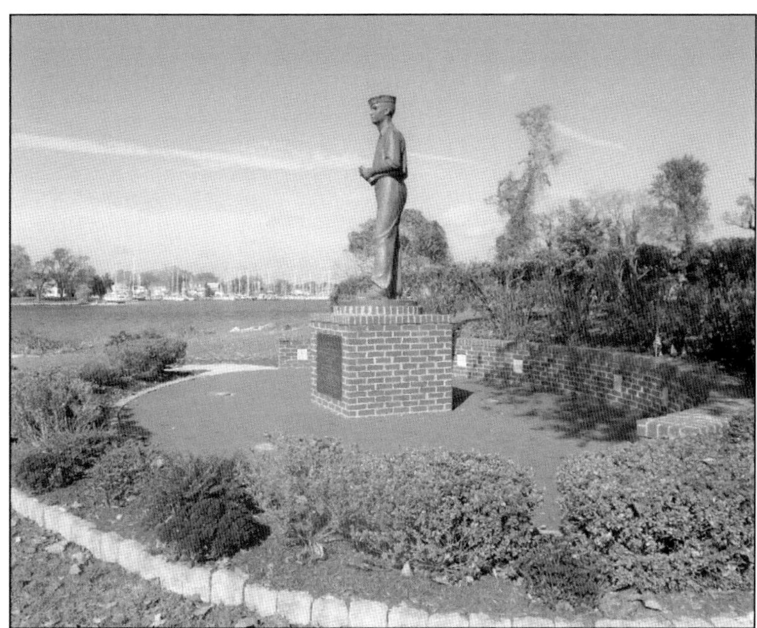

Dedicated in 2007, the *On Watch* sculpture by artist Antonio Tobias Mendez commemorates the US Amphibious Training Base that existed to the east of Solomon's Island, across Back Creek. It was the nation's first amphibious training base during World War II (1942–1945), and over 68,000 members of the US Armed Forces trained here for landings during the invasions of North Africa, Sicily, Normandy, and the Pacific Islands.

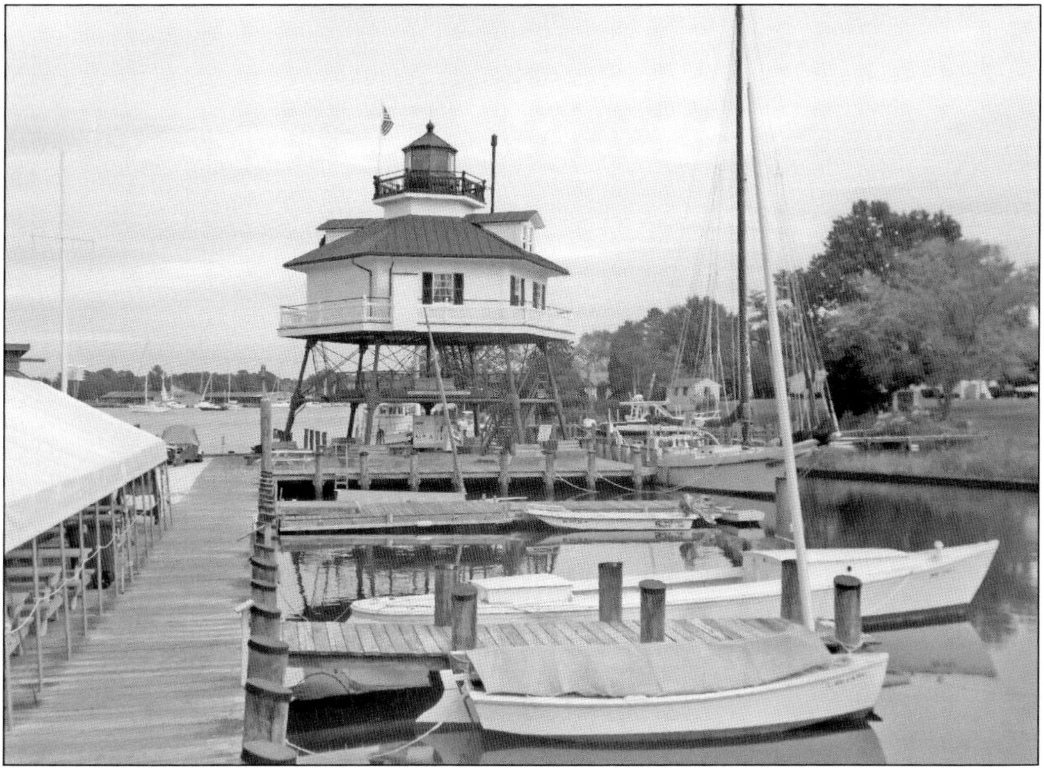

Built in 1883, the Drum Point Lighthouse is a hexagonal structure with wooden keeper's quarters. One of 42 lighthouses of its type built in the Chesapeake area after 1854, the metal-framed, screw-piled structure stood at the north side of the mouth of the Patuxent River on the Potomac until it was decommissioned in 1962, then moved to the Calvert Marine Museum in 1975 to prevent its demolition.

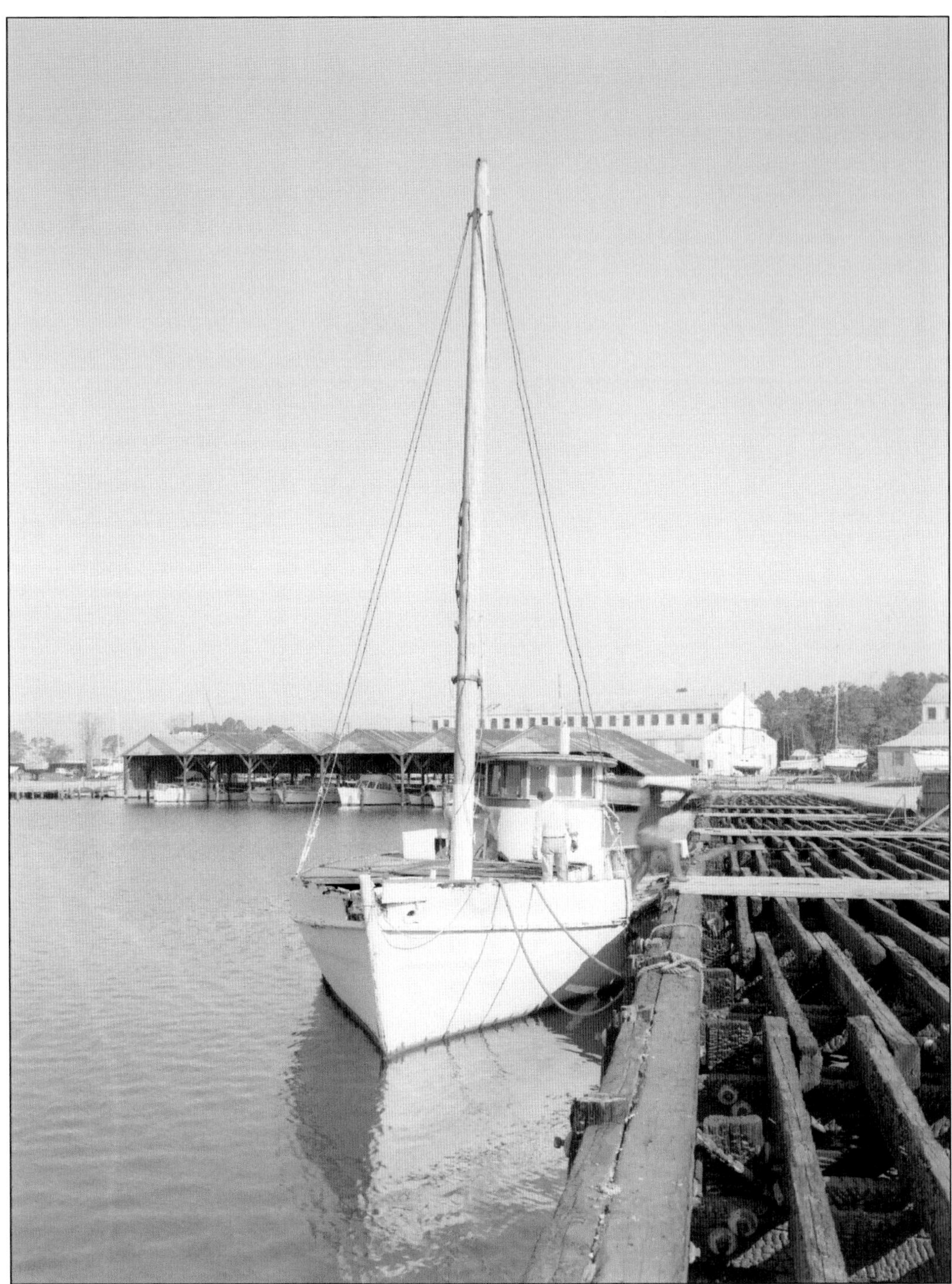

Once a common sight along Southern Maryland's waterways, the bugeye was a type of oyster-dredging boat developed on the Chesapeake Bay in the 1860s and 1870s to carry large loads with a shallow draft and a small crew. James T. Marsh built the *Louise Travers*, shown here, at Solomon's Island in 1896, and the Historic American Engineering Record (HAER) had documented the boat before it burned in 1986. (Jet Lowe, HAER.)

Three

Charles County

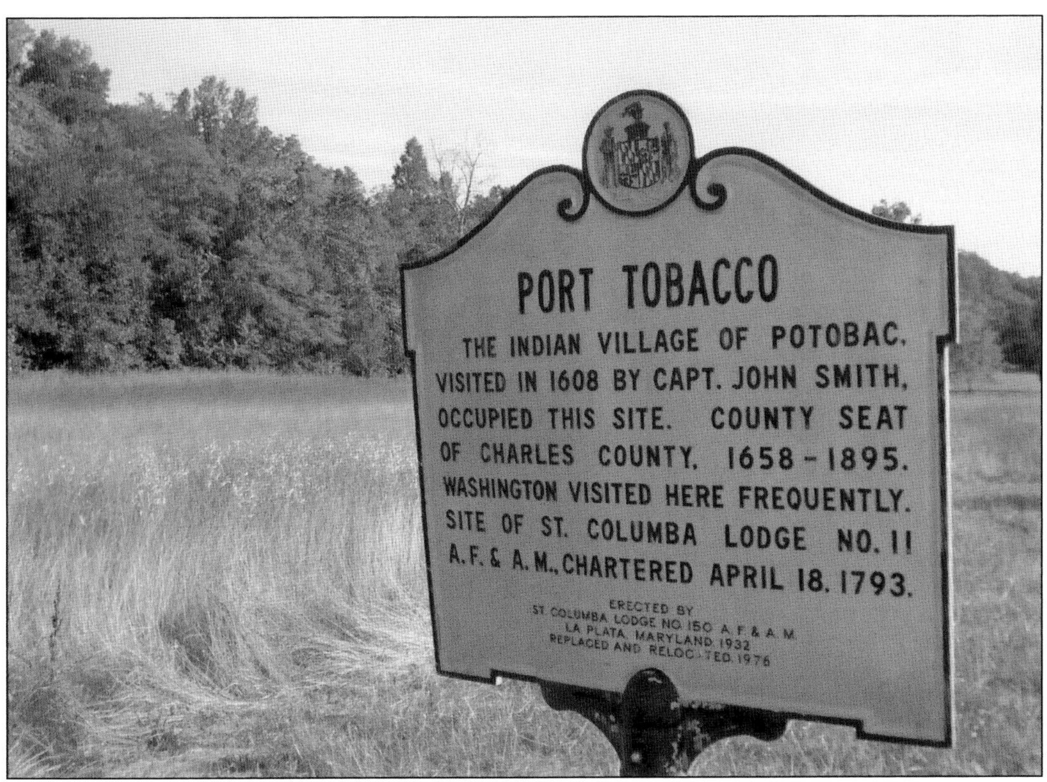

Located at the southern end of the Port Tobacco Valley, the Port Tobacco Creek drains into the Potomac River as a bay called the Port Tobacco River. The name *Port Tobacco* comes from the Algonquian Indian village called Potobac, located here for centuries prior to the arrival of Virginia colonist Capt. John Smith in 1608. Included on his famous map of the region, the native village remained into the 1640s.

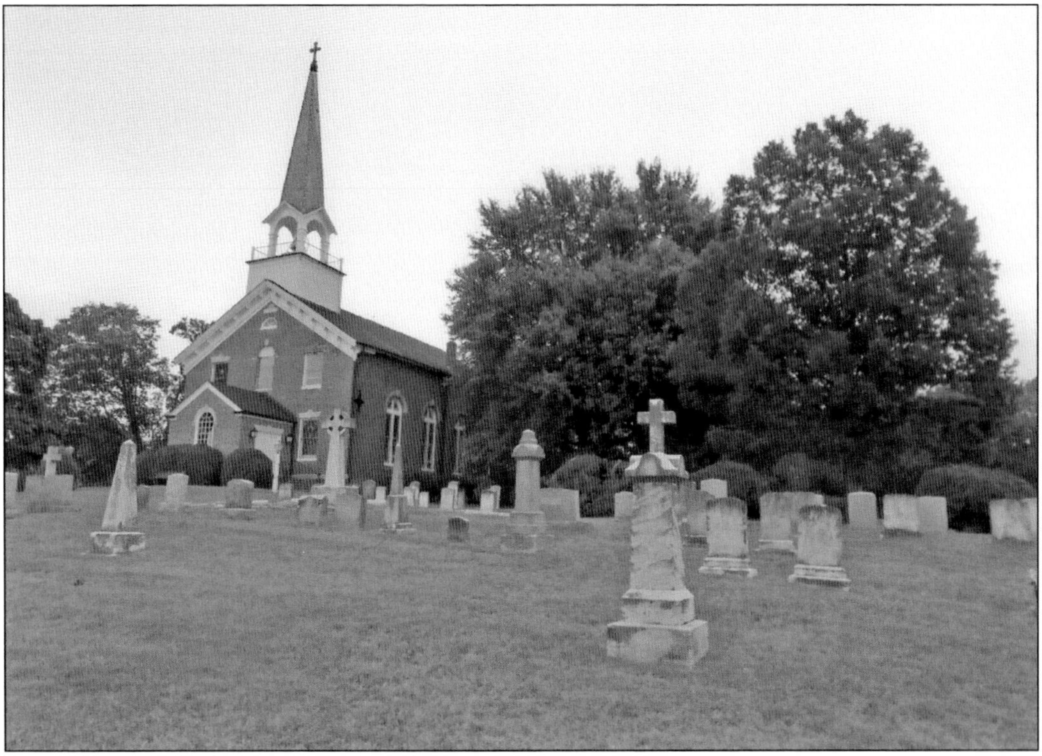

In 1641, Jesuit missionary Fr. Andre White established the St. Ignatius Catholic Church on St. Thomas Manor, four miles south of the Indian village of Potobac. It is the oldest continuous English-speaking Catholic parish in the country since 1662. Built atop a high hill overlooking the Port Tobacco River at Chapel Point, the church consists of a complex of buildings that was once the center of Jesuit ministry in Charles County.

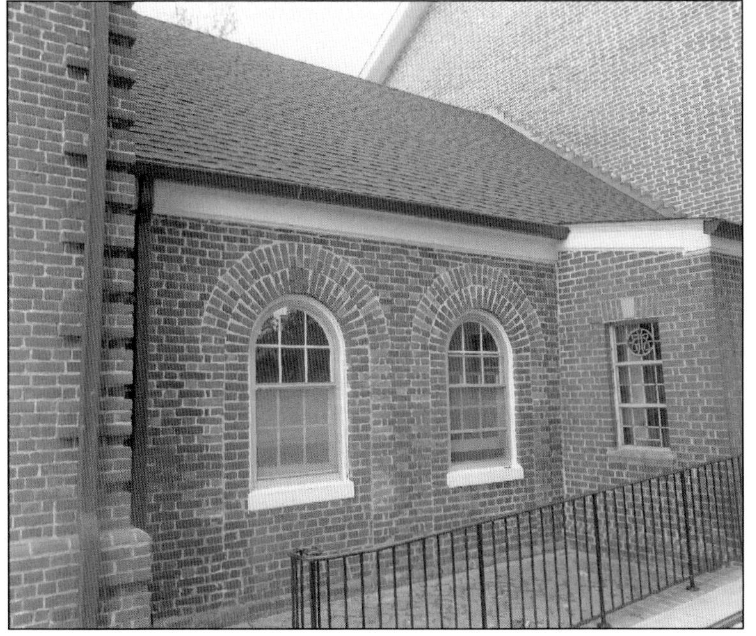

This small hyphen connecting St. Ignatius Church with the manor house of St. Thomas Manor is what remains of the brick chapel, built atop the hill by 1692 after the original wooden chapel along the shore was no longer in use. What was once an open structure graced by arched portals has been enclosed with windows to create the area that now contains the sacristy and part of the altar for St. Ignatius.

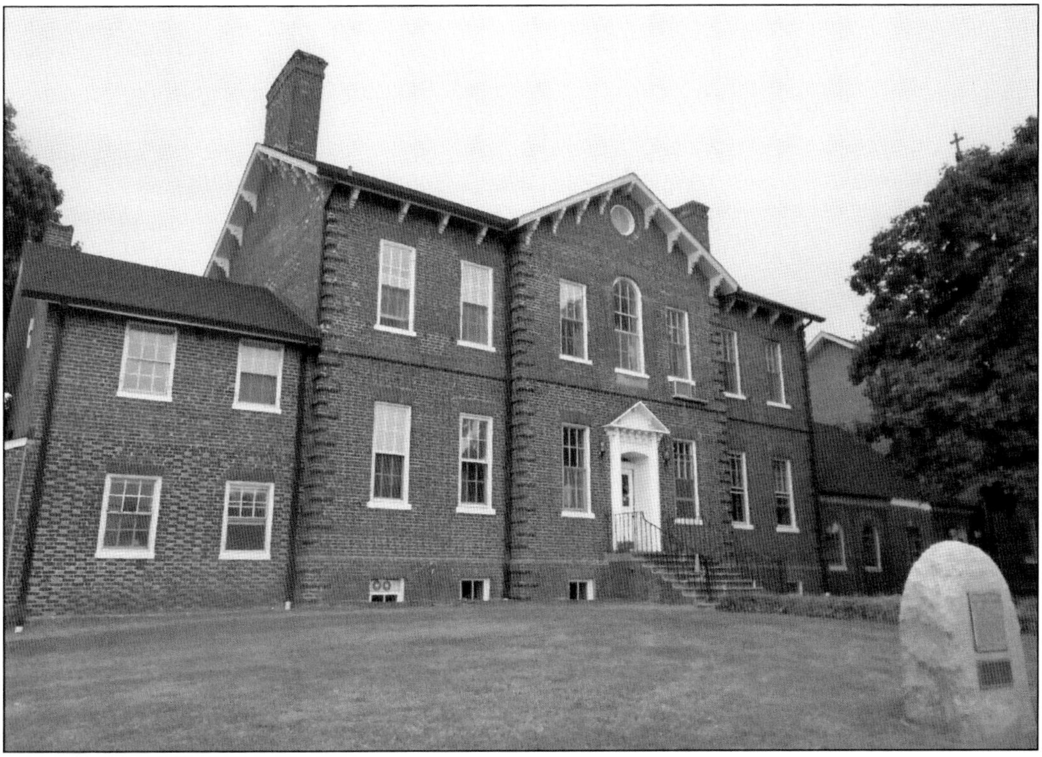

Built in 1741 as the main residence for the Jesuits on the 4,000-acre land grant surveyed in 1649, the manor house at St. Thomas Manor is considered one of the best surviving examples of Georgian architecture in Maryland. Originally built with a hipped roof, the manor house and the attached church survived a massive fire in 1866, after which they were reconstructed with the gable roof and Italianate brackets seen today.

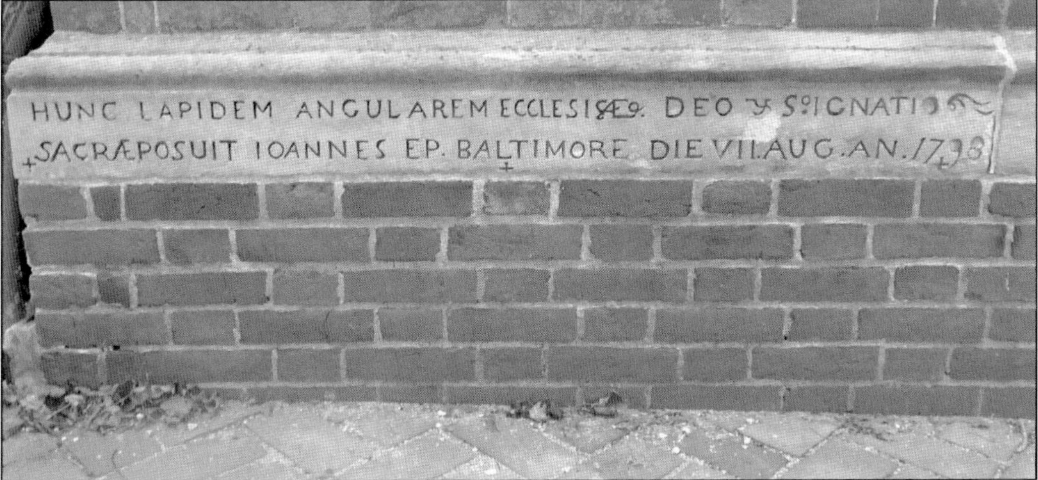

The first American-born Catholic bishop and archbishop of the United States, Rev. John Carroll, placed the cornerstone of St. Ignatius Catholic Church on August 7, 1798. Born in Upper Marlboro in 1735, John Carroll was the brother of Constitution signer Daniel Carroll and a cousin of Declaration of Independence signer Charles Carroll of Carrollton. Reverend Carroll once served here as a priest.

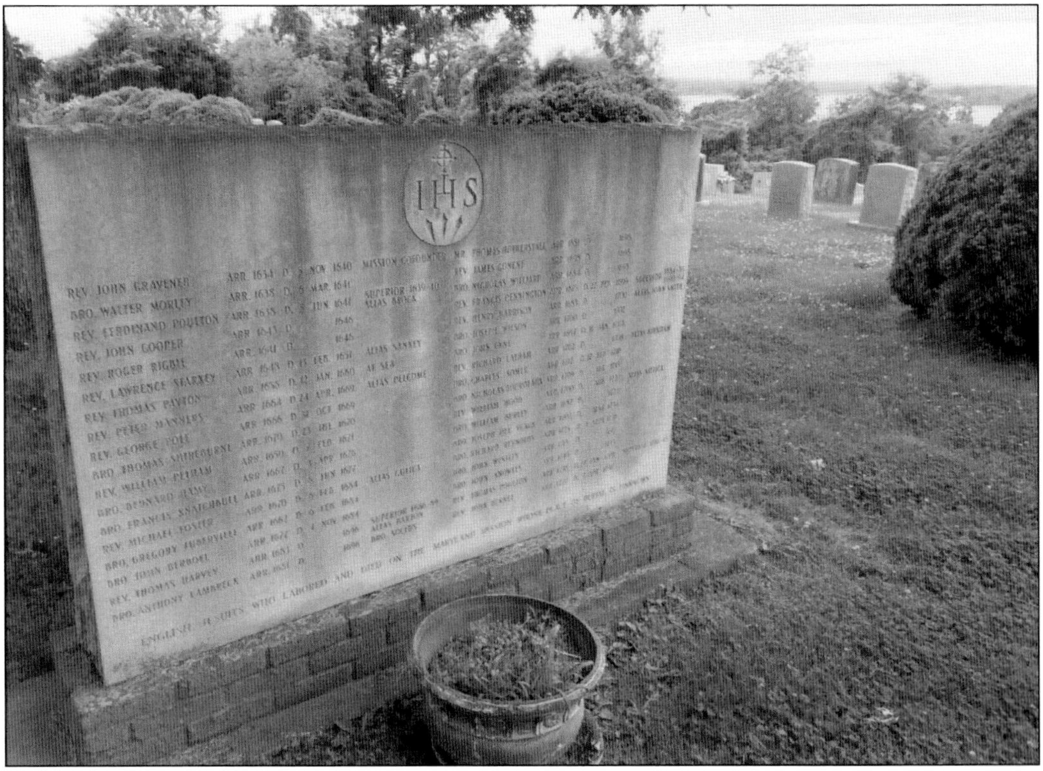

In the churchyard to the southeast of St. Ignatius is a memorial to the many "English Jesuits who labored and died on the Maryland Mission whose place of burial is unknown," with deaths beginning in 1634. It stands among the dozens of marked Jesuit burials and the hundreds of parishioner graves in the cemetery and remains a place of quiet reflection for visitors to the site.

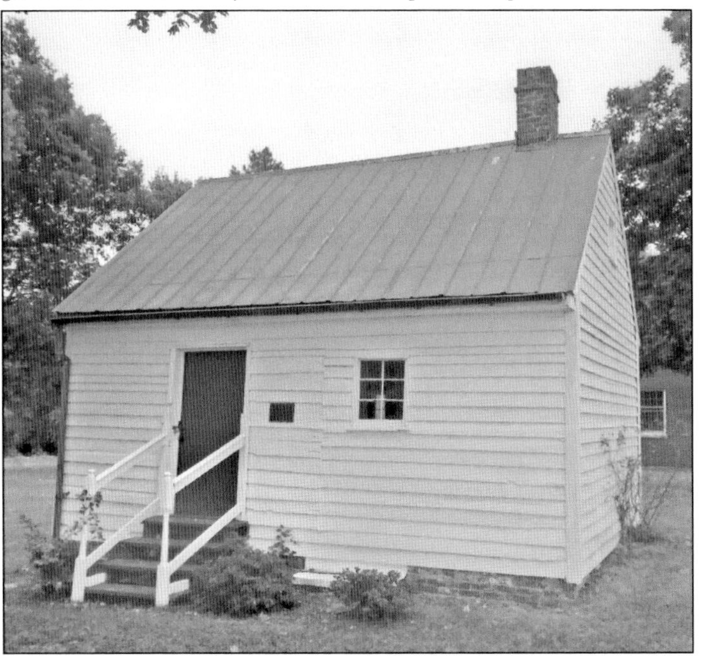

East of the manor is a small cabin that is believed to have been the home for a slave family before 1830. It was originally constructed as a single open room with a fireplace on the main floor and a sleeping room in the attic. After the manor house and church burned in 1866, it was the priests' residence until repairs on the church and manor were finished in 1868.

Once believed to have been built from a ship's ballast, Blossom Point Farm at Cedar Point Neck was actually constructed of locally made bricks around 1805. Situated on the eastern bank of Nanjemoy Creek at the Potomac River, it was first leased to Bennet Semmes, then to the Army in 1942. The federal government purchased the property in 1980. Long neglected, it was demolished in 1995. (Walter Smalling, HABS.)

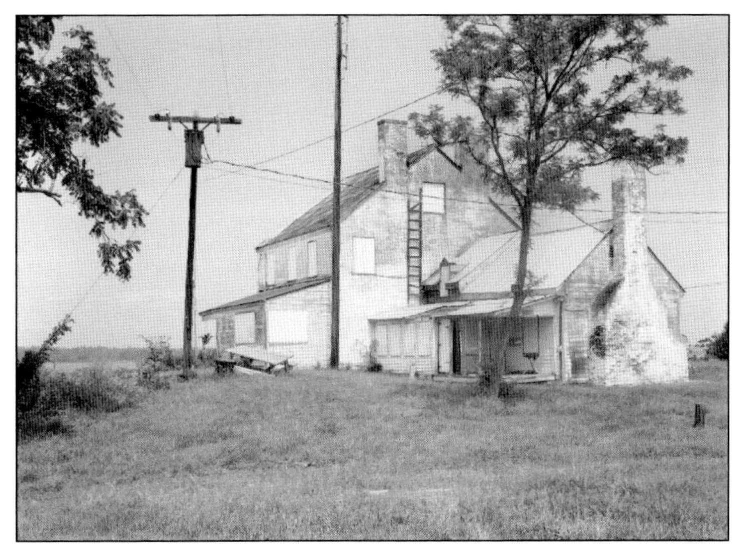

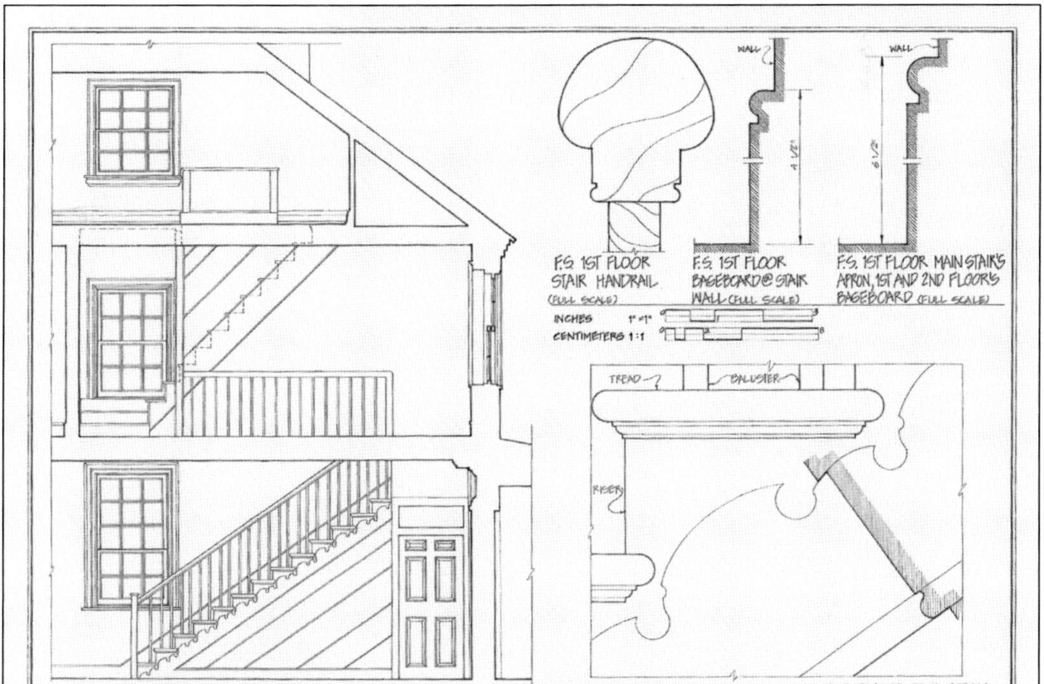

Blossom Point Farm was the site of ordnance testing during World War II, and the house was initially used as offices. Bennet Semmes was a successful plantation owner in the area who leased 186 acres of the land from the Jesuits while serving as their subagent to collect rents from other tenants. Prior to its demolition, the house's original woodwork and Federal period detailing were remarkably intact. (Alma R. Plummer, HABS.)

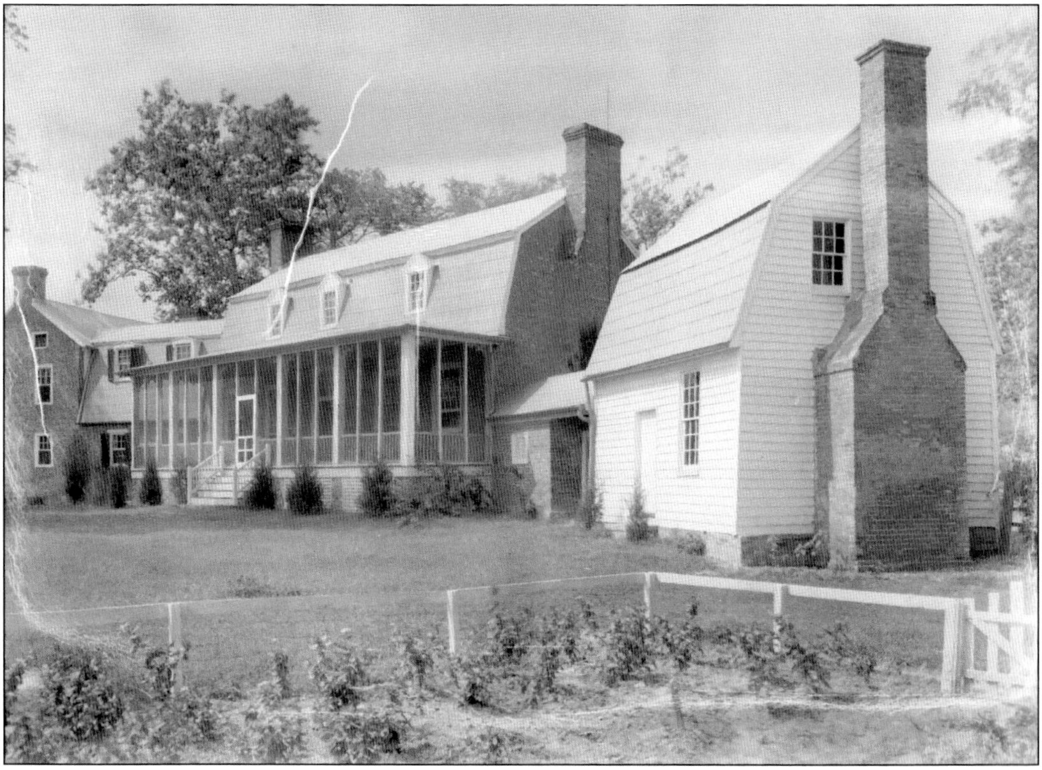

The centerpiece of the Thomas Stone National Historic Site is the mansion house called Habre de Venture. Thomas Stone (1743–1787), a successful lawyer and signer of the Declaration of Independence, built the house in an arching five-part plan between 1771 and 1773. Practicing mostly in Annapolis, Stone returned after his wife, Margaret, died in June 1787. He died, reportedly of a broken heart, four months later. (FBJPC, LOC.)

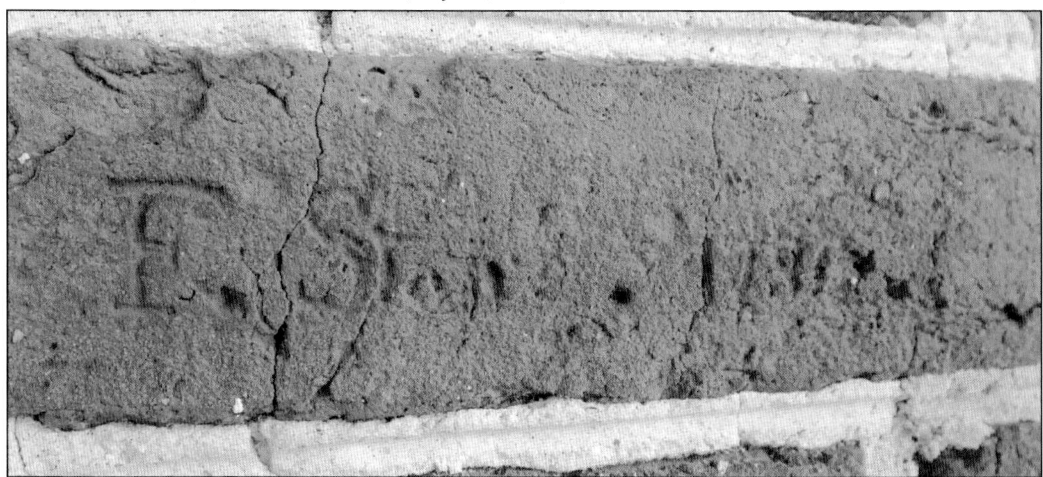

The nephew of Constitution signer Daniel of St. Thomas Jenifer (1723–1790), who lived less than three miles away, Thomas Stone was surrounded by a close network of related families. His wife, Margaret, was the daughter of Dr. Gustavus Brown, who lived at nearby Rose Hill. Over the years, the names and initials of many family members were scratched into its brick walls, such as Thomas Stone's son Frederick in 1780.

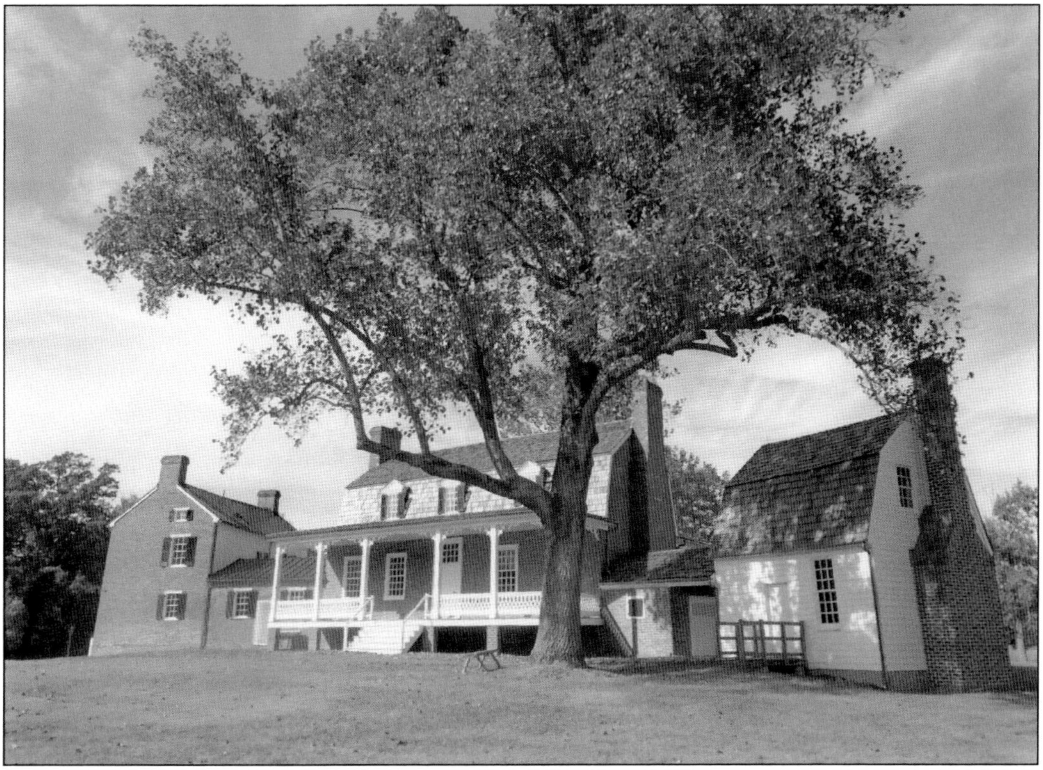

After Thomas Stone's death, his brother Michael Jenifer Stone, a member of the first Congress and later a judge, became the guardian of his orphaned children and ran the estate. Michael's son William Briscoe Stone, a lawyer and a judge, purchased the estate in 1831 and added the east and west wings. It was damaged by fire in 1977, acquired by the National Park Service in 1978, and finally restored in the 1990s.

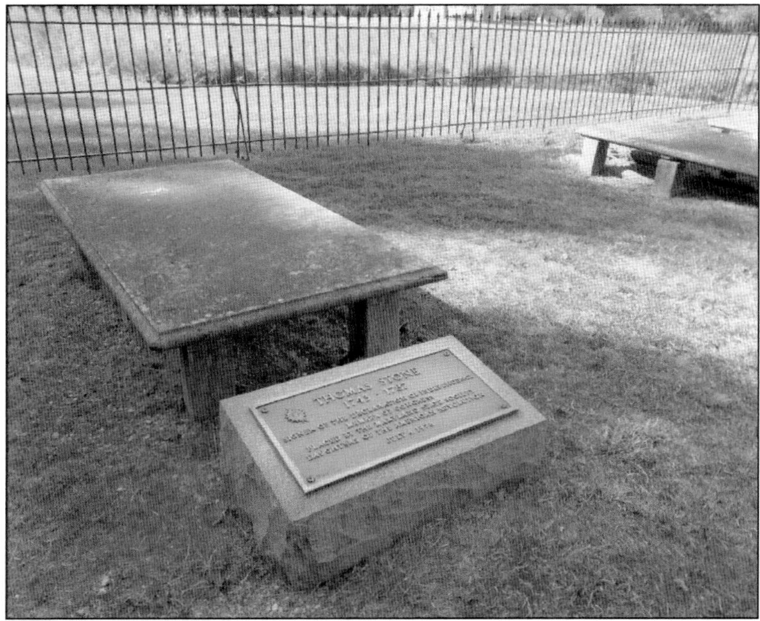

Thomas Stone was interred next to his wife in Habre de Venture's family cemetery, which was enclosed by an iron fence in 1860. Family members continued to be buried here until 1913, with burials dating from the 18th to the 20th centuries. African Americans who worked for the family after the Civil War were buried in a secluded area of the nearby woods.

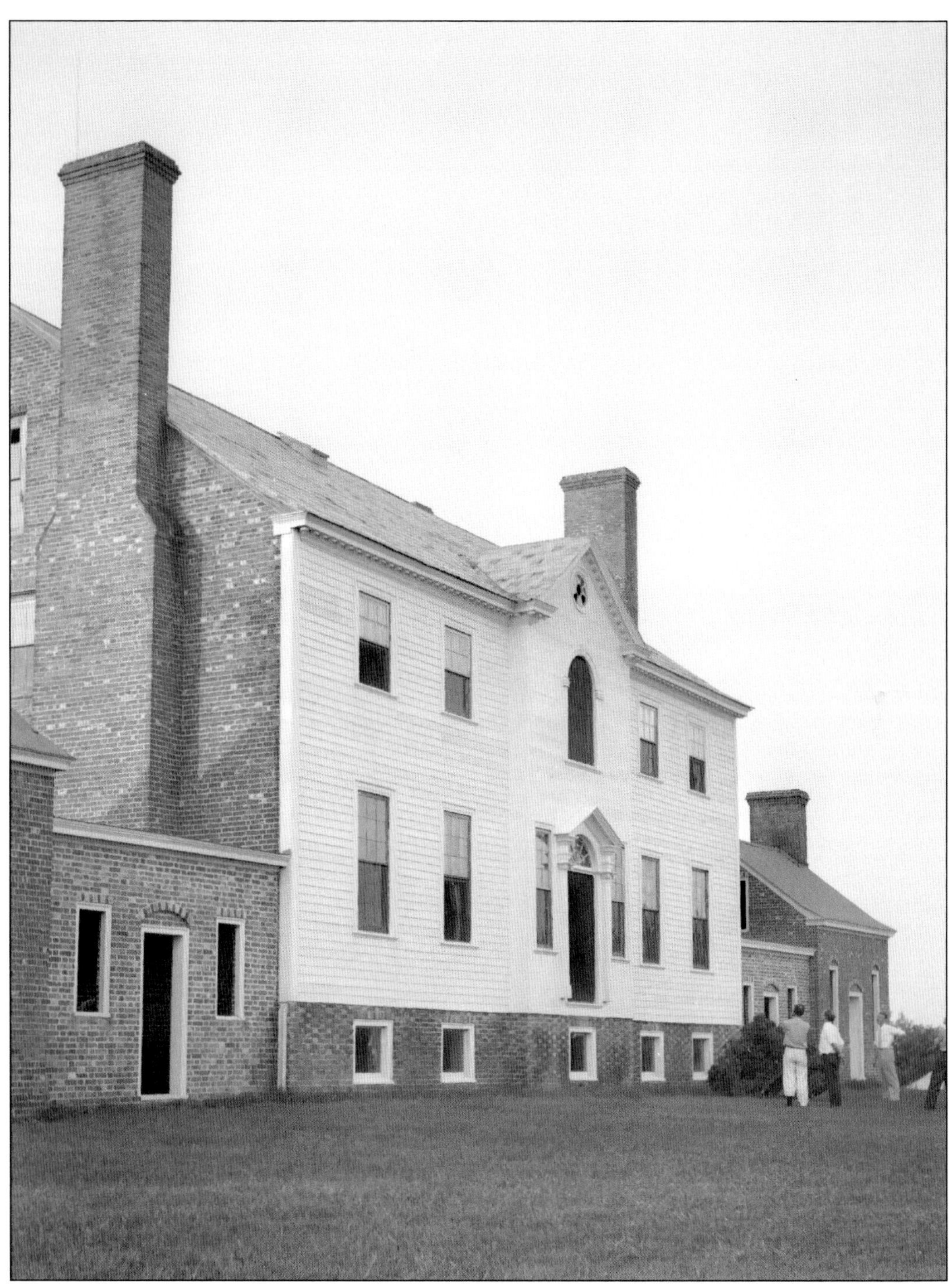

Built on an estate consisting of parcels acquired after the American Revolution, Rose Hill was the home of patriot Dr. Gustavus Richard Brown, the father-in-law of Thomas Stone and friend and physician of George Washington. The frame home was constructed on an elevated brick foundation in 1783. It was two and a half stories high and five bays wide with brick chimney ends. (Thomas T. Waterman, HABS.)

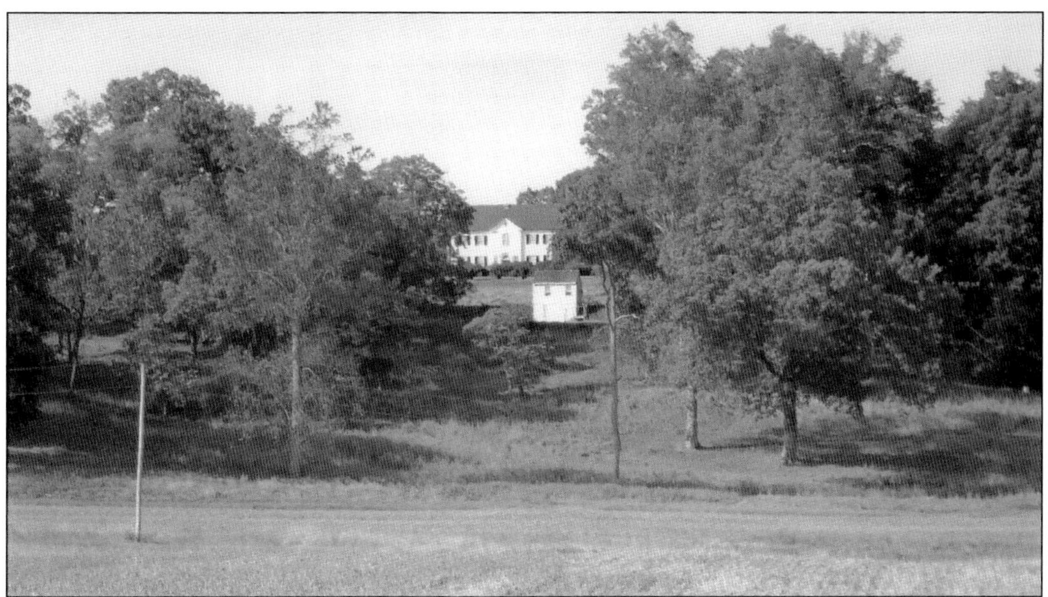

By the early 1930s, Rose Hill had been severely neglected. In the early 1940s, Herbert E. Ryerson, a veteran World War I Army officer and the European director for the US Rubber Company, and his wife, Virginia Woodward Ryerson, completed the home's restoration. Commanding an impressive view of the Port Tobacco Valley, the Rose Hill mansion was the centerpiece of the Ryersons' tobacco farm.

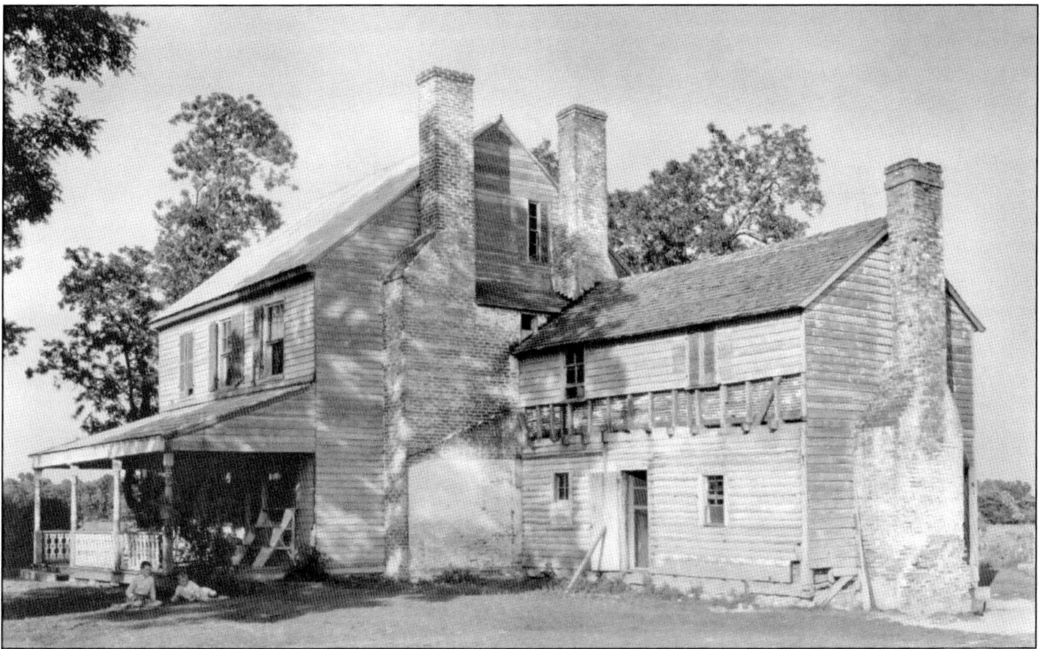

Locust Grove is a two-and-a-half-story frame house that has been constructed in various stages over time. Ralph Falkner of Virginia built its oldest section between about 1739 and 1749. A subsequent owner, Thomas A. Davis, a vestryman at Christ Church Episcopal in Port Tobacco, built the central block of the house after 1815. After a long period of neglect, the house was renovated and further expanded in the 1990s. (FBJPC, LOC.)

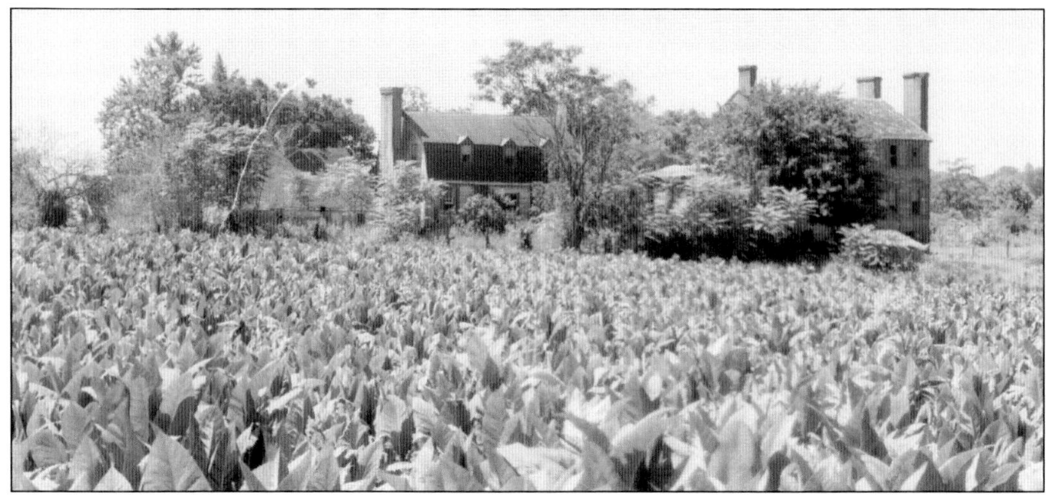

In 1936, famed photographer Frances Benjamin Johnston visited the remnants of the once thriving Port Tobacco village to document it for the Carnegie Survey of the Architecture of the American South. Still standing in the former center of the community were Stagg Hall (left) and the Chimney House (right), which are shown in this photograph taken across a tobacco field. (FBJPC, LOC.)

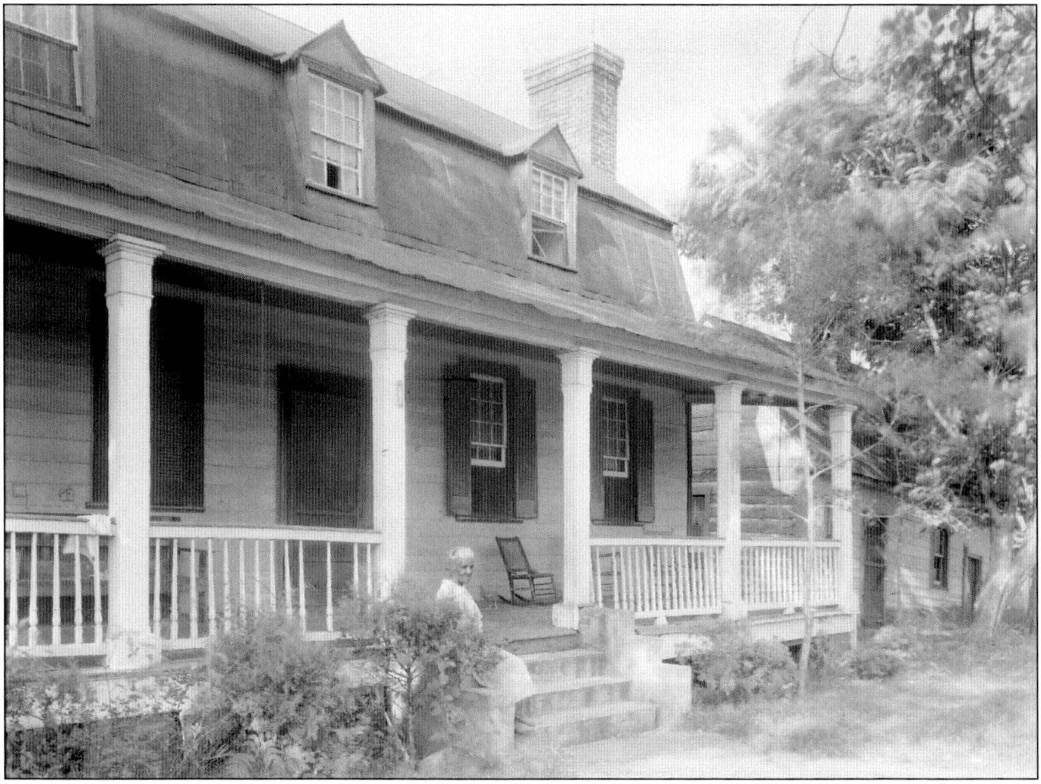

Built between 1739 and 1746, Stagg Hall was among the most substantial houses in Port Tobacco after it became the seat of Charles County in 1727. Constructed of frame and weatherboard siding over a full stone and brick masonry cellar, the main block of the house is five bays wide and one and a half stories high with a gambrel roof and porch running along the front. (FBJPC, LOC.)

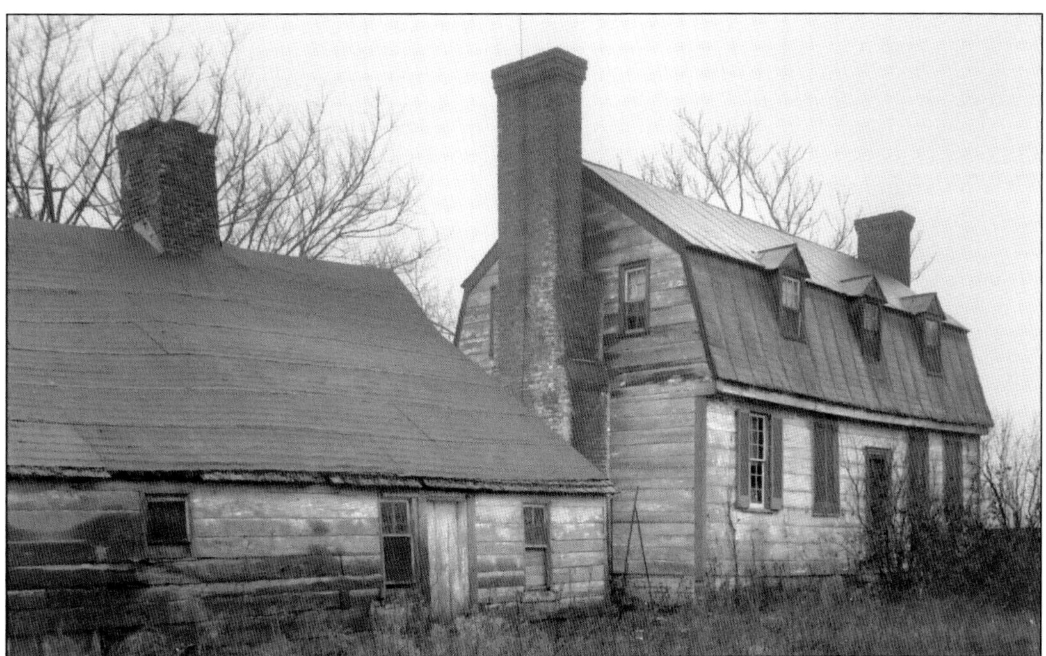

As with many historic homes, Stagg Hall's finely preserved 18th-century wood paneling was removed for exhibition at the Art Institute of Chicago in 1932. It was returned in 1972 and reinstalled. This 1936 image shows the rear of the home with its catslide roof and the kitchen wing built in the 1750s. The kitchen wing itself was rebuilt in the 1950s using its original foundation, chimney, and other materials. (E.H. Pickering, HABS.)

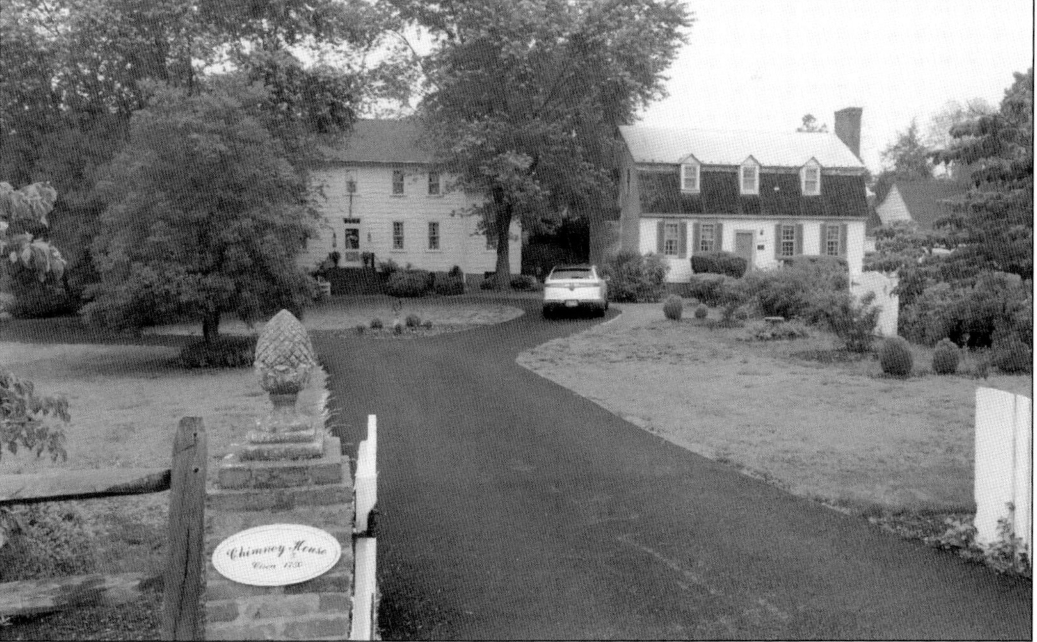

Due to the efforts of local preservationists beginning in the 1930s, Port Tobacco village retains an air of its 18th-century ambiance as a result of the restoration of the Chimney House and Stagg Hall, which stand adjacent to the east side of the reconstructed Port Tobacco Courthouse.

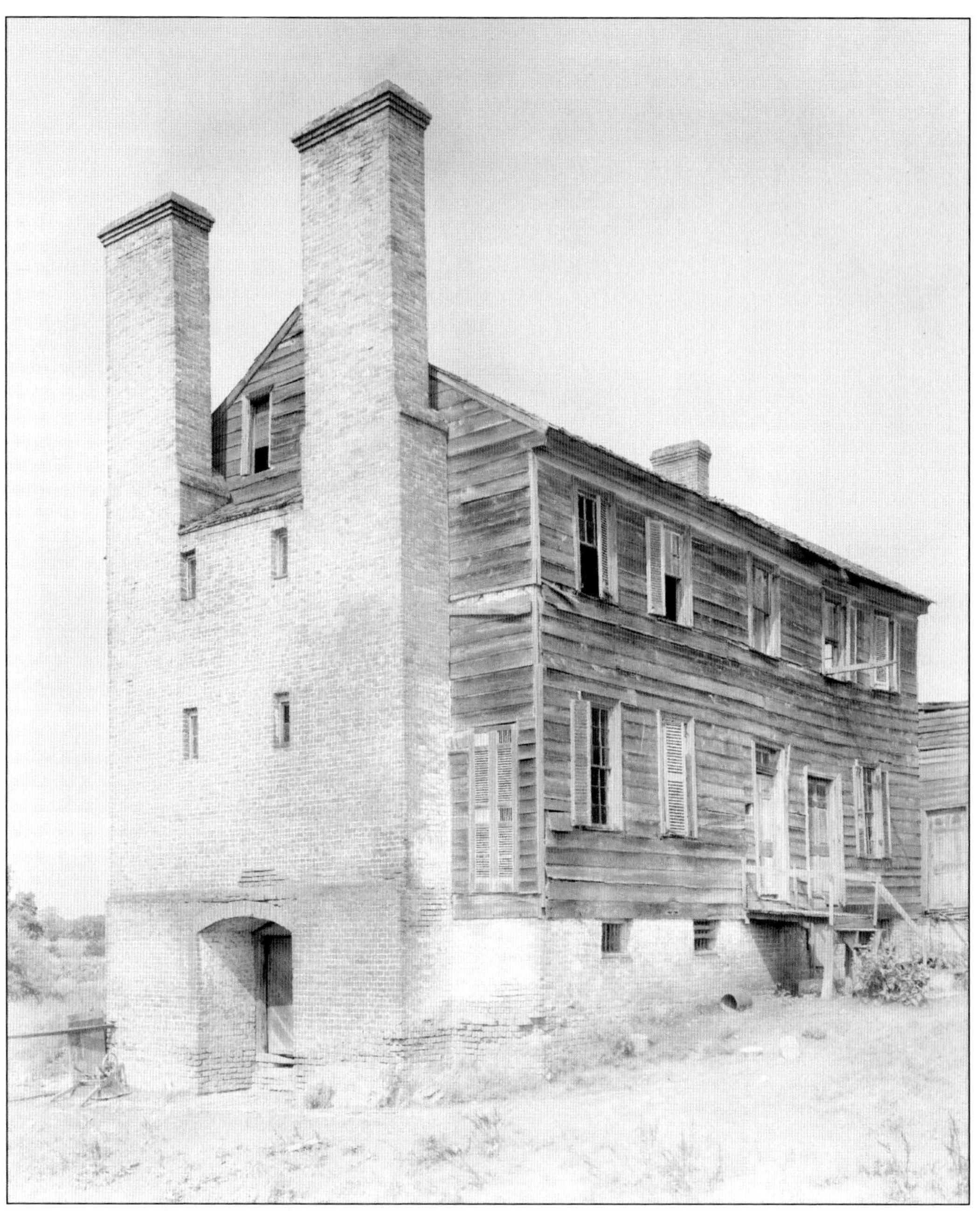

Built for Scottish-born merchant Thomas Howe Ridgate before his death in 1789, the Chimney House is another survivor from Port Tobacco's heyday as a bustling waterfront village. It was named for its massive two-story double chimney, and it has a doorway underneath it that leads into its English basement. In the 1930s, local philanthropist Alice Ferguson purchased the property and restored it as one of the first historic village houses to be saved. (FBJPC, LOC.)

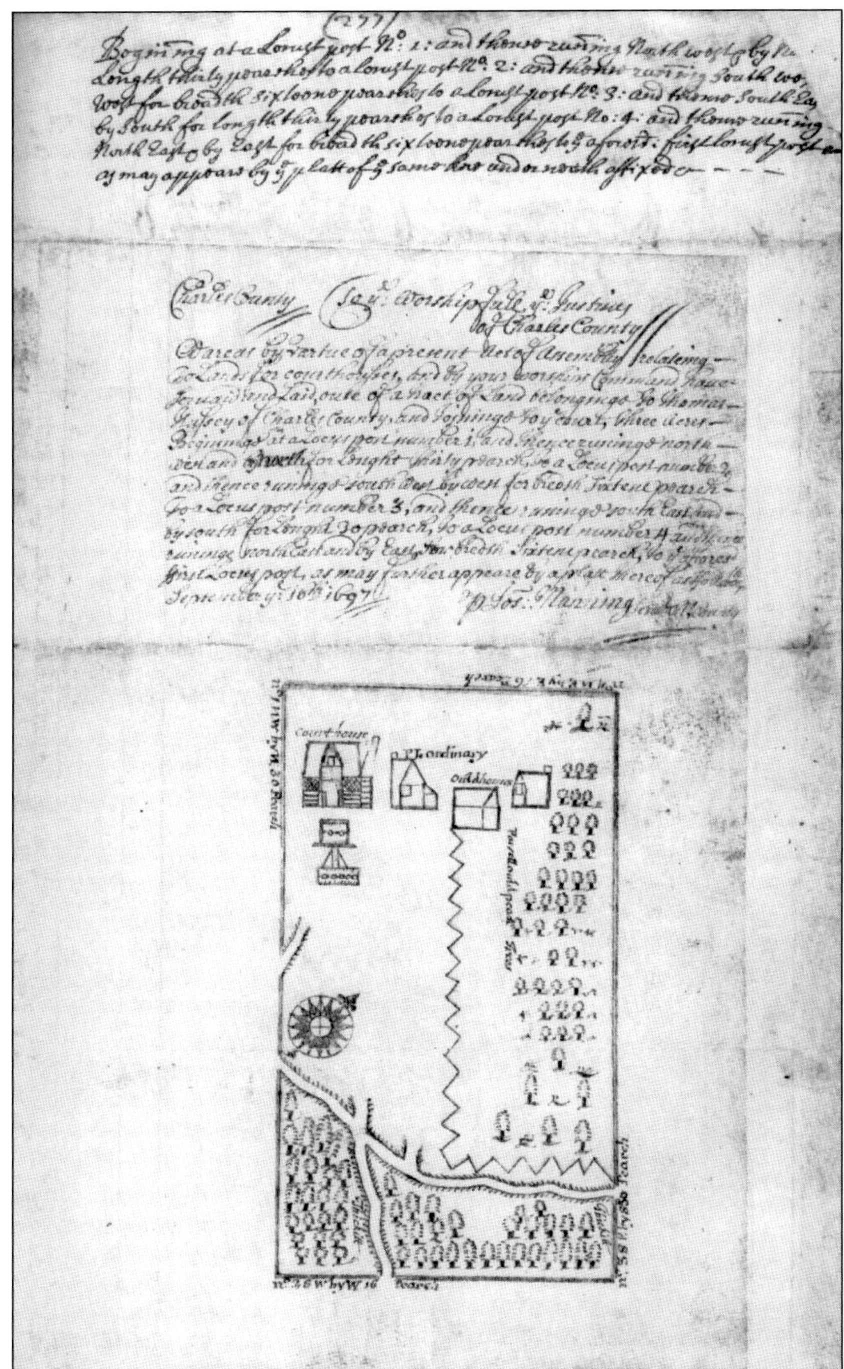

Charles County was established in 1658 and named for Lord Cecil Calvert's son. In 1674, Moore's Lodge was established as the first county courthouse several miles east of Port Tobacco. Shown on this 1697 plat map, it later was demolished in 1731. Though its location had long been forgotten, genealogist Dianne Giannini and land surveyor Kevin Norris traced its remains, which were uncovered by archaeologist Dr. Julia King in 2008, the county's 350th anniversary. (Maryland State Archives.)

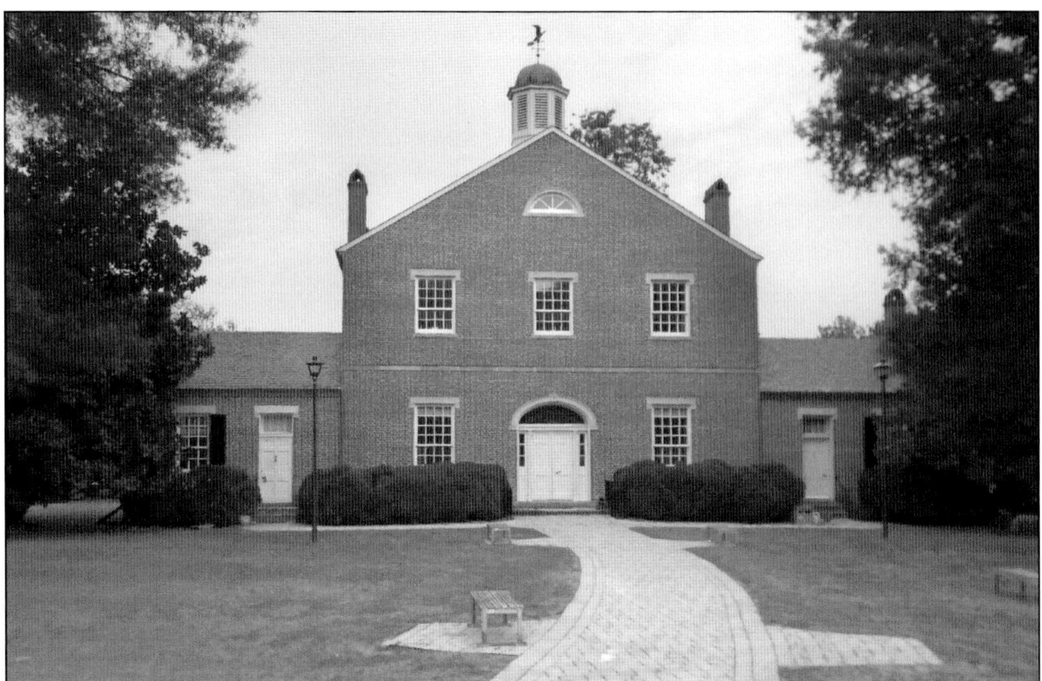

In 1972, Port Tobacco's 1821 courthouse was reconstructed using state funds. The original building was destroyed by fire in 1892, which provided another catalyst for moving the county seat to La Plata after the railroad came through there in 1872. It is operated by the Society for the Restoration of Port Tobacco and now serves as a place to educate the public about the region's past.

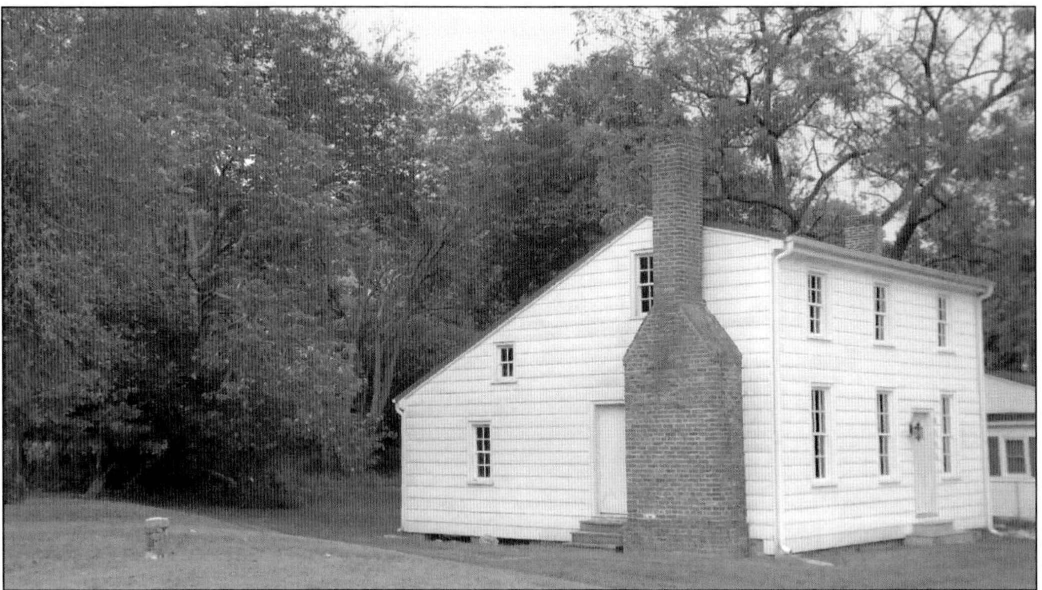

The Catslide House, or Burch House, was built between 1720 and 1730, and it may be the only village structure predating Port Tobacco becoming the county seat in 1727. Originally constructed as a one-story frame house with an attic, it was expanded to its present shape in the early 1800s. Once languishing, it was restored by the Society for the Restoration of Port Tobacco and now houses an archaeological exhibit.

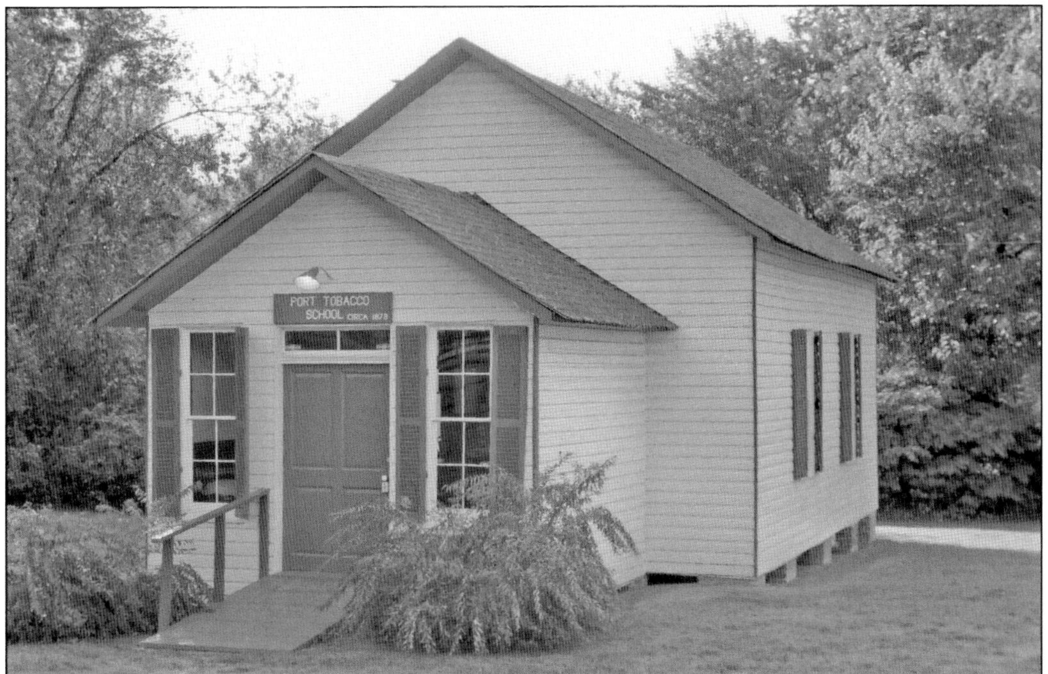

Built around 1878 to serve the children near Port Tobacco village, the Port Tobacco School is typical of Southern Maryland's wood-frame and clapboard-covered one-room schoolhouses. No longer in use and in severe disrepair in the 1960s, it was restored by the Society for the Restoration of Port Tobacco and now hosts visits from the county's schools to demonstrate the conditions in which earlier generations received their education.

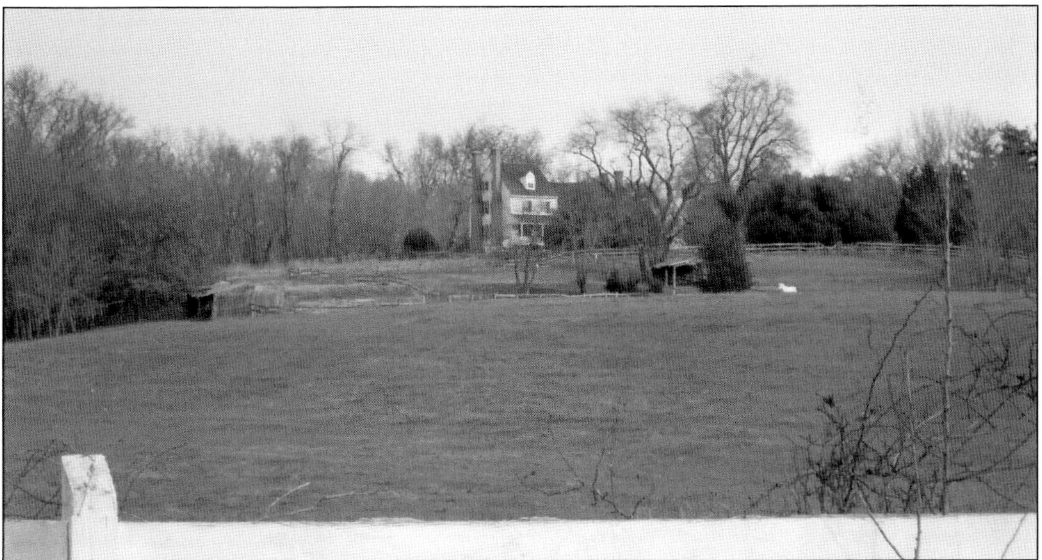

Capt. John Mitchell, an officer under Gen. William Smallwood in the American Revolution, built Linden around 1785. The two-and-a-half-story frame structure was expanded in 1840 to include a one-and-a-half-story wing, with double chimneys at each end of the house. Overlooking the Port Tobacco Valley, it became the home to Captain Mitchell's son "General" Walter H.J. Mitchell, who was an unsuccessful candidate for the governorship in the 1850s.

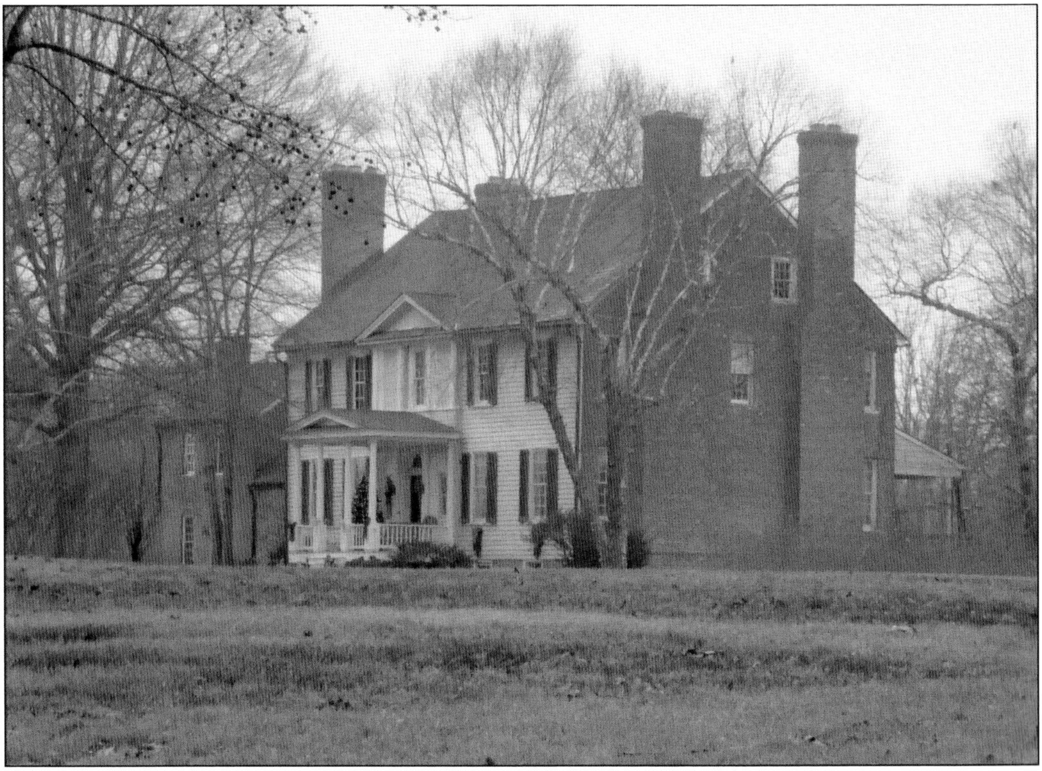

Dr. James Craik built La Grange near La Plata in 1765. The Georgian mansion is a two-story, brick-ended frame structure with a Palladian-style pedimented pavilion and entry. Craik was a Scottish-born physician and former British Army surgeon who first immigrated to Virginia in the 1750s. He served as the Continental Army's chief physician and, along with Dr. Gustavus Brown of Rose Hill, was attending George Washington when he died.

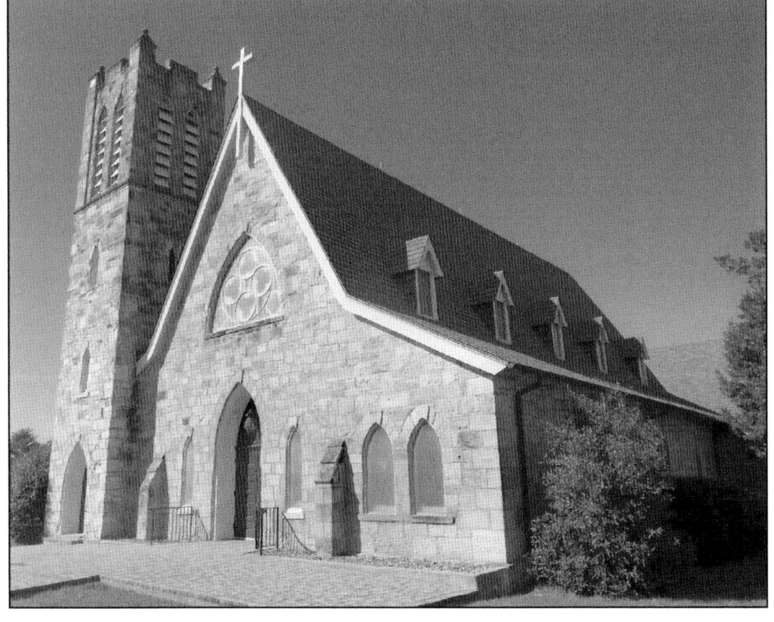

First established as a parish for Port Tobacco village in 1692, the earliest Christ Episcopal Church was built of wood near the site of the Port Tobacco Courthouse. In 1818, it was replaced by a stone church, which was later remodeled to its present Victorian Gothic style in 1884. As Port Tobacco declined, the church was dismantled and rebuilt in downtown La Plata in 1904.

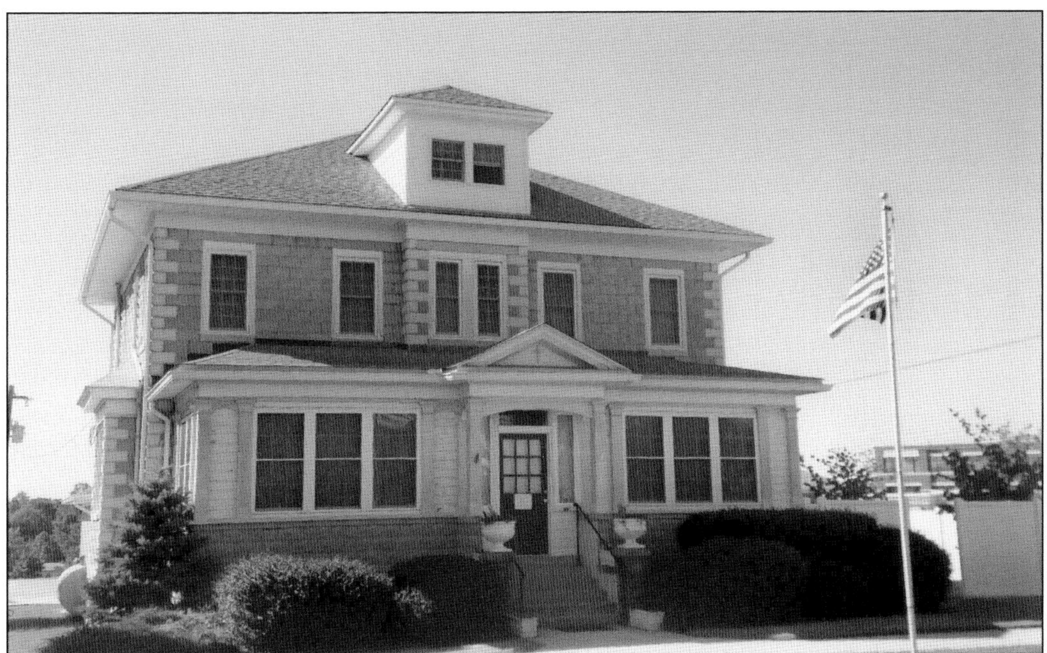

This American Foursquare house serves as the rectory for Sacred Heart Catholic Church in La Plata. The two-and-a-half-story home was built of rusticated concrete block to resemble stone for the Stonestreet family in 1900 as the town of La Plata developed. Once construction on Sacred Heart commenced, the archdiocese of Washington purchased it in 1963, following the Jesuits' relinquishment of their mission there.

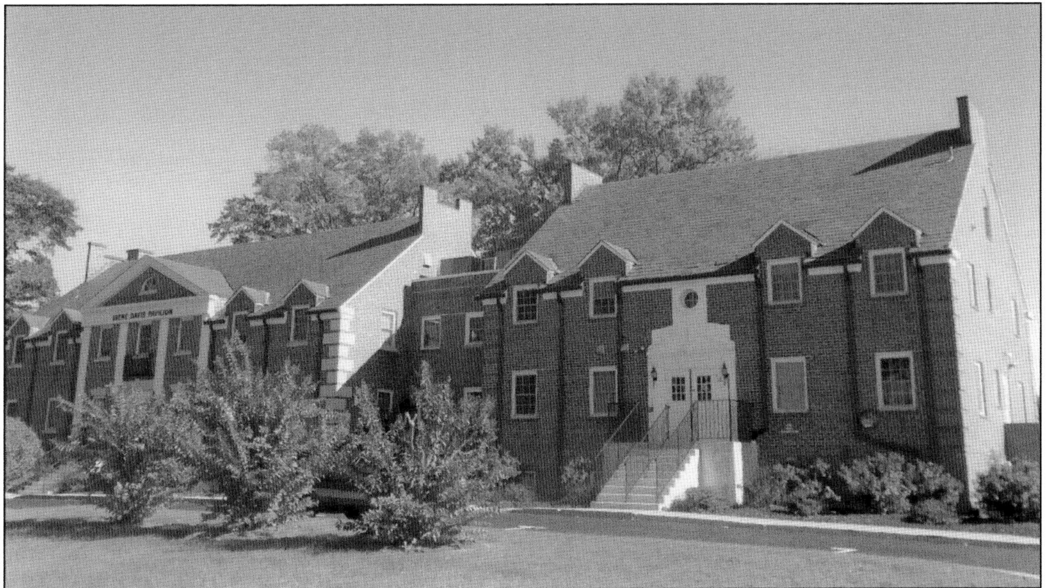

Following a deadly 1926 tornado that killed 15 people and injured 40 others at a time when there was no local medical facility, the construction of the two-part, two-story, Colonial Revival–style Physicians Memorial Hospital in 1938 was a significant event in La Plata history. The adjoining wing was built in 1940, starting what would become the University of Maryland's Charles Regional Medical Center, serving all of Southern Maryland.

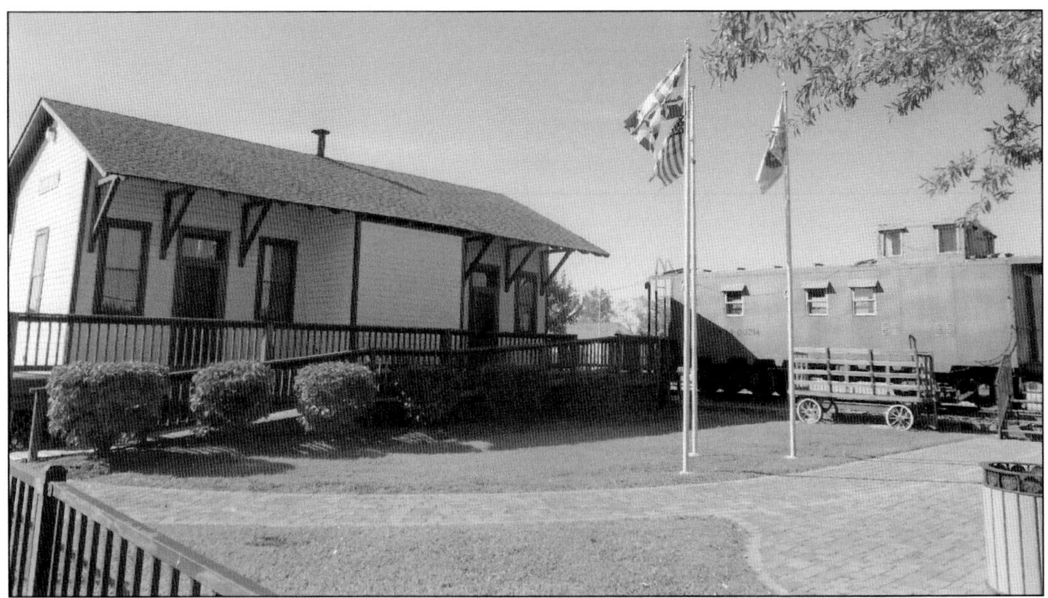

The Baltimore & Potomac Railroad built the La Plata railroad station on part of the Chapman family's La Plata farm in 1873, at which time it served a largely rural area. The coming of the railroad, however, encouraged the rapid development of the town of La Plata and the removal of the county seat from Port Tobacco. This is the last 19th-century train station remaining in Charles County.

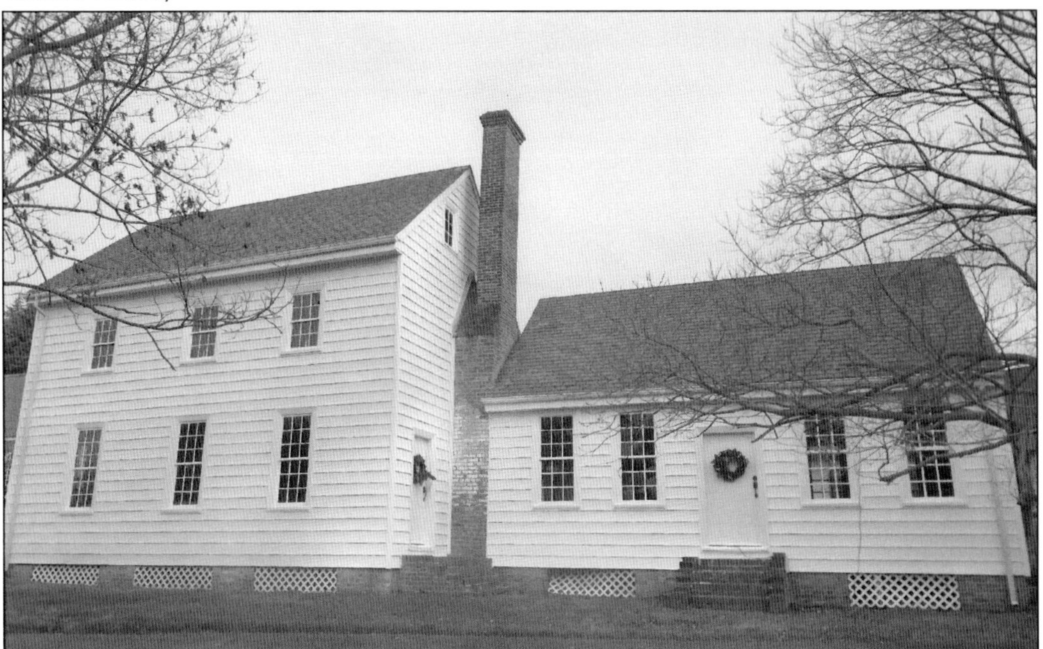

Belgian Catholic nuns of the Discalced Carmelite Order founded the Mount Carmel Monastery near La Plata in 1790. The prioress, Mother Mary Margaret Brent, was a Southern Marylander who persuaded her cousin Jesuit father Charles Neale to sponsor them. After the sisters moved to Baltimore in 1831, the monastery was abandoned until a group of locals, calling themselves the Restorers of Mount Carmel, restored the site for Maryland's 1933 tercentenary.

Nanjemoy Baptist Church began in 1790 when four Virginian Baptists crossed the Potomac to preach, and it is now the oldest Baptist congregation in the county. George Dunnington secured the land for the church in 1791, and the first meetinghouse was built in 1793. Incorporating the location and some framing of the earlier structure, this simple, rural Victorian Gothic church was built in 1905. Today, Dunnington is honored with a granite memorial.

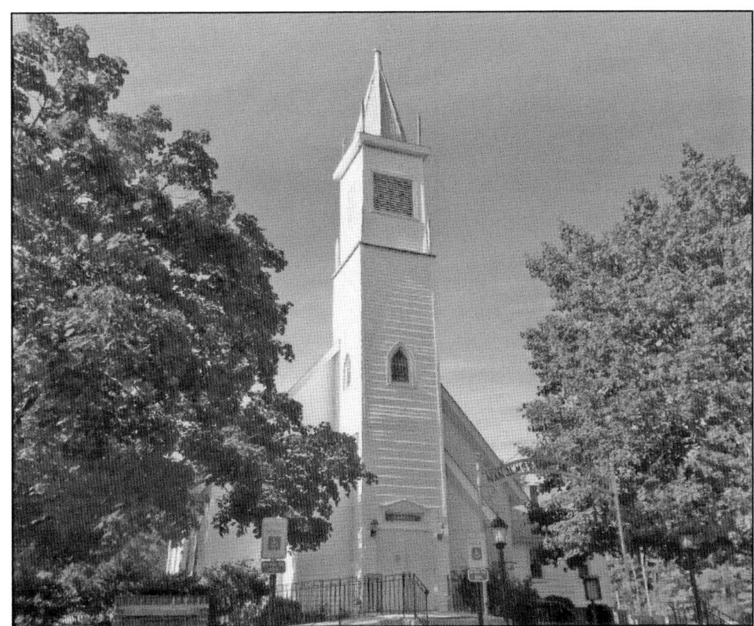

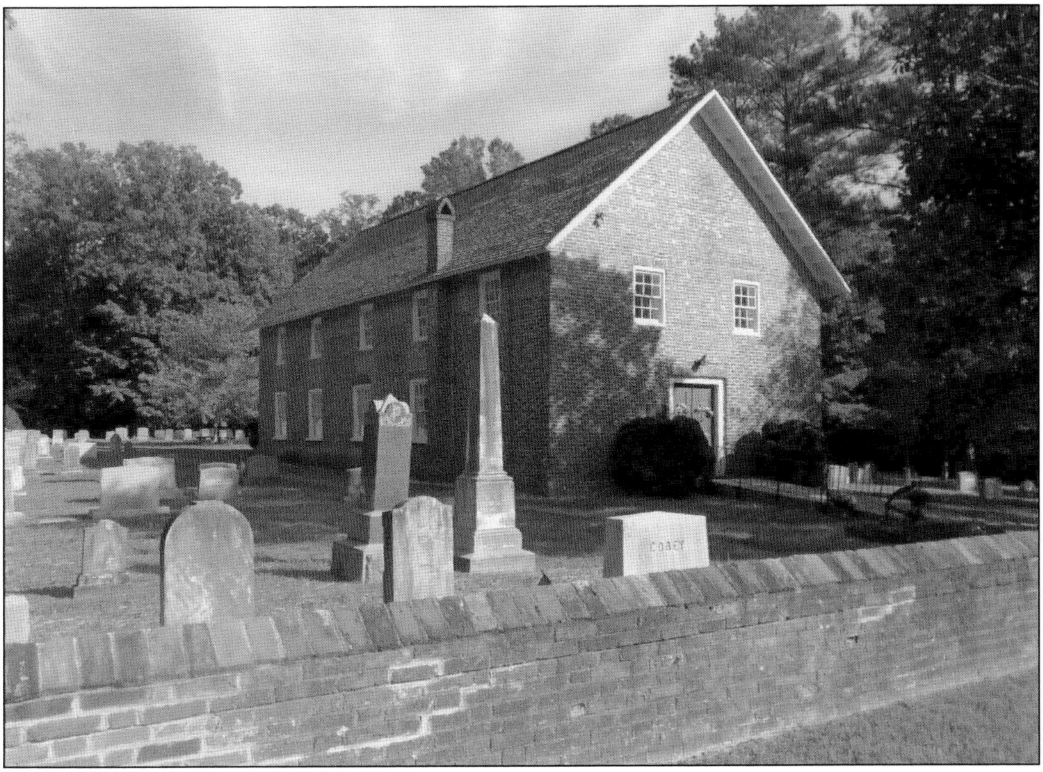

In a parish created in 1692, the Old Durham Church of Ironsides, also known as Christ Church Episcopal, was built in 1732 as a one-story brick structure that replaced an earlier log chapel. It was raised to its present height between 1791 and 1793, with extensive renovations in 1843. Gen. William Smallwood was a parishioner here, and George Washington is known to have attended services with his old Revolutionary War comrade.

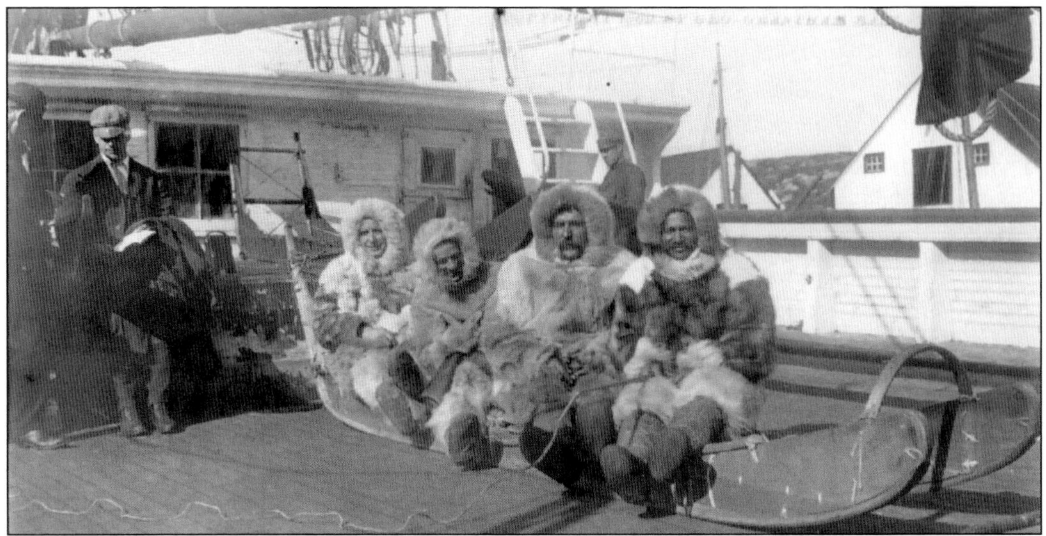

Born on Nanjemoy farm in 1866, African American Arctic explorer Matthew Henson (far right) was an orphan who moved to Baltimore at age 12 and became a sailor. In 1887, he met Navy officer and explorer Robert E. Peary, who hired Henson for all his expeditions, including one to the North Pole in 1909. Henson was interred at Arlington National Cemetery, and an historically African American middle school in Bryans Road, built in 1958, was named in his honor in 1969. (LOC.)

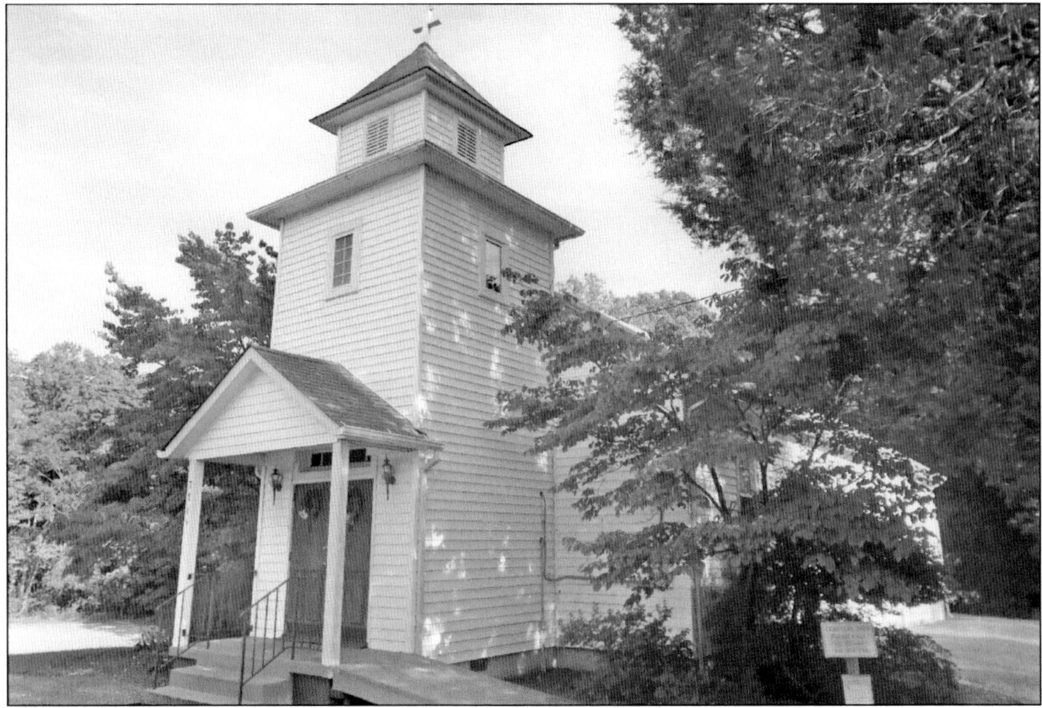

Built in 1911 on land deeded by Lemuel B. Owen for African American Catholics around McConchie, St. Catherine's Catholic Church has historically shared a pastor with the nearby church of St. Ignatius, Hilltop. Constructed of wood on a rectangular, six-bay-long plan with a tiered bell tower above the entrance, St. Catherine's is representative of a number of rural churches built in Southern Maryland during the early 20th century.

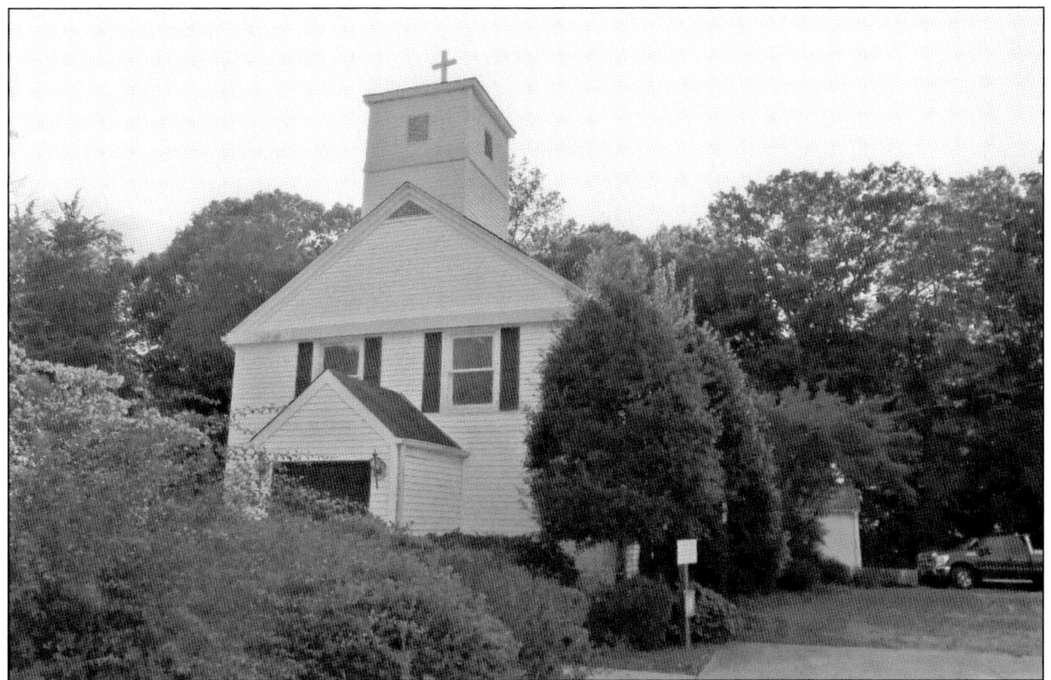

St. Ignatius of Loyola in Hilltop was a mission for the Jesuit priests of St. Thomas Manor at Chapel Point. The two-story frame structure was built around 1859. Unlike a parish, no rectory was established here. Instead, there were modest accommodations for visiting priests at the rear. The small square belfry was added in 1878. There is a small churchyard on the south side and a cemetery across the street.

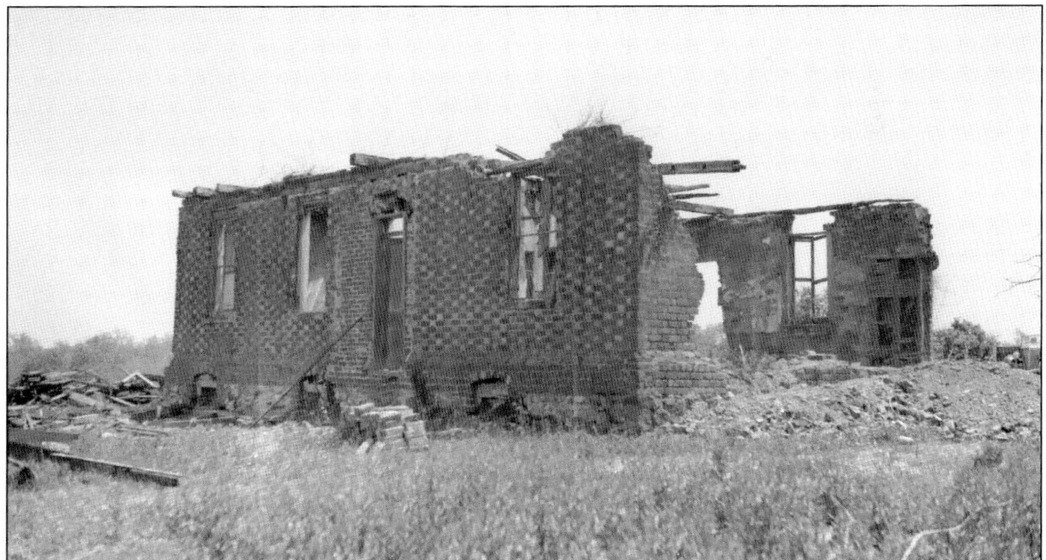

Smallwood's Retreat in Marbury was the home of Revolutionary War officer and Maryland governor Gen. William Smallwood (1732–1792). Educated at Eton College, Smallwood built his modest four-bay, one-and-a-half-story brick home around 1760 after returning from England. Decrepit but still intact before 1900, the house was collapsing in the 1930s. The Smallwood Foundation, formed in 1939, purchased the property to save it. (Thomas T. Waterman, HABS.)

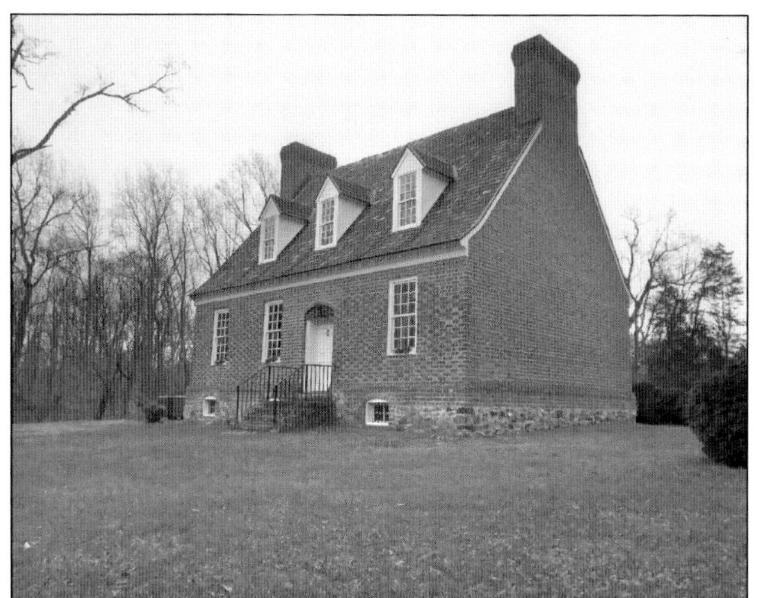

In 1940, the Smallwood Foundation purchased the house and the 10 acres surrounding it, stabilized it, and prepared for its restoration. However, the state legislature did not provide funds for its restoration until 1954. With the assistance of Col. Walter L. Simpson, retired military engineer and owner of Bachelor's Hope in Chaptico, and Baltimore architect H.P. Hopkins, among others, the house was restored in 1958 and donated for a state park.

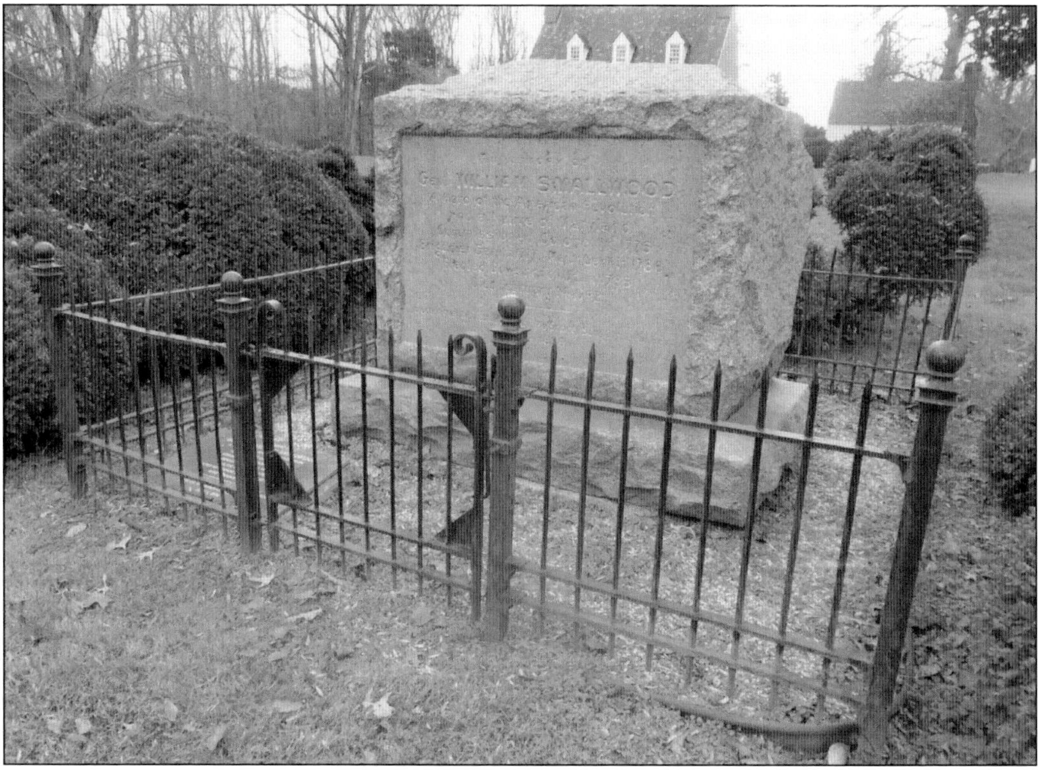

In 1898, before Smallwood's Retreat began collapsing, the Sons of the American Revolution honored the memory of Gen. William Smallwood with a large granite monument commemorating his life. As a participant of the fierce fighting in the Battle of Brooklyn, in which his Maryland soldiers defended Washington's retreat, Smallwood was recognized for his pivotal role and bravery in the war. After the war, Smallwood served as the first president general of the Maryland Society of the Cincinnati.

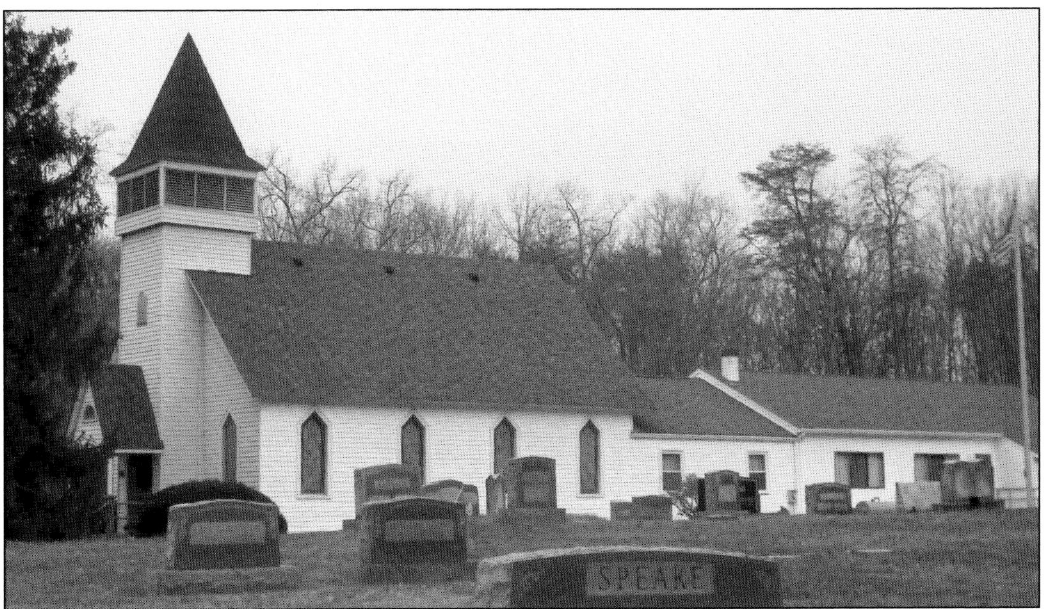

Built on land acquired for the congregation's first frame church in 1841, the Chicamuxen United Methodist Church is a four-bay-long, simplified frame, vernacular Victorian Gothic structure with an engaged bell tower above the entrance. The present church was constructed in 1905. Its predecessor was the site of Union general Joseph Hooker's Civil War headquarters from October 1861 through March 1862, with almost 12,000 soldiers camped in the area.

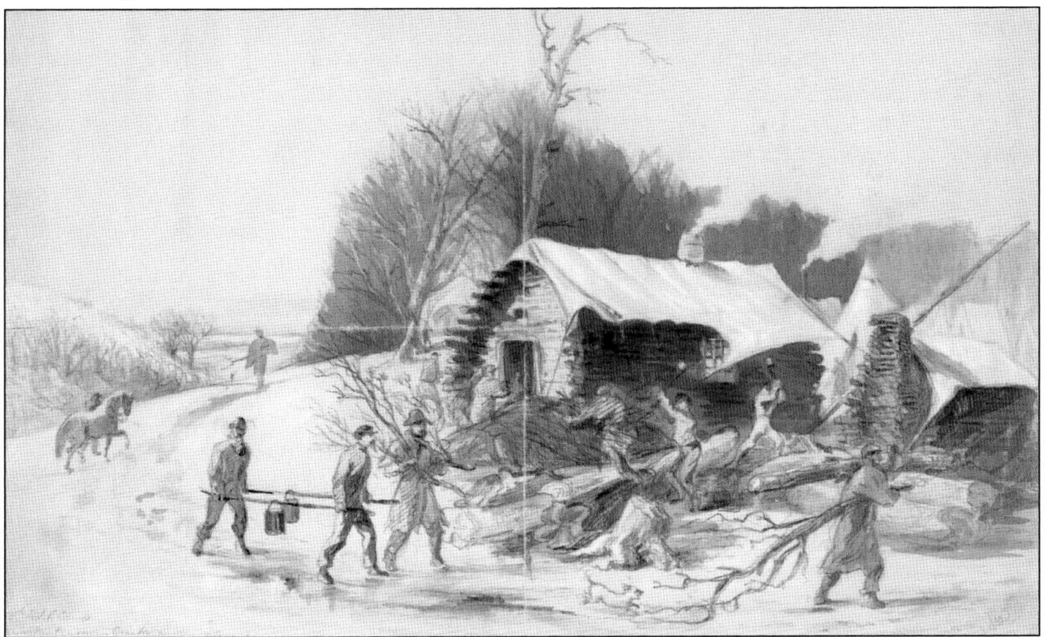

Born in Dublin in 1837, Irish American artist Arthur Lumley studied at the National Academy of Design before the Civil War. Sent to Washington as a newspaper illustrator in April 1861, he was the first special artist "embedded" in the Army of the Potomac, living among Gen. Joseph Hooker's troops near Chicamuxen. His illustration shows some of Hooker's 8th New Jersey Volunteers preparing their winter quarters around Mattawoman Creek. (Arthur Lumley, LOC.)

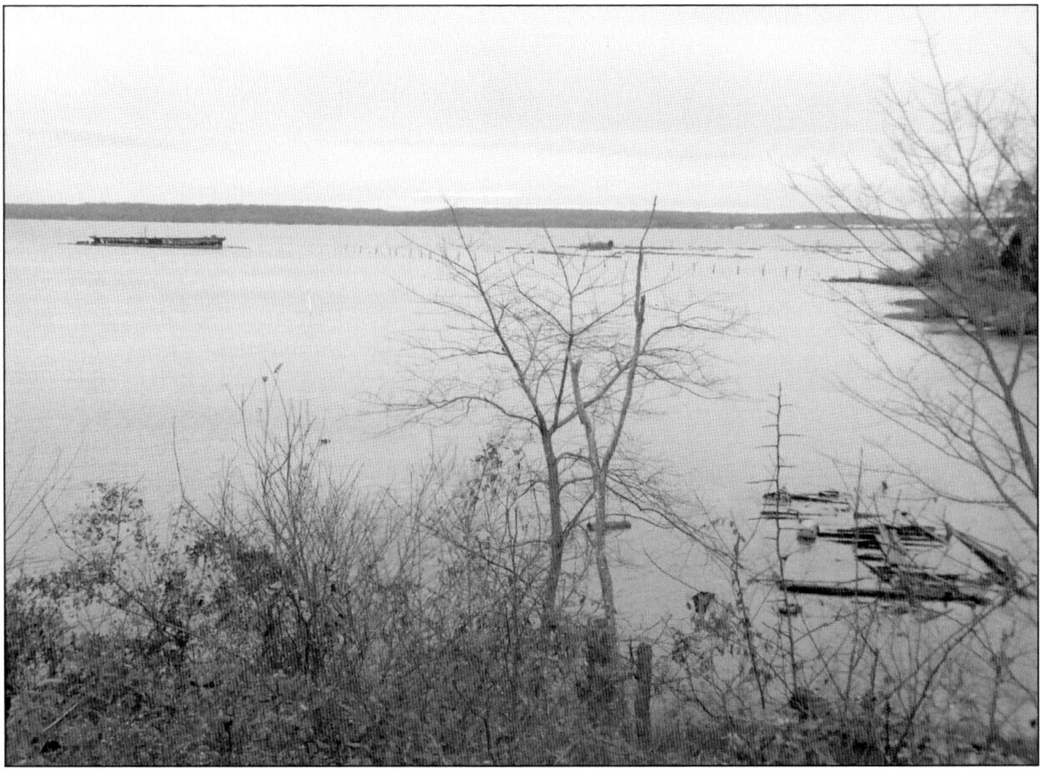

When World War I ended, the Navy had hundreds of surplus cargo steamships that had been made for service in the war. Brought up the Potomac to Mallows Bay (originally Marlow's Bay, after a local family), the Navy ordered the fleet of surplus ships to be burned to the waterline in November 1925. This unique collection of riverine shipwrecks is now a county park and a favorite spot for kayakers and birders.

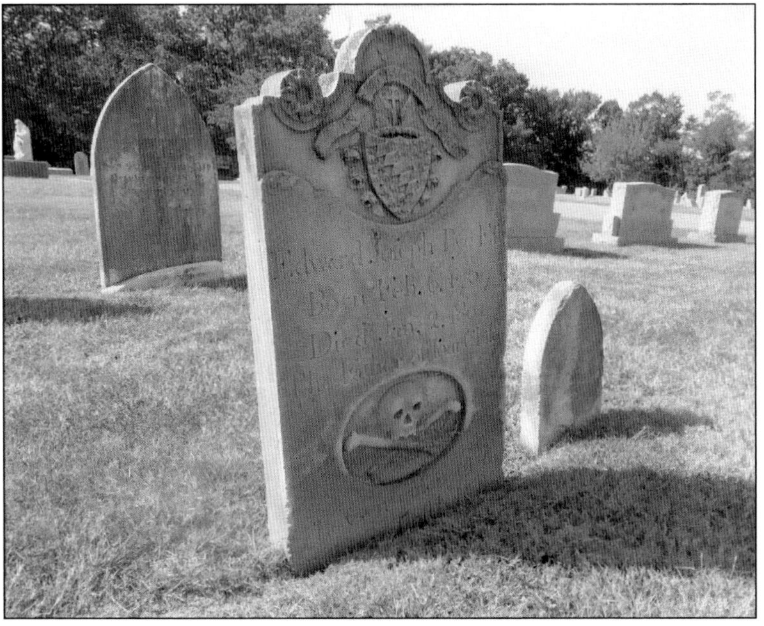

In a complex deal with the duke of Norfolk in 1767, Charles Pye acquired 5,000 acres once granted to Thomas Cornwaleys for the area around Indian Head. He built the Pye Chapel on the Cornwallis Neck peninsula, where it was served by Jesuits from St. Thomas Manor and became St. Charles Catholic Church (razed 1913). The elaborate armorial 1801 gravestone of Edward Pye is a masterpiece of stone carver's art.

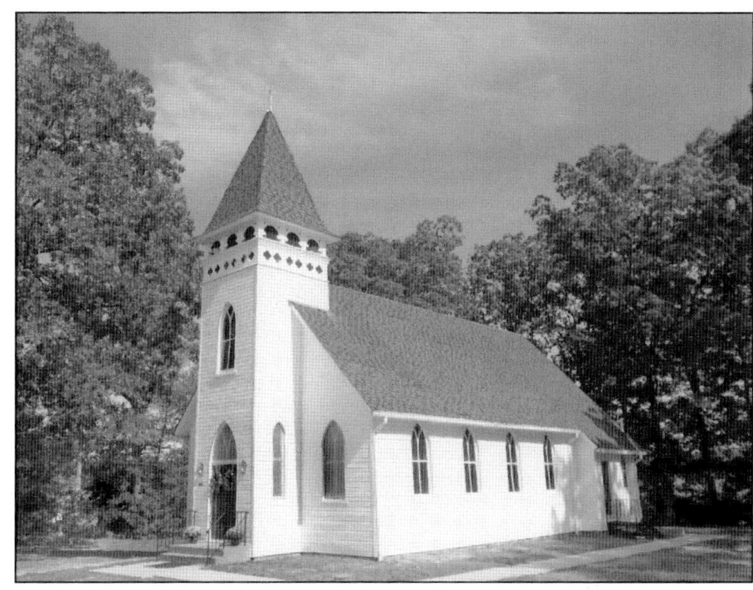

Recently converted to Calvary Road Baptist Church in Pomonkey, this modest Victorian Gothic frame church began its life as St. John's Episcopal Chapel. The first chapel was constructed a half mile south on Bumpy Oak Road, where St. John's Cemetery is located, in 1842. Built in 1901, this was the second church for its members. In 1966, it was moved back slightly to accommodate a new basement.

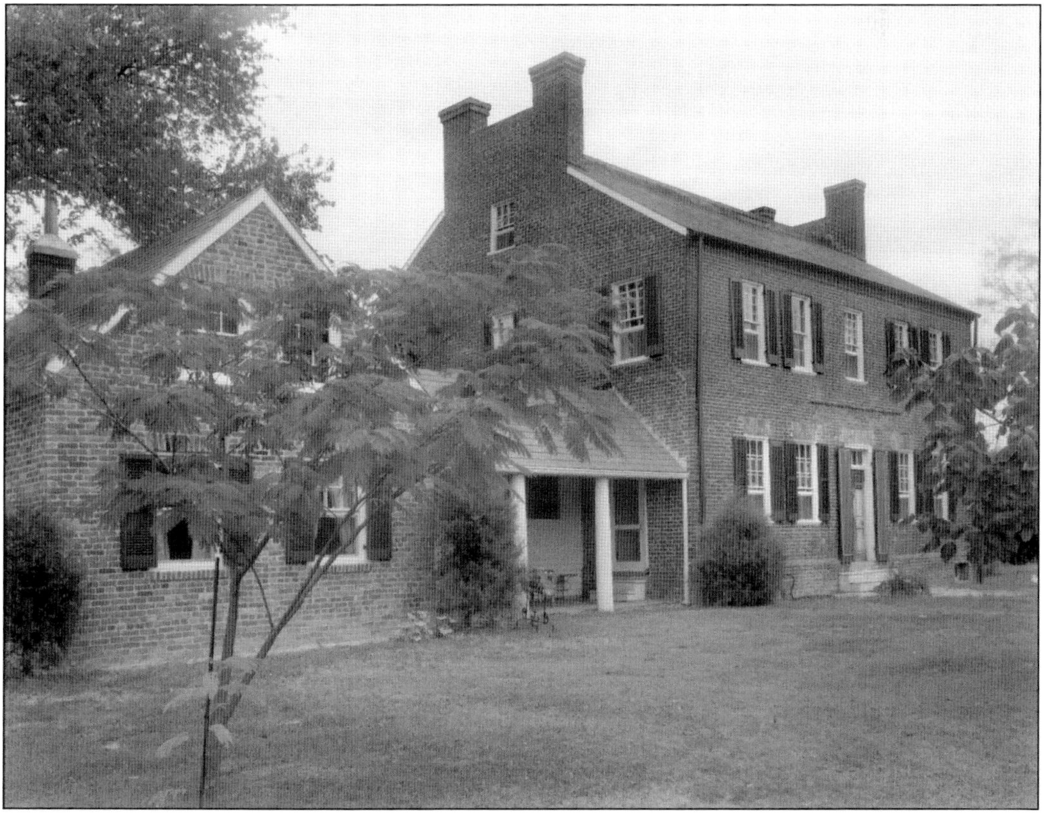

Built in 1720 as a one-and-a-half-story brick estate, Araby was extensively enlarged in the early 19th century with a second floor and a frame hyphen connecting a brick kitchen. In 1750, George Mason, the Virginia patriot living across the Potomac, married Ann Eibeck of Araby. Mason owned land adjacent to Araby, and the couple lived there until their Virginia mansion, Gunston Hall, was completed in 1759. (FBJPC, LOC.)

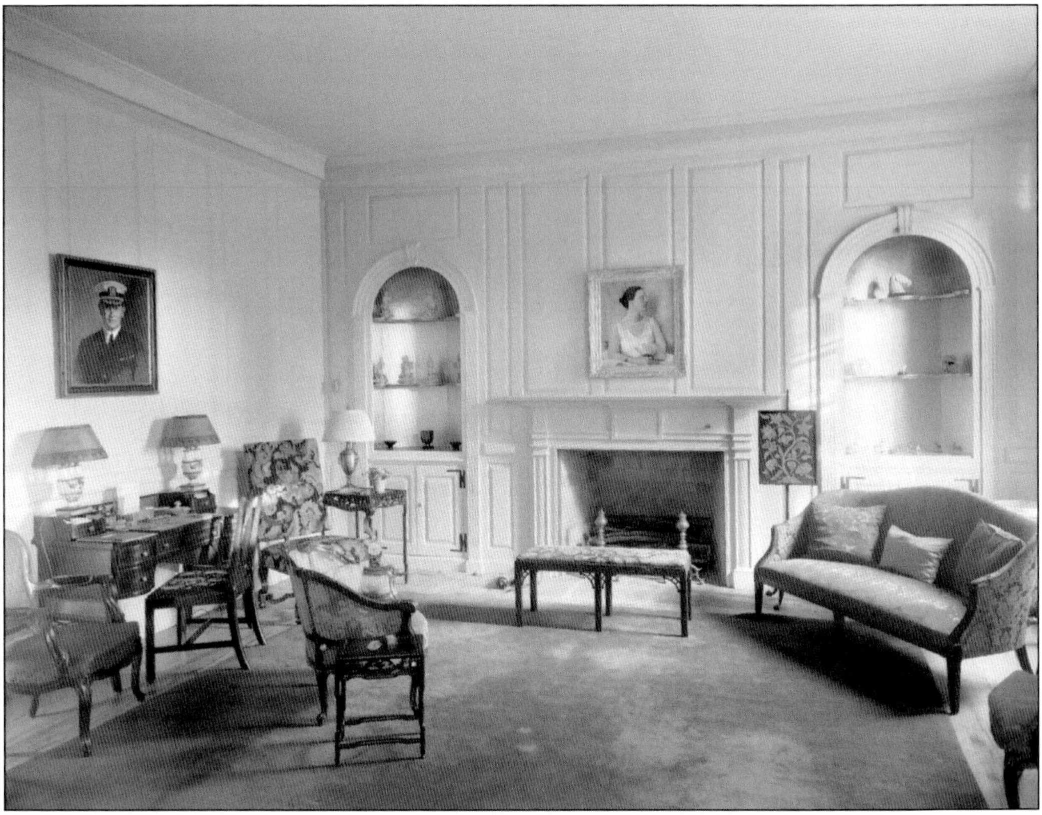

Visited by George Mason's Virginia neighbor George Washington on several occasions, Araby is rare among the surviving 18th-century houses in Charles County in having managed to maintain a great deal of its original interior woodwork. Until the 1960s, Araby also had preserved an 18th-century gristmill among its dependencies, but that was demolished because of a road-widening project. (FBJPC, LOC.)

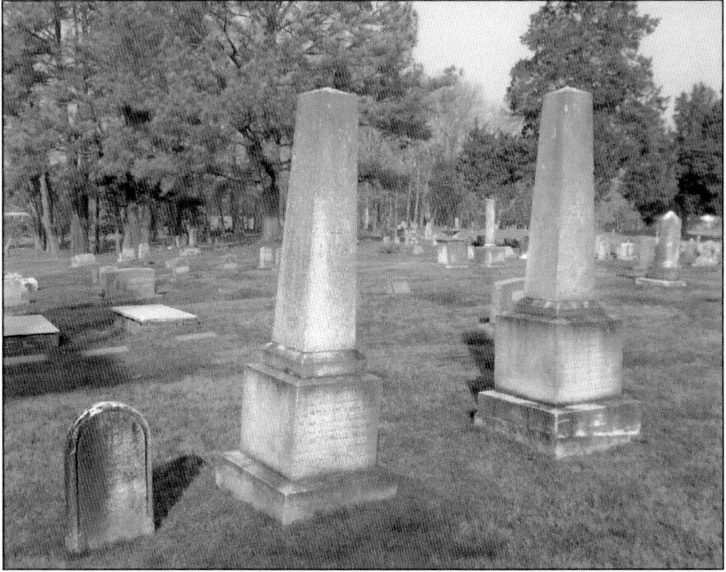

In the cemetery of St. Joseph's Catholic Church in Pomfret, a pair of stone obelisk grave markers mark the burial sites of Col. William Thompson and his wife, Mary Grace Davis Thompson, who owned Araby after 1849. After joining the militia in 1810, Thompson rose to the rank of colonel. Though they died in 1853 and 1850, respectively, Araby remained in the Thompson and related Wills family for over a century.

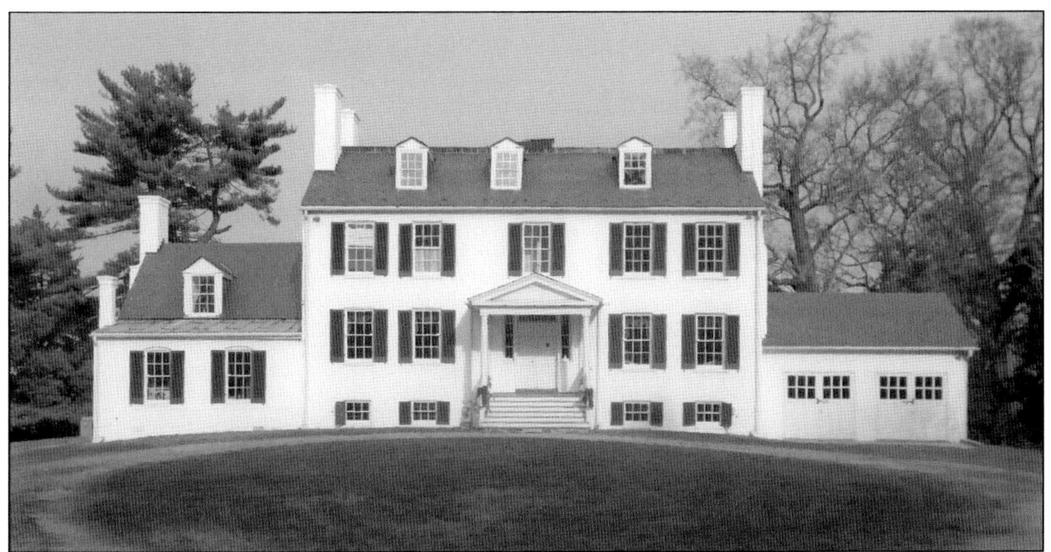

Situated on a high hill overlooking the Potomac about five miles downriver from Mount Vernon, the land upon which Mount Aventine was built was acquired by the Chapman family in 1750 and remained in the family until 1916. The two-and-a-half-story home was constructed of brick over an English basement. Mount Aventine was greatly expanded between 1840 and 1860, replacing an earlier house built nearby around 1760.

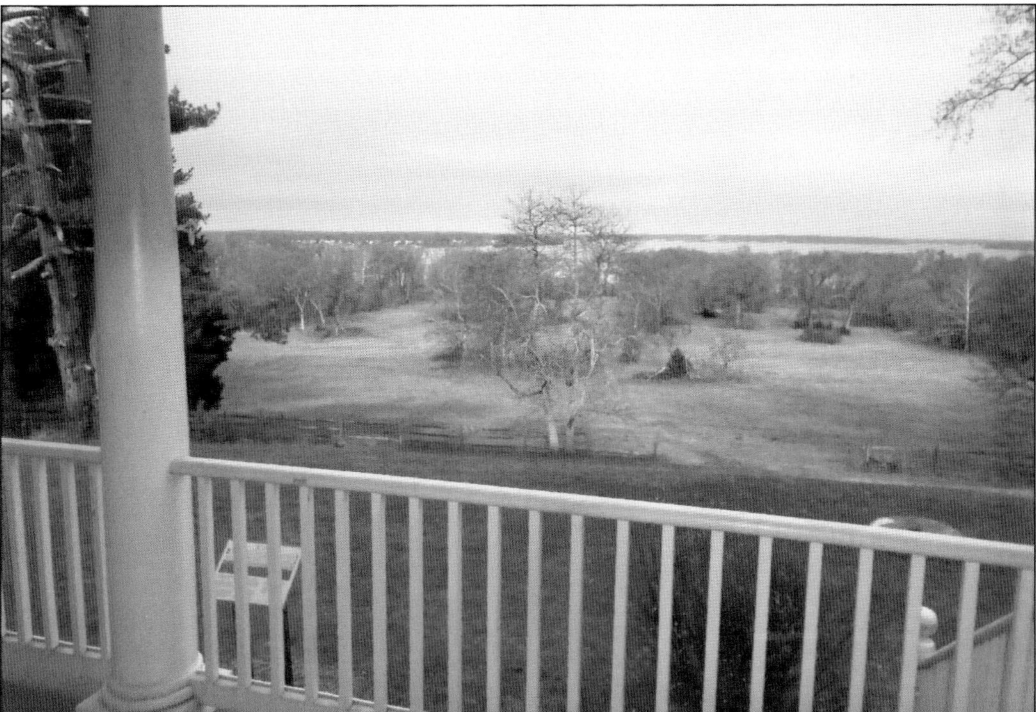

Along the western elevation facing the river is a porch that runs the full length of the main block of the house. The lawn drops off rapidly toward the river, providing Mount Aventine with a majestic view of the Potomac, the sites of both Gunston Hall and Mount Vernon, and the location of the lucrative ferry that the Chapman family once ran from the property.

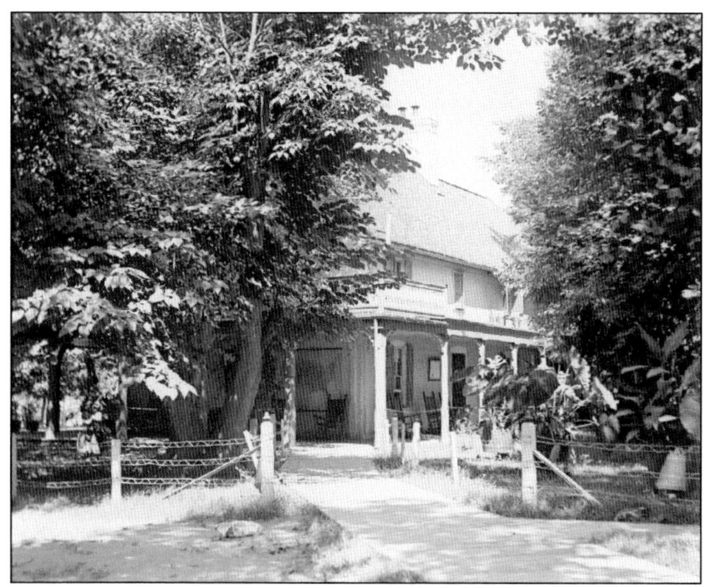

Built by Thomas Marshall in 1728, Marshall Hall was the largest house in Southern Maryland through the mid-18th century. Located along the Potomac about a mile southeast of Mount Vernon, it was originally a five-bay, two-story brick home that was expanded to seven bays around 1760. The Marshalls sold the property in 1866 due to postwar hardships, and it became a Victorian steamboat resort in 1895. (National Photo Company, LOC.)

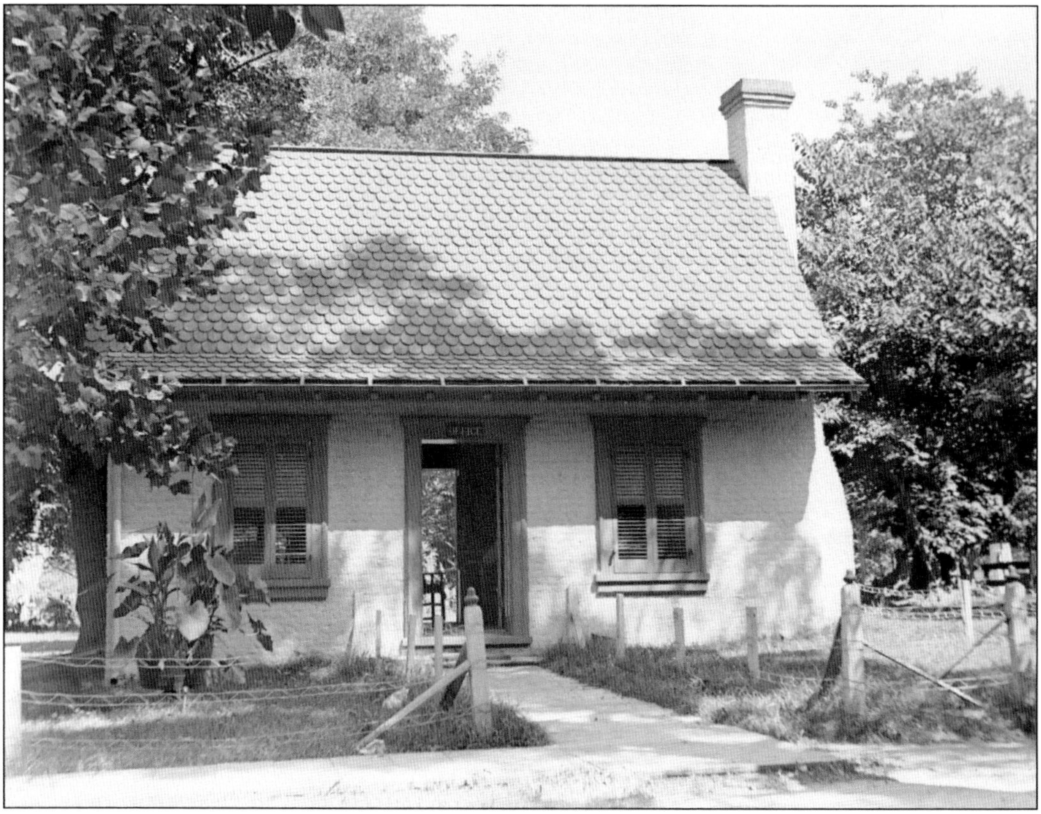

About 30 feet south of Marshall Hall is its last standing dependency. The one-story, three-bay brick building is reported to have been the office of Dr. Thomas Marshall II (1731–1801), the son of the builder. He was also a friend of George Washington, a member of Charles County's Committee for Correspondence, a Revolutionary War militia captain, and a signer of the Maryland Oath of Allegiance. (National Photo Company, LOC.)

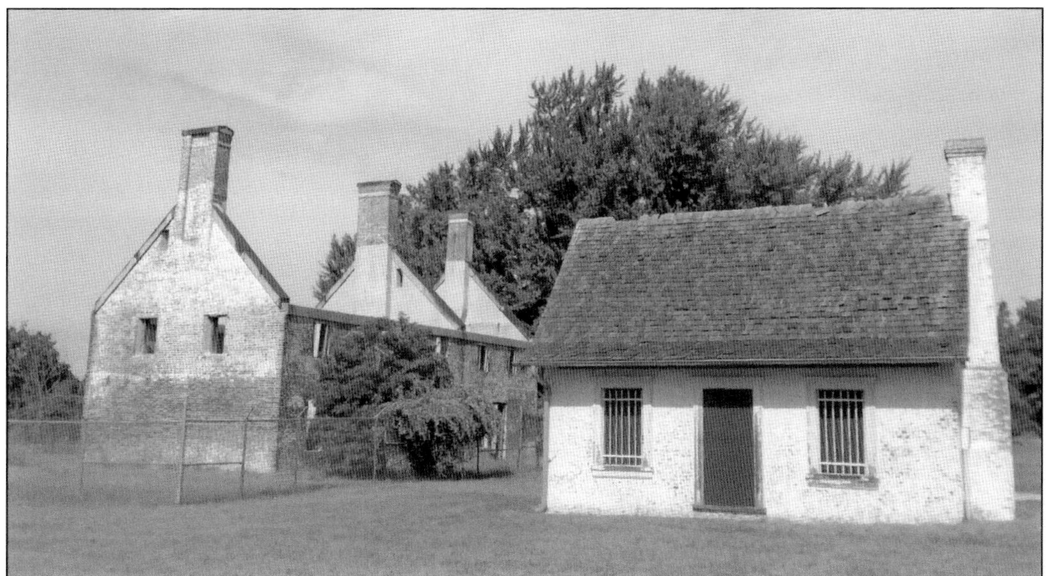

Today, Marshall Hall is a mere shell of its former grandeur. In 1976, the National Park Service acquired the property with the intent to restore it while it was still intact. In October 1981, an arsonist torched the house, gutting it. The home had been stabilized but not restored when a large truck lost control and drove straight through the walls of the house in January 2003. Having suffered these indignities, the home and its adjacent office await restoration.

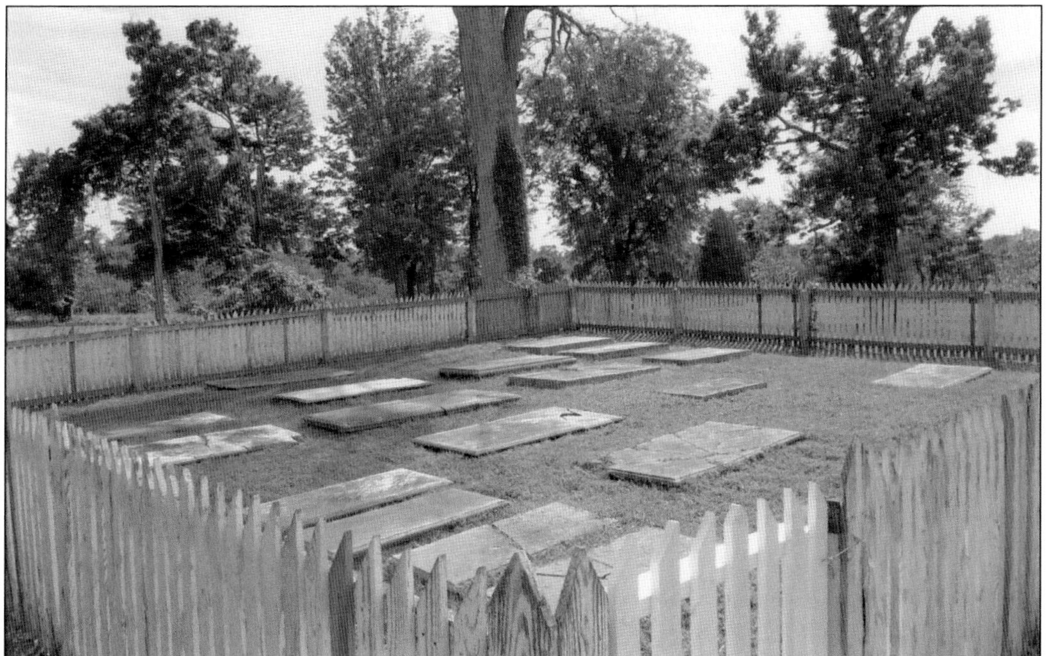

About 200 yards northeast of Marshall Hall is the Marshall family cemetery, enclosed by a small white picket fence. The burial site of Thomas Marshall and 17 other marked graves remain within the small compound for the family who was considered the third wealthiest in the county for generations. Marshall Hall, the cemetery, and the grounds are within the westernmost portion of Piscataway Park, owned by the National Park Service.

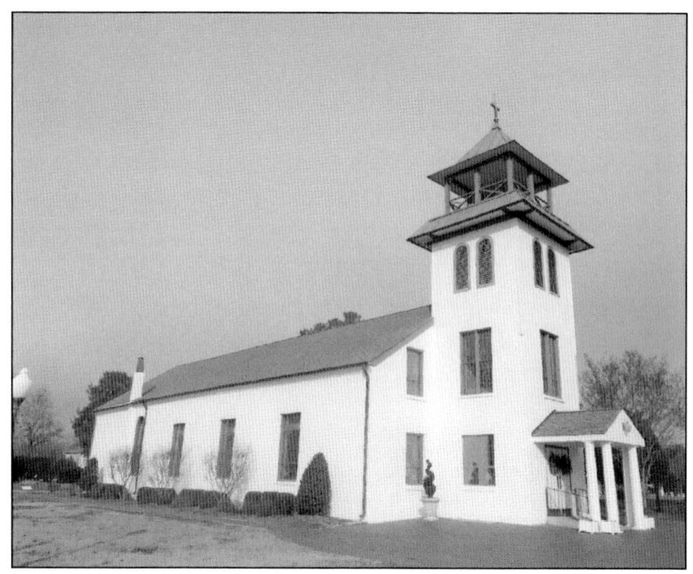

Rev. George Hunter, SJ, founded St. Joseph's Catholic Church in Pomfret in 1763. Razed in 1835 because of deterioration, the first 18th-century frame church stood in the churchyard, about 100 yards north of the current brick church, which opened in 1849. The one-story stuccoed church with its three-story bell tower was closed for restoration in 1974, then reopened with a mass led by Washington archbishop William Cardinal Baum in 1977.

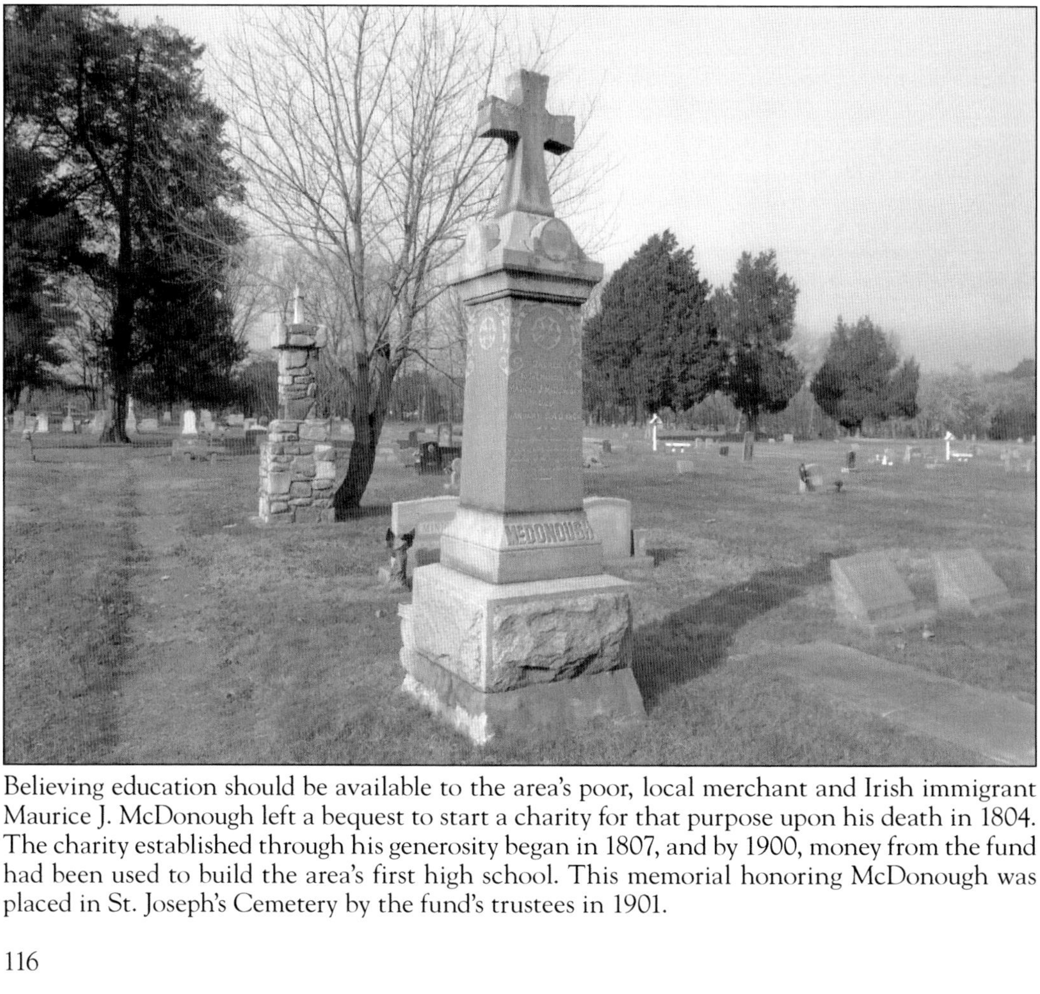

Believing education should be available to the area's poor, local merchant and Irish immigrant Maurice J. McDonough left a bequest to start a charity for that purpose upon his death in 1804. The charity established through his generosity began in 1807, and by 1900, money from the fund had been used to build the area's first high school. This memorial honoring McDonough was placed in St. Joseph's Cemetery by the fund's trustees in 1901.

The Dent family built this typical Southern Maryland Tidewater hall and parlor home with brick noggin between the wood beams in the mid-18th century. Rescued from collapse by the Historical Society of Charles County in 1968, the Friendship House was removed from its original site along Nanjemoy Creek and reconstructed on the College of Southern Maryland's La Plata campus, where it is now a museum.

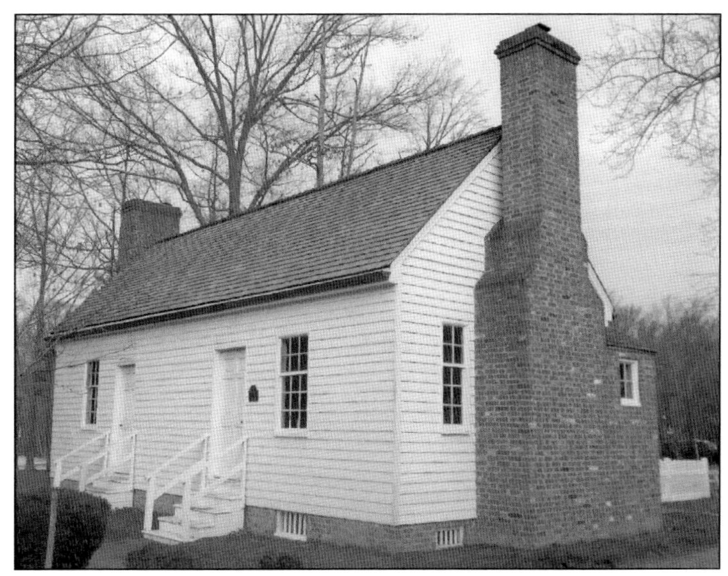

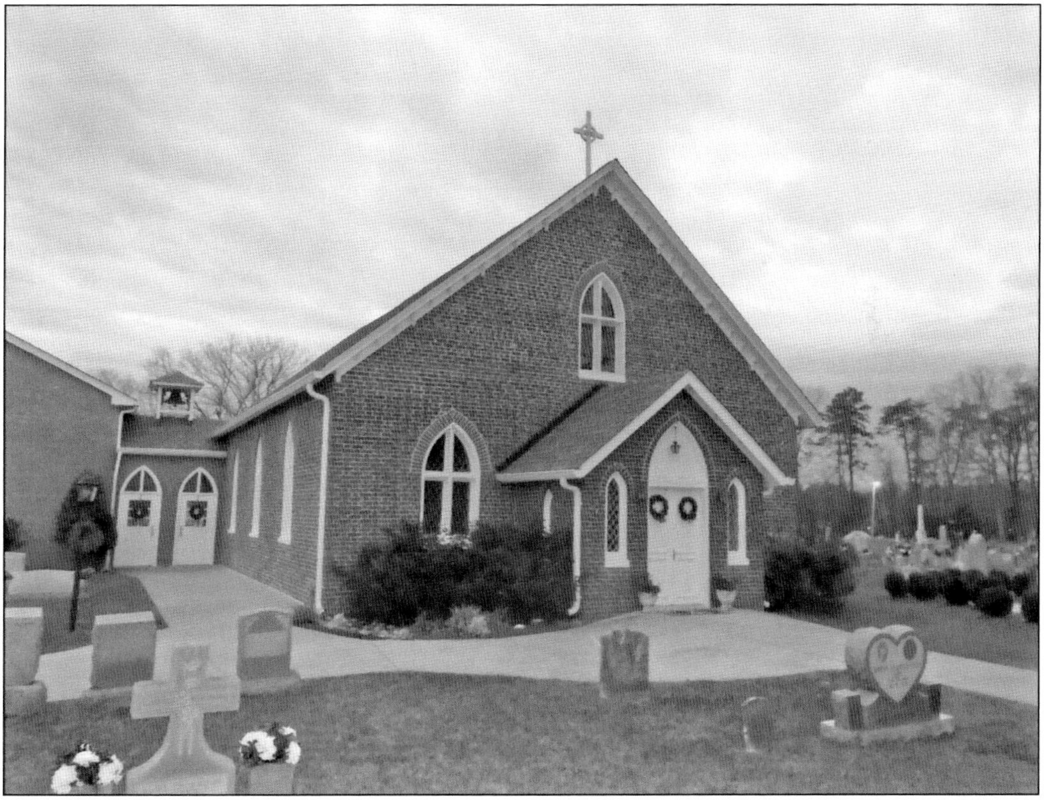

Originally organized as a chapel of ease for the Episcopal parish of Port Tobacco in 1754, the first St. Paul's Episcopal Church in Waldorf was made of hewn logs, but it burned before 1823. Ignatius Spalding of Washington, DC, then built a brick chapel with lancet windows for a cost of $1,550 in 1831. The replacement chapel was partly incorporated into the present church.

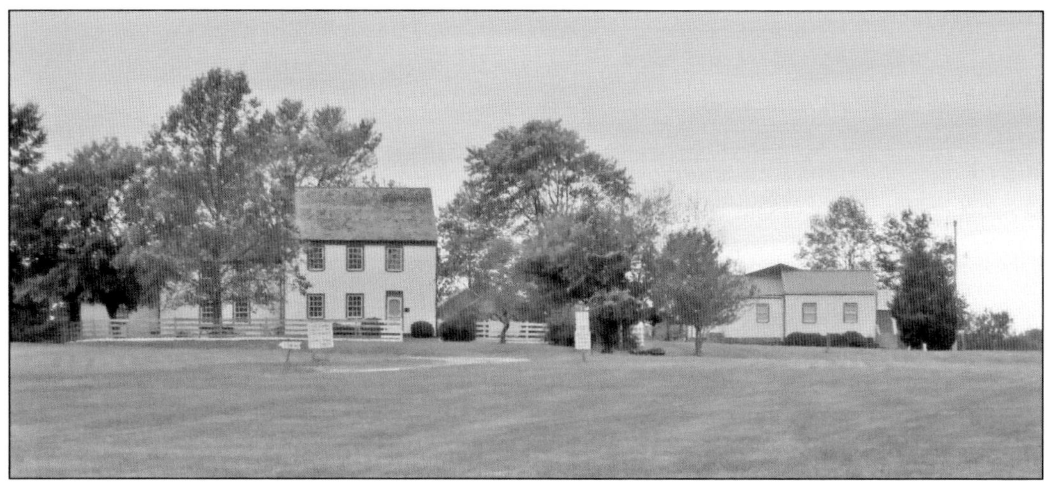

Thomas Mudd purchased the manor named St. Catherine in 1696, but it is best known as the site of the Dr. Samuel A. Mudd House. The house was built around 1857 as a typical wood-frame, three-part telescoping farmhouse by Dr. Mudd (1833–1883), known for setting the broken leg of John Wilkes Booth after Pres. Abraham Lincoln's assassination. Located between Waldorf and Bryantown, the house is open for tours and is still owned by the Mudd family.

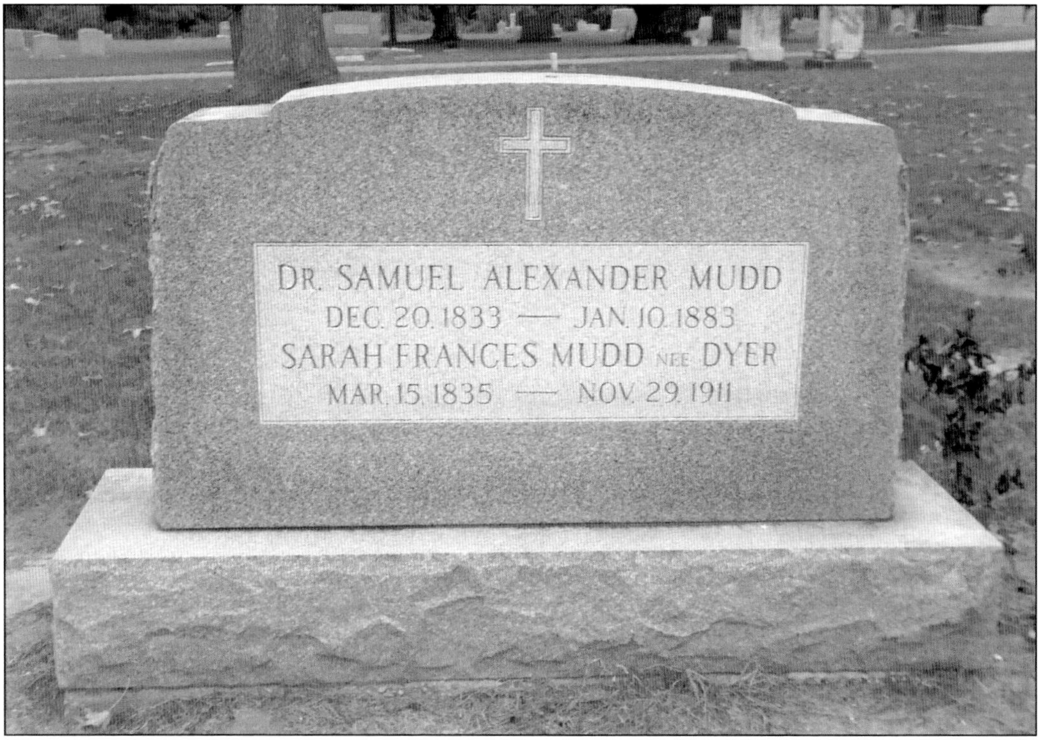

Dr. Mudd attended Georgetown College, then the University of Maryland for medical school, and practiced in Charles County. Convicted by a military tribunal for assisting Booth, he was sentenced to life imprisonment at Fort Jefferson, an island fortress in the Dry Tortugas west of Key West, Florida. However, he was pardoned by Pres. Andrew Johnson for saving people at the fort during an epidemic. Mudd died at his home and is buried at St. Mary's Catholic Church cemetery in Bryantown.

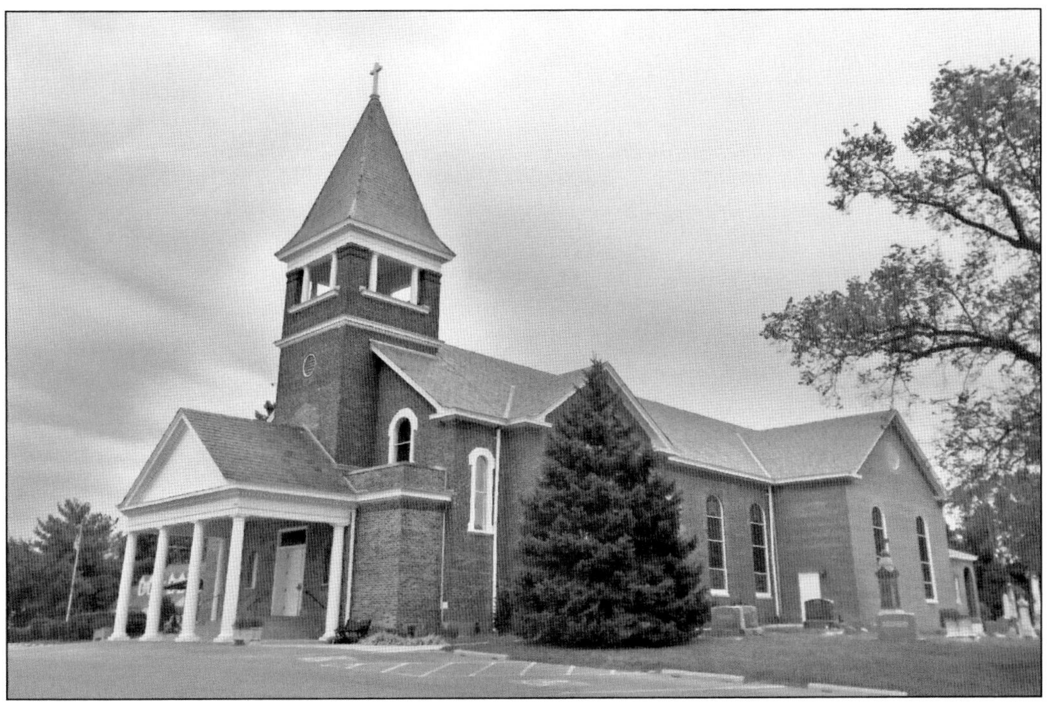

In 1793, the first St. Mary's Catholic Church was built on the site of an 18th-century Catholic log chapel situated within Boarman's Manor, which was established in 1674. The large brick cruciform church was constructed in 1846, replacing the older building. The engaged bell tower over the entrance was added in 1895, and the church was extensively renovated after a fire in 1963.

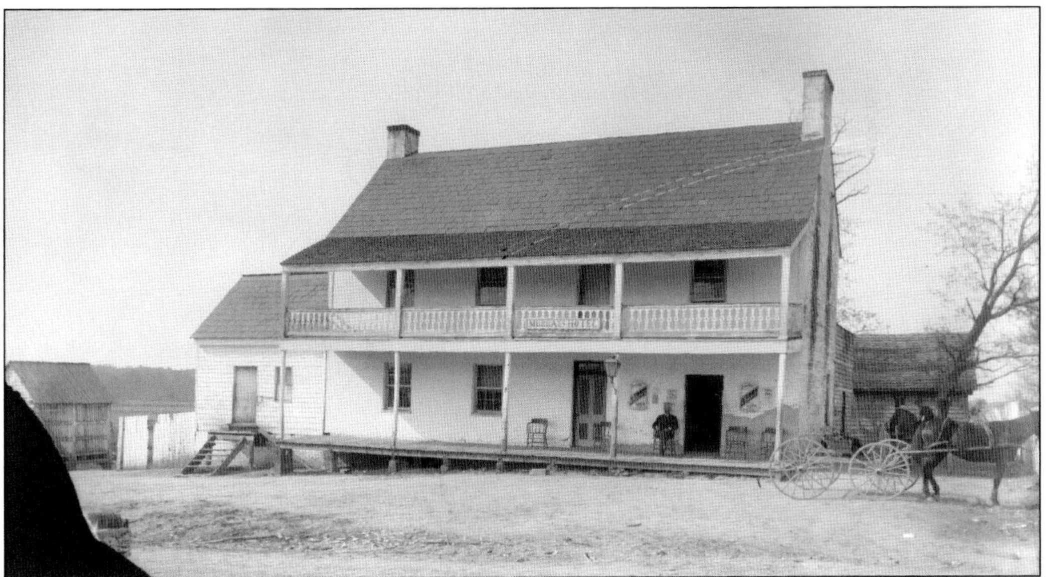

Built around 1820, the Bryantown Tavern was a two-story, Federal-style building with a second-story balcony running the length of its brick facade. After President Lincoln's assassination in 1865, Federal troops stopped here in the search for John Wilkes Booth. It was known as Murray's Hotel when this photograph was taken around 1890. It is currently a private home. (Brady-Handy Photograph Collection, LOC.)

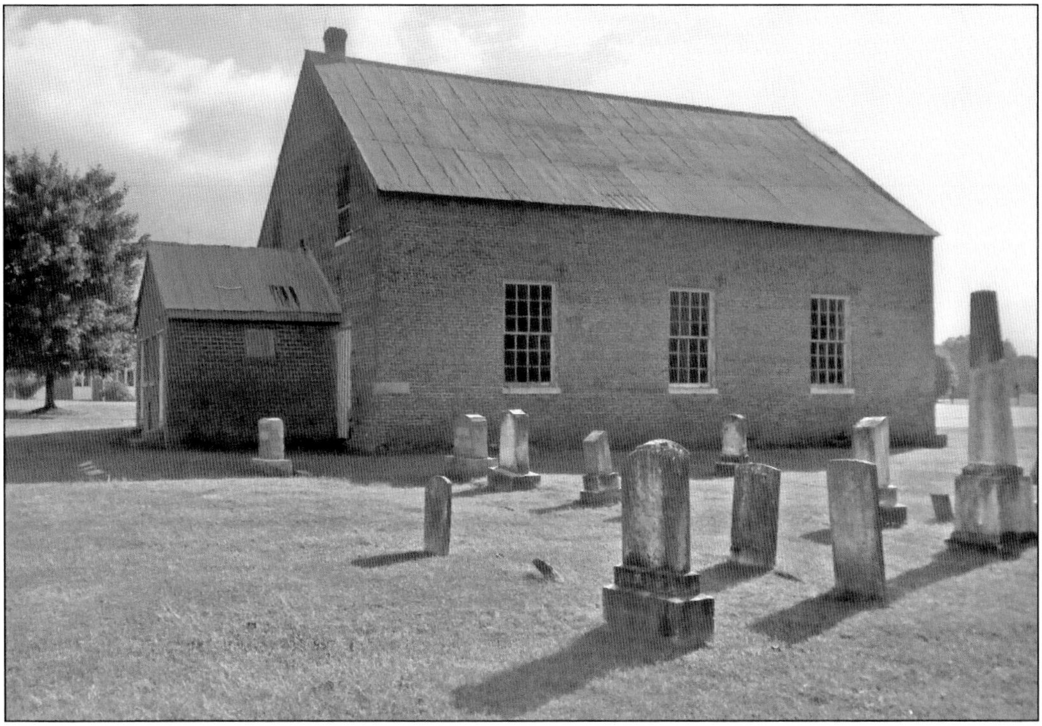

In 1674, Maj. William Boarman gave the land and materials to Rev. Richard Hobart, a Franciscan, for the construction of a chapel on this site in Newport, the first Franciscan mission in the English colonies. The old St. Mary's Catholic Church was built in 1840, replacing the colonial chapel, and it was converted into the parish hall in 1906, when a new church was built. It is now in need of repair.

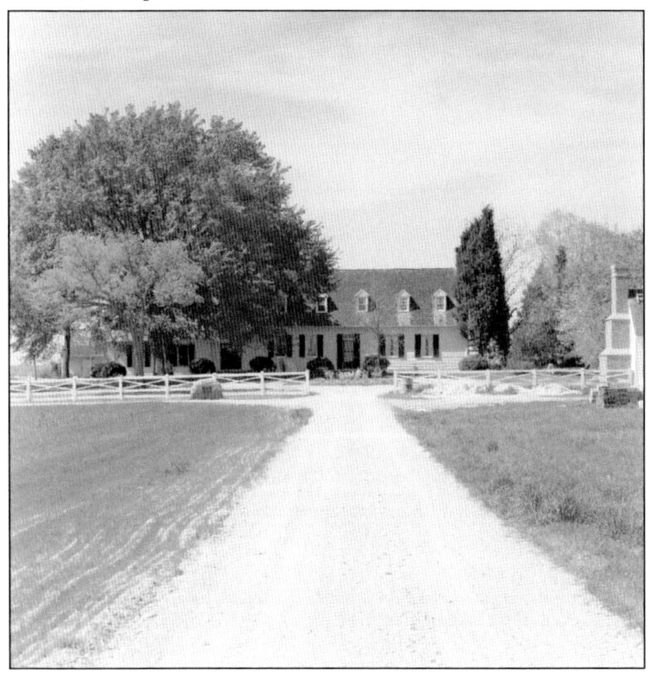

Built on a 1,000-acre patent issued to John Pile by Lord Calvert in 1653, Sarum in Newport is among the earliest houses in Charles County. Based on tested wood samples, the oldest part of the one-and-a-half-story, clapboard-sided residence was built in 1717 by Joseph Pile, John's grandson, to replace the 17th-century house. In 1736, it was expanded with its catslide roof and dormers. (R. Randolph Langenbach, HABS.)

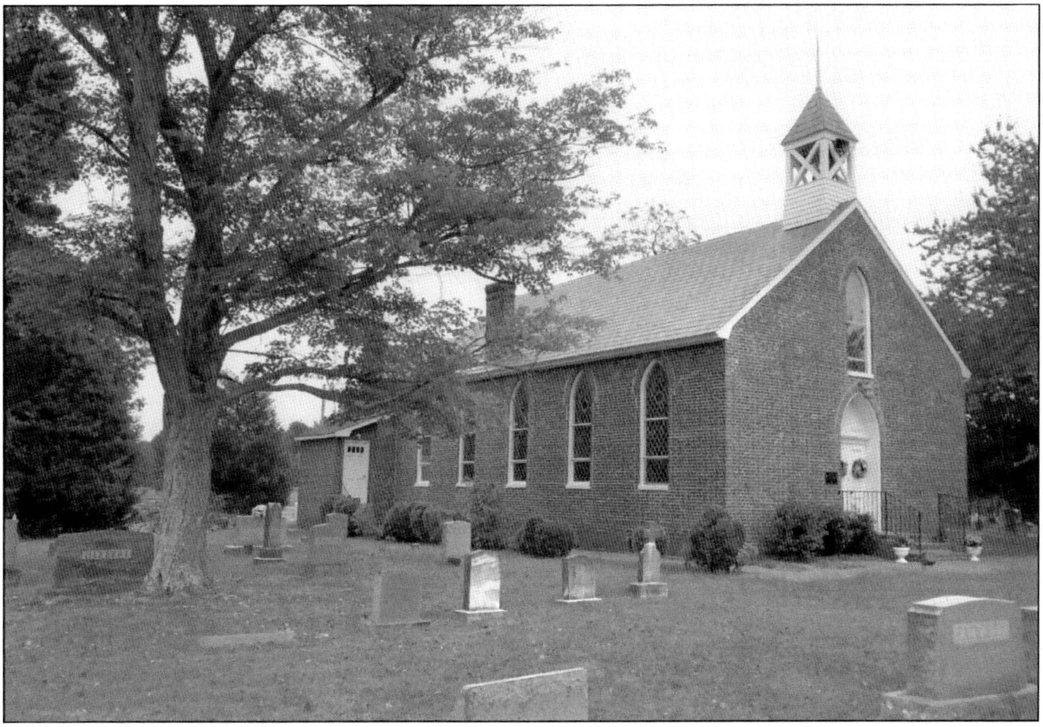

Established as a parish in 1744, Trinity Episcopal Church in Newport was built of brick on a five-bay plan in 1756. In the 19th century, the windows and entryway were modified to form lancet arches, the interior was renovated, the roof was raised, and a small wooden belfry was erected. Other changes include a brick chancel, sanctuary, and sacristy added to the rear of the building in the 1920s through the 1930s.

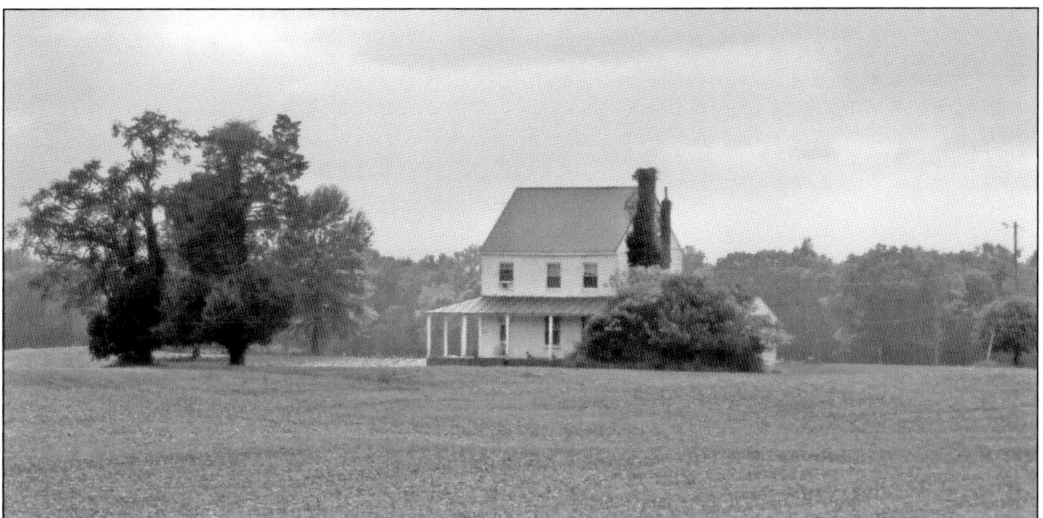

Michael Jenifer Stone built Equality in Bel Alton around 1795 to serve as his residence after he left Congress and while he served as the chief judge of Maryland's 1st Judicial District. The two-and-a-half-story, three-bay frame farmhouse was constructed on a side-parlor plan in a vernacular adaptation of the Federal style. Stone and other relatives are buried in a cemetery on the estate.

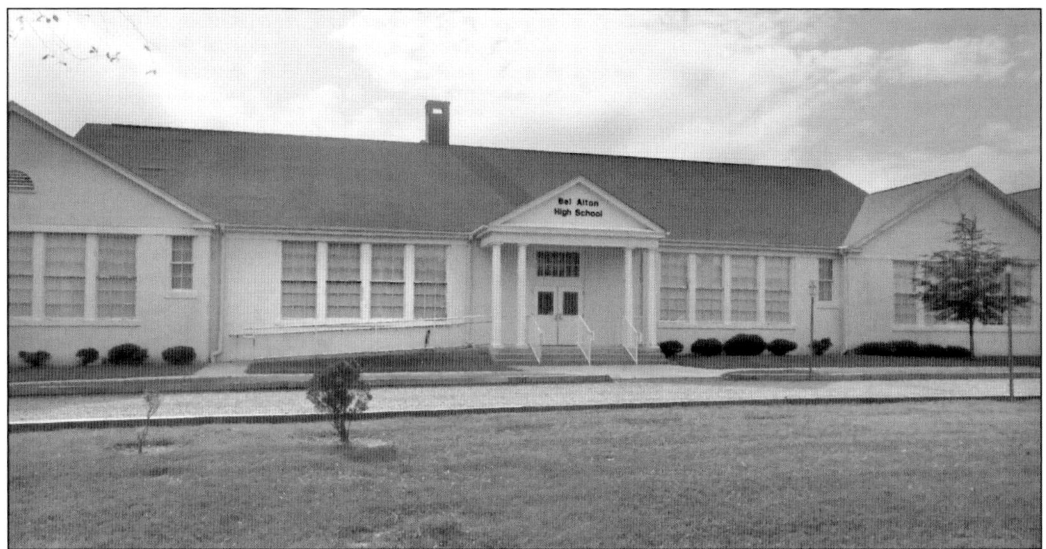

Built of stuccoed concrete block in 1937 and opened for students in 1938, Bel Alton High School was the first public high school in Charles County for African American children. It was the centerpiece of a campus that encompassed an auditorium, gymnasium, agricultural building, and elementary school. Bel Alton High School was expanded in 1948 and operated until schools were desegregated in 1965.

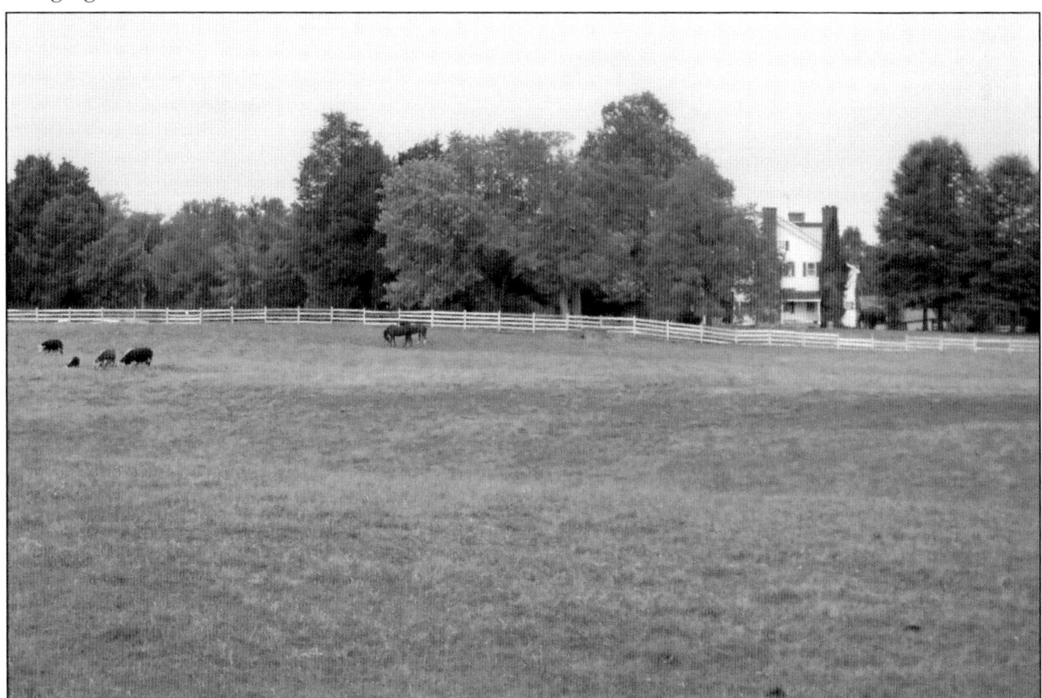

Built in 1840 on land acquired by the Wills family in 1839, Preference is a Federal-style farmhouse that was the center of a 1,122-acre tobacco plantation. The three-bay-wide, two-and-a-half-story frame and clapboard structure was constructed on a brick foundation with galleries and double end chimneys. It remained in the family until Thomas Wills sold it in 1894. The property has maintained its agricultural roots.

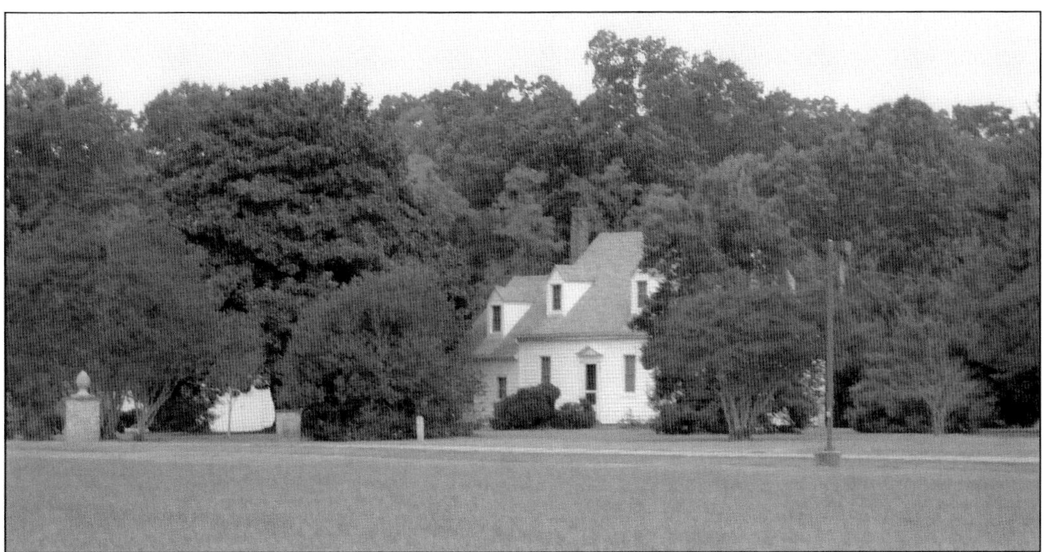

Huckleberry is a one-and-a-half-story, three-bay-wide residence built in the early 1800s. Now a Jesuit-run retreat house, it is best known as the home of Confederate chief signal agent Thomas A. Jones. When John Wilkes Booth and accomplice David Herold were seeking to evade the Union military dragnet after President Lincoln's assassination, it was Jones who aided them and ferried them across the Potomac to Virginia.

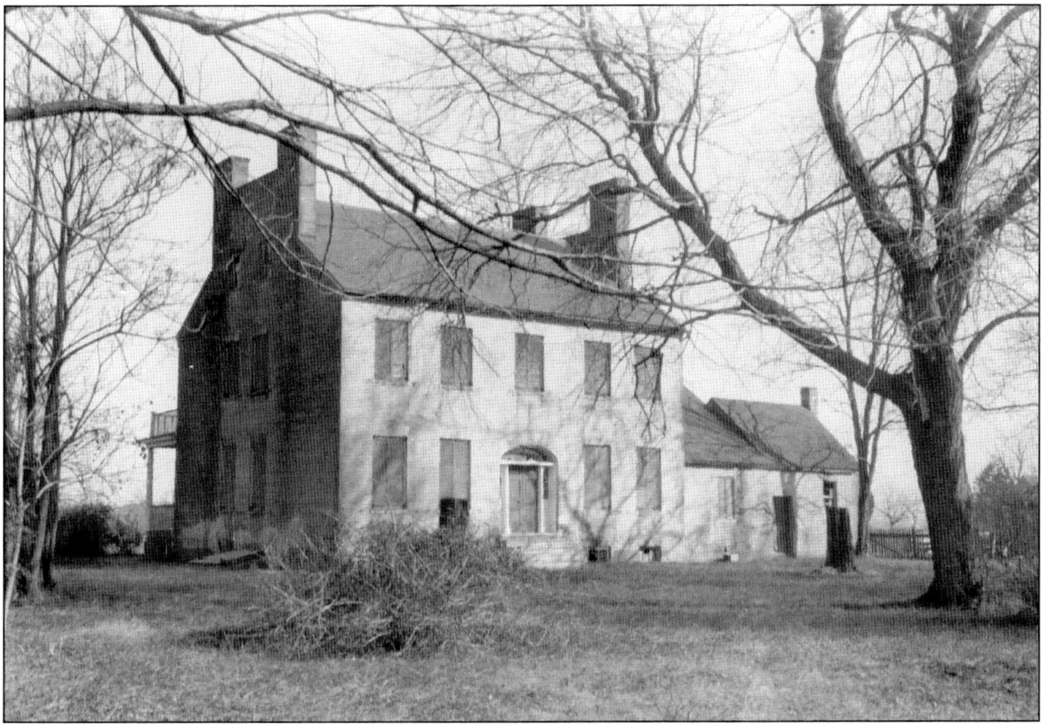

Built in 1795 on land called Bowles Purchase of St. George, Waverly is situated near the Potomac River, south of Newburg. Waverly acquired its Federal-style form between 1823 and 1826 after Dr. Morgan A. Harris inherited the property. The two-story brick home, which was restored in the 1960s, sits atop a full basement with dual chimneys built into each end. (Delos H. Smith, HABS.)

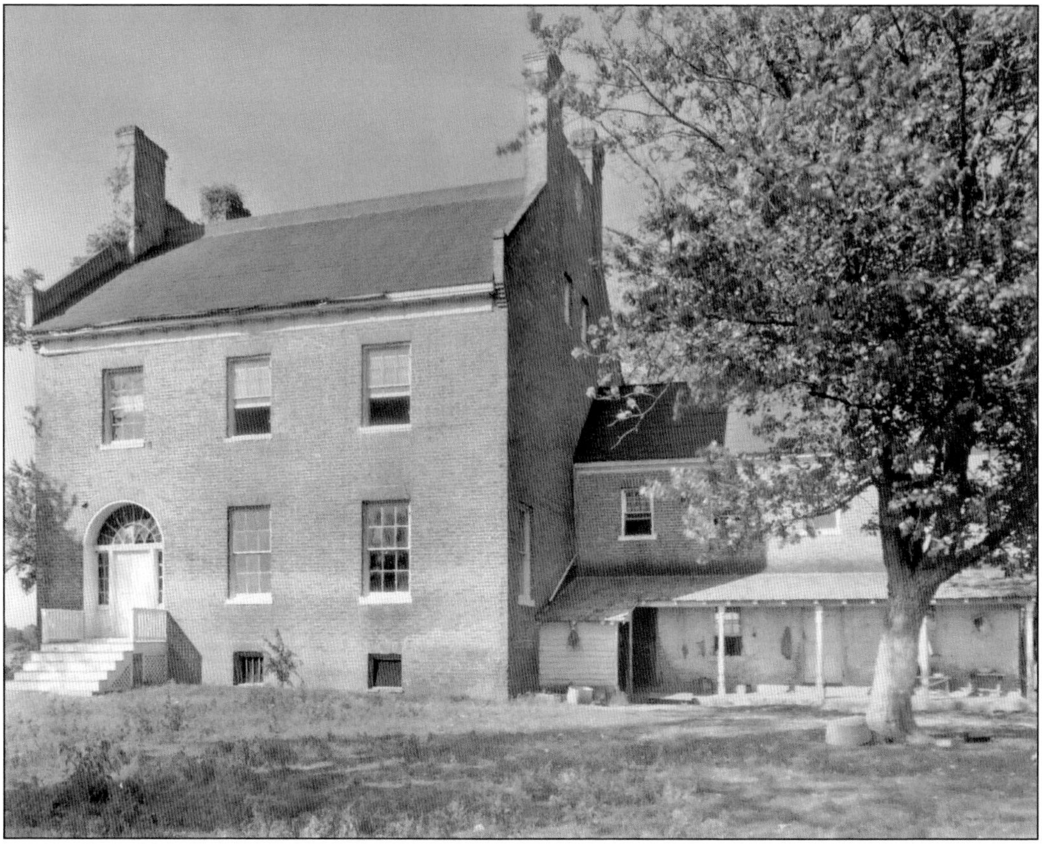

Mount Republican, near Newburg in Piccowaxen, is believed to be the work of the same master builder as Waverly. The main block of this two-story, two-part brick house was built over a full basement around 1790. The Federal-style home was once thought to have been constructed for Theophilus Yates, a successful planter who died in 1781, but it was likely built for one of his children. (FBJPC, LOC.)

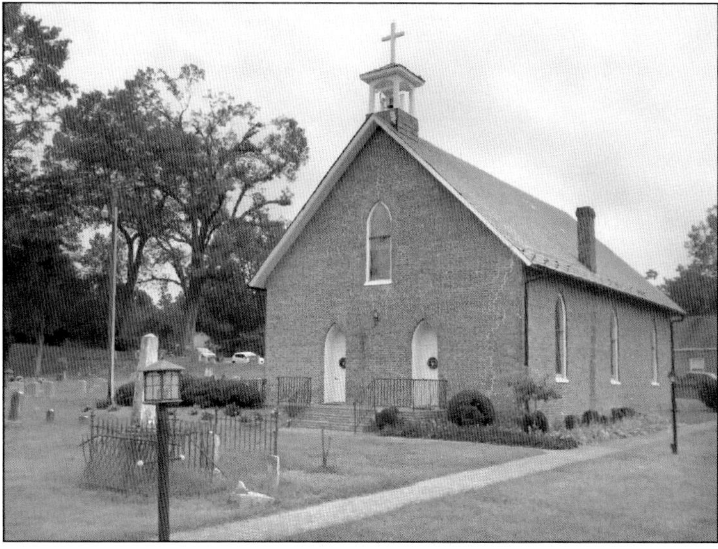

Established as William and Mary Parish in 1692, Christ Church in Wayside was constructed after 1750. At one story high and three bays long, it is the smallest of the county's several colonial Episcopal churches. It was also the boyhood church of Rev. Thomas John Claggett, the first American-born Episcopal bishop. Damaged by Union troops during the Civil War, the church was heavily renovated in the 19th century.

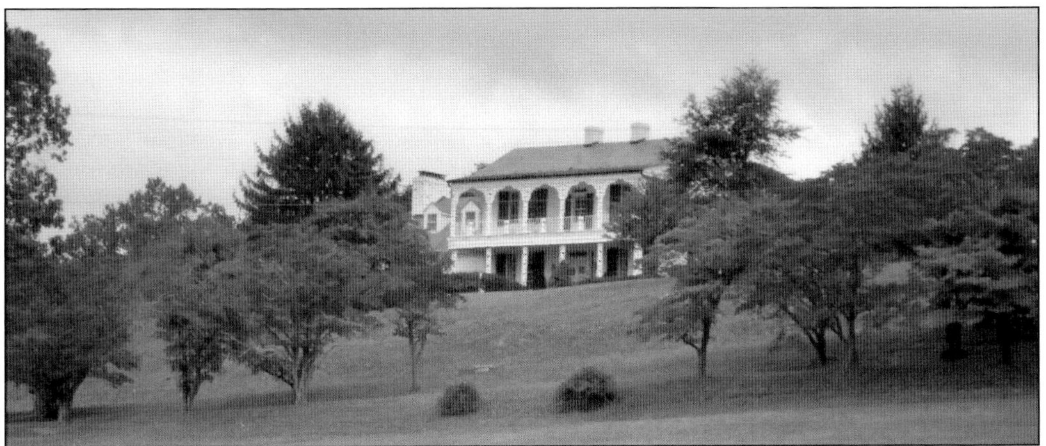

Elmwood was built atop a hill facing Piccowaxen Creek around 1850. With a double gallery front and decorative wrought iron porches, the two-story, five-bay house is more reminiscent of New Orleans than Maryland. In the early 1900s, it was home to Adrian Posey, a state senator and state attorney, and his wife, Mamie Howard Posey, daughter of the owners of the Chapel Point steamboat resort.

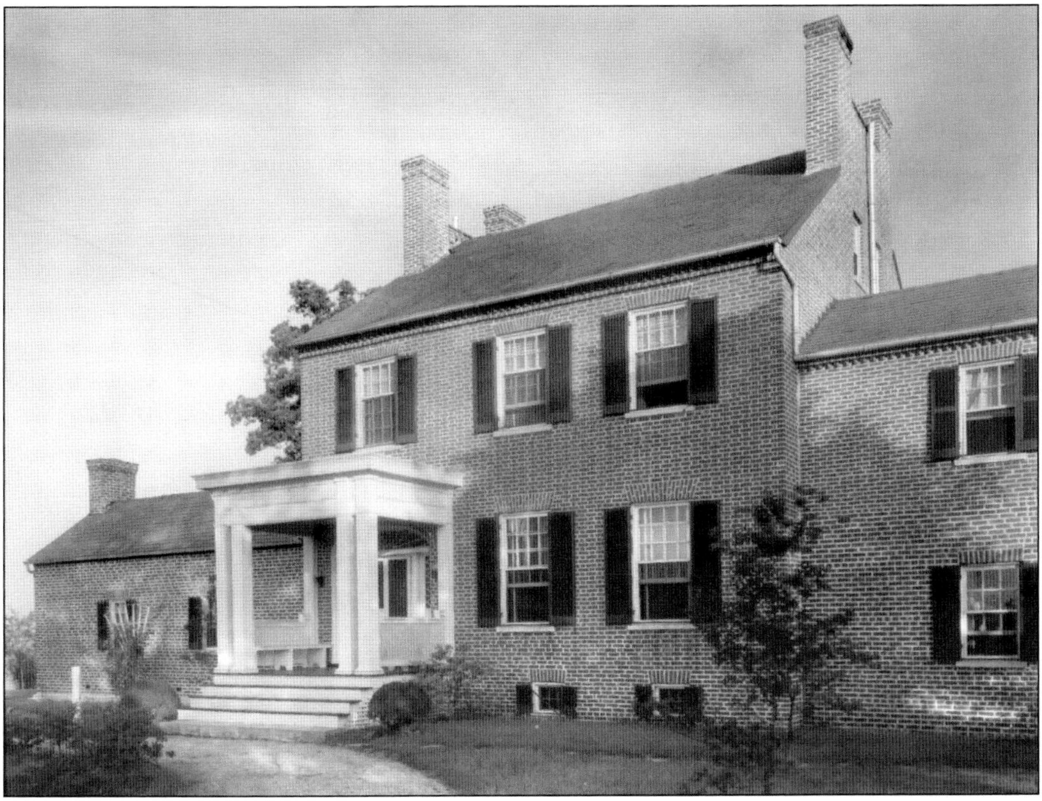

Overlooking the Wicomico River from Stoddert Point, West Hatton was built on land that was part of a 500-acre patent secured by Thomas Hatton in 1650. The two-story, side-hall, double-pile Federal residence with flanking wings is likely the work of the same master builder as Waverly and Mount Republican. It was once the home of John Truman Stoddert, a War of 1812 officer, state delegate, and congressman. (FBJPC, LOC.)

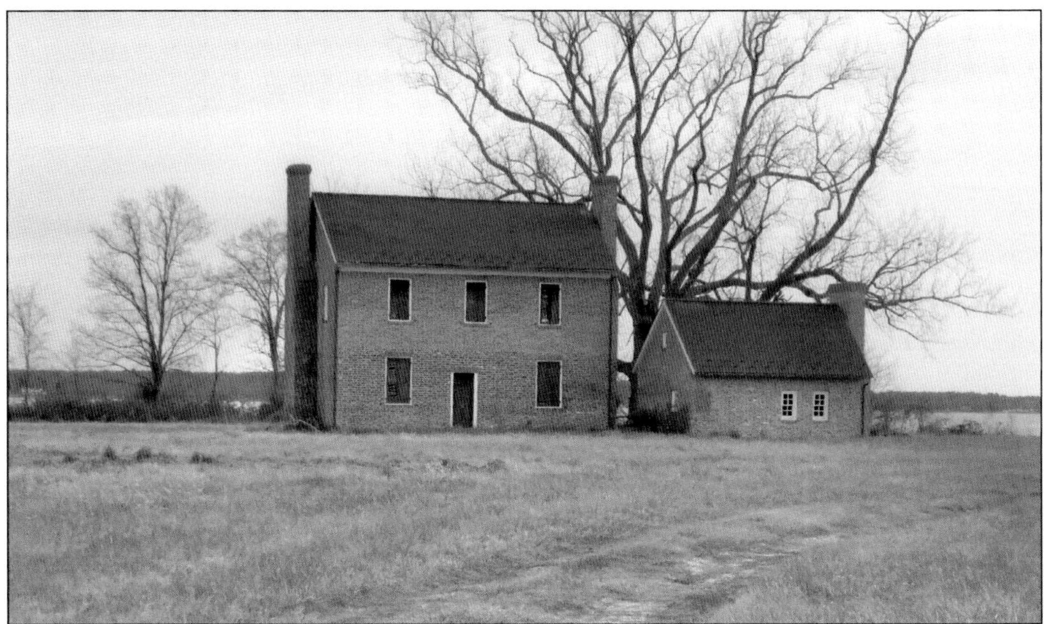

Built around 1800, Rock Hall is a Federal-style residence overlooking the Wicomico River near Rock Point. The plain two-story structure is flanked by brick exterior chimneys. A two-story frame addition on the south gable end has been removed, but a detached brick kitchen remains just steps away from the residence. This was the birthplace and home of Simon Spearman Lancaster (1859–1940), a Maryland delegate and senator.

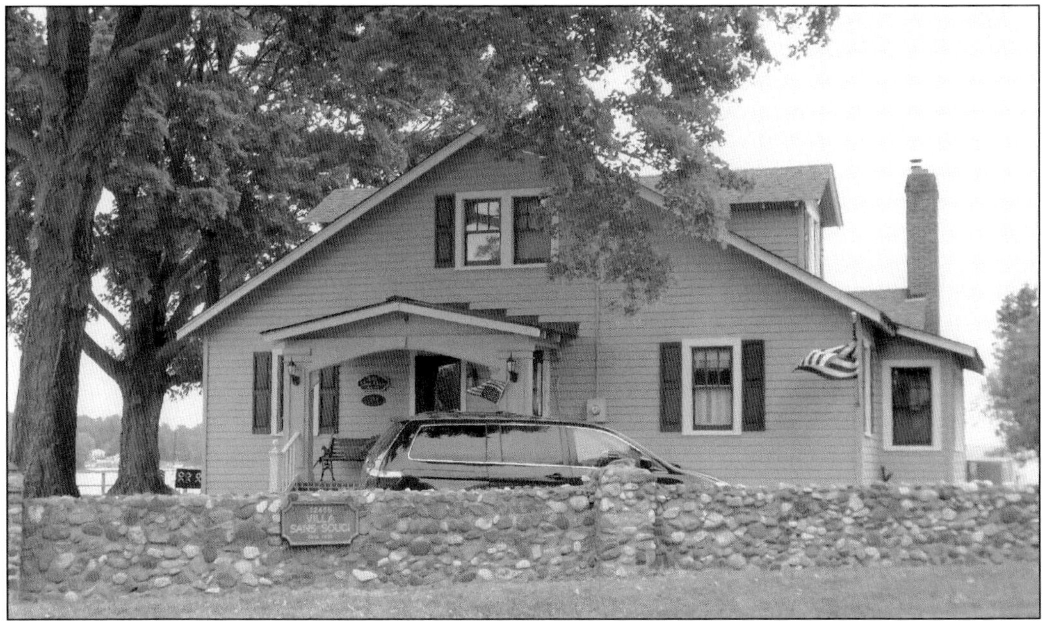

In 1897, George Vickers of Philadelphia purchased Cobb Island at the confluence of the Wicomico and Potomac Rivers and soon began construction of Villa Sans Souci. Using local contractors, the one-and-a-half-story residence was frame built and clapboard sided. Completed in 1899, it is the oldest structure on Cobb Island. Canadian inventor Reginald Aubrey Fessenden broadcast the first successful radio transmission of speech here in December 1900.

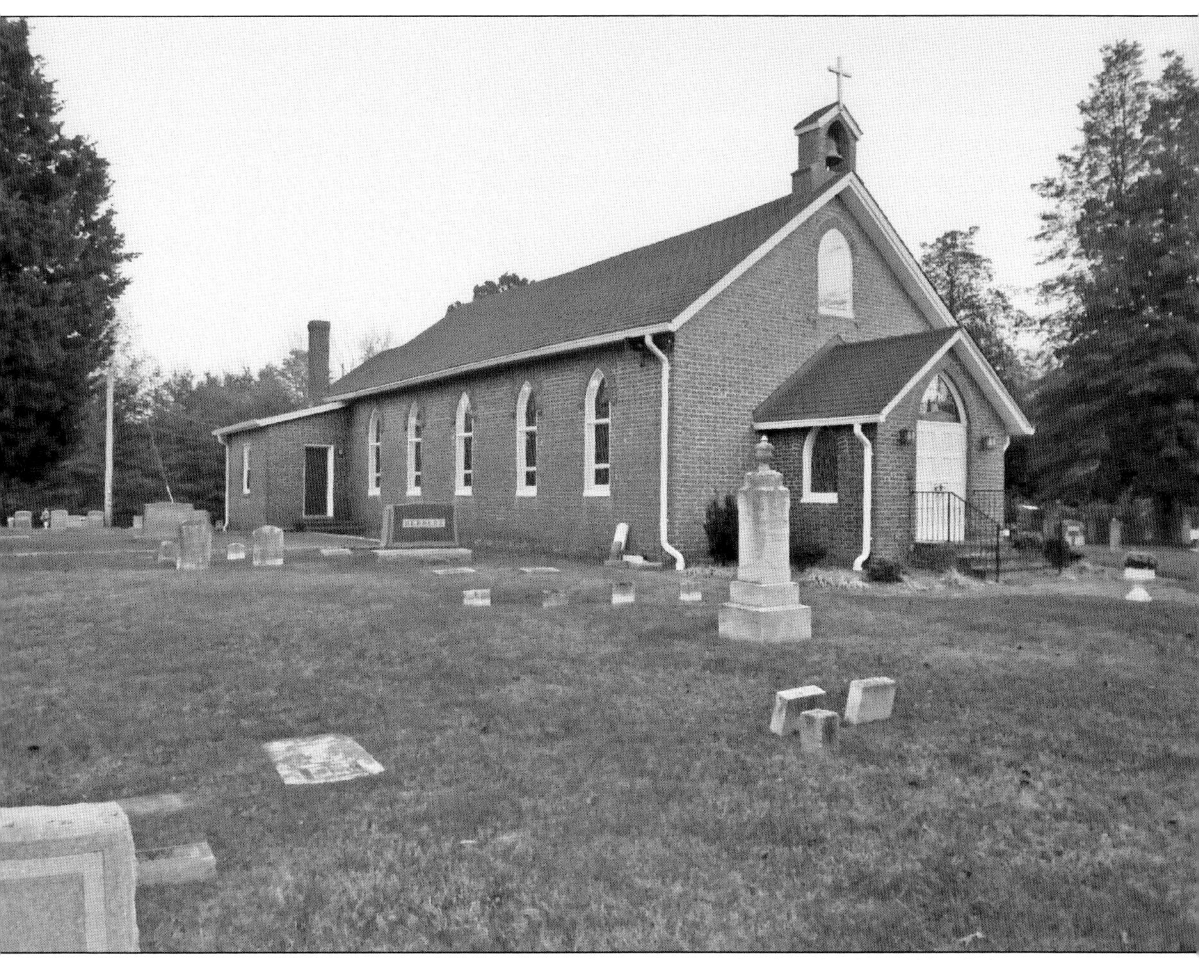

Oldfields Episcopal Chapel is a one-story, five-bay rectangular brick church built between Hughesville and Benedict in 1769. Like most local Episcopal churches, it was modified in the 19th century by raising the roof and adding lancet windows and a small brick belfry above the entrance. Other additions were made in the early 1900s. The churchyard holds the graves of several British soldiers who died during the War of 1812.